Colors
Steve Buccellato
and Colorgraphix (#153)

Letters
Richard Starkings
& Comicraft

Original Series Editor
Mark Powers

Book Design:
JG and Comicraft's
Eng Wong

Assistant Editor
Matty Ryan

Collections Editor
Ben Abernathy

Editor In Chief
Joe Quesada

*Special thanks to
Doreen Mulryan

WOLVERINE®: BLOOD DEBT, Contains material originally published in magazine form as WOLVERINE, Vol. 1, #'s 150-153. Published by MARVEL COMICS, Bill Jemas, President; Frank Fochetta, Senior Vice President, Publishing; Joe Quesada, Editor-in-Chief; Stan Lee, Chairman Emeritus. OFFICE OF PUBLICATION: 387 PARK AVENUE SOUTH, NEW YORK, N.Y. 10016. Copyright © 2000, 2001 Marvel Characters, Inc. All rights reserved. WOLVERINE (including all prominent characters featured in this issue and the distinctive likenesses thereof) is a registered trademark of MARVEL CHARACTERS, INC. No part of this book may be printed or reproduced in any manner without the written permission of the publisher. Printed in Canada First Printing, July, 2001. ISBN: 0-7851-0785-1. GST #R127032852. MARVEL COMICS is a division of MARVEL ENTERPRISES, INC. Peter Cuneo, Chief Executive Officer; Avi Arad, Chief Creative Officer.

10 9 8 7 6 5 4 3 2 1

Stan Lee presents

WOLVERINE

BLOOD DEBT

by STEVE
SKROCE

writer & artist

LARY
STUCKER

inks

Collecting
Wolverine
issues #150 - 153

CHAPTER ONE

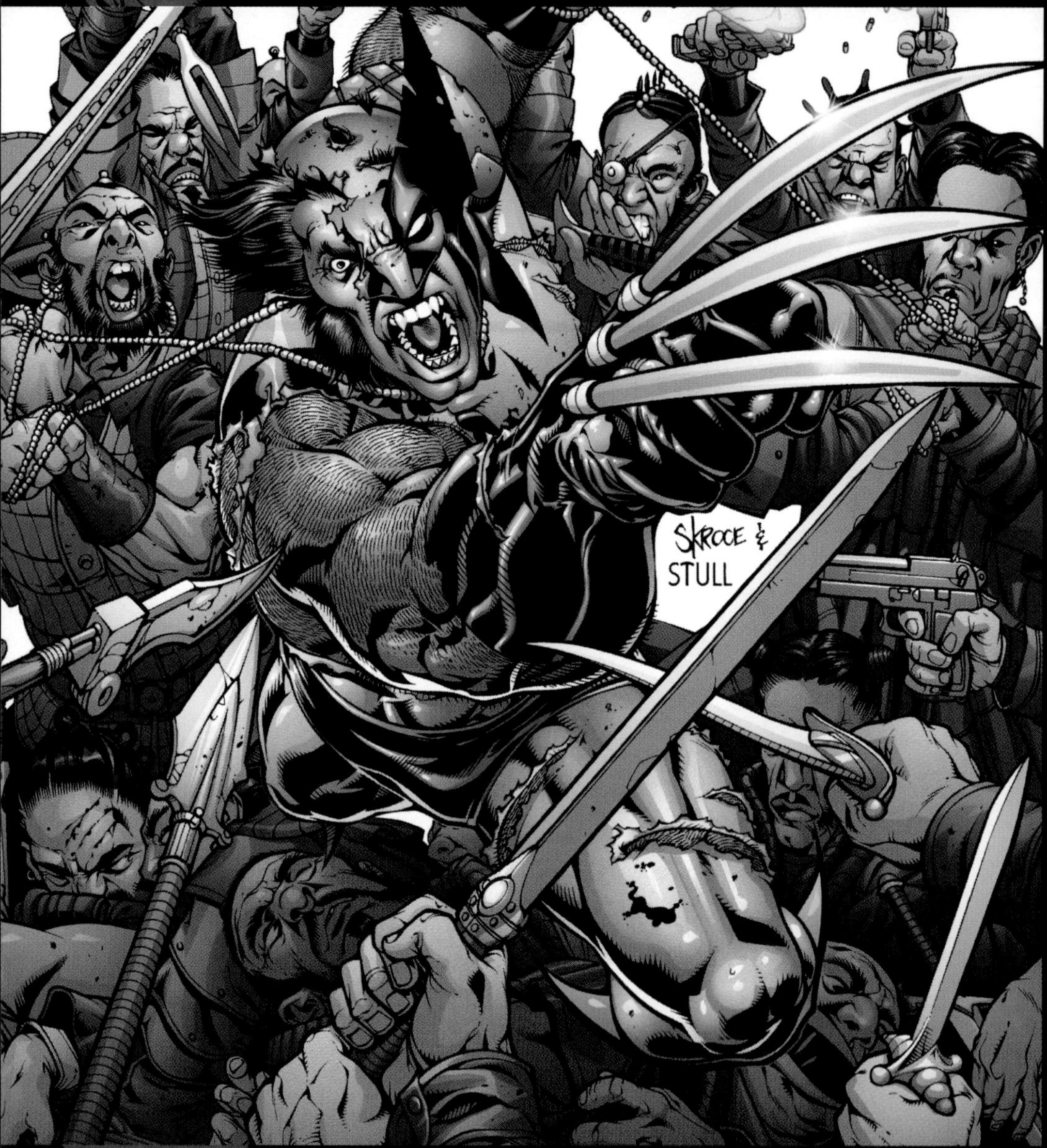
SKROCE &
STULL

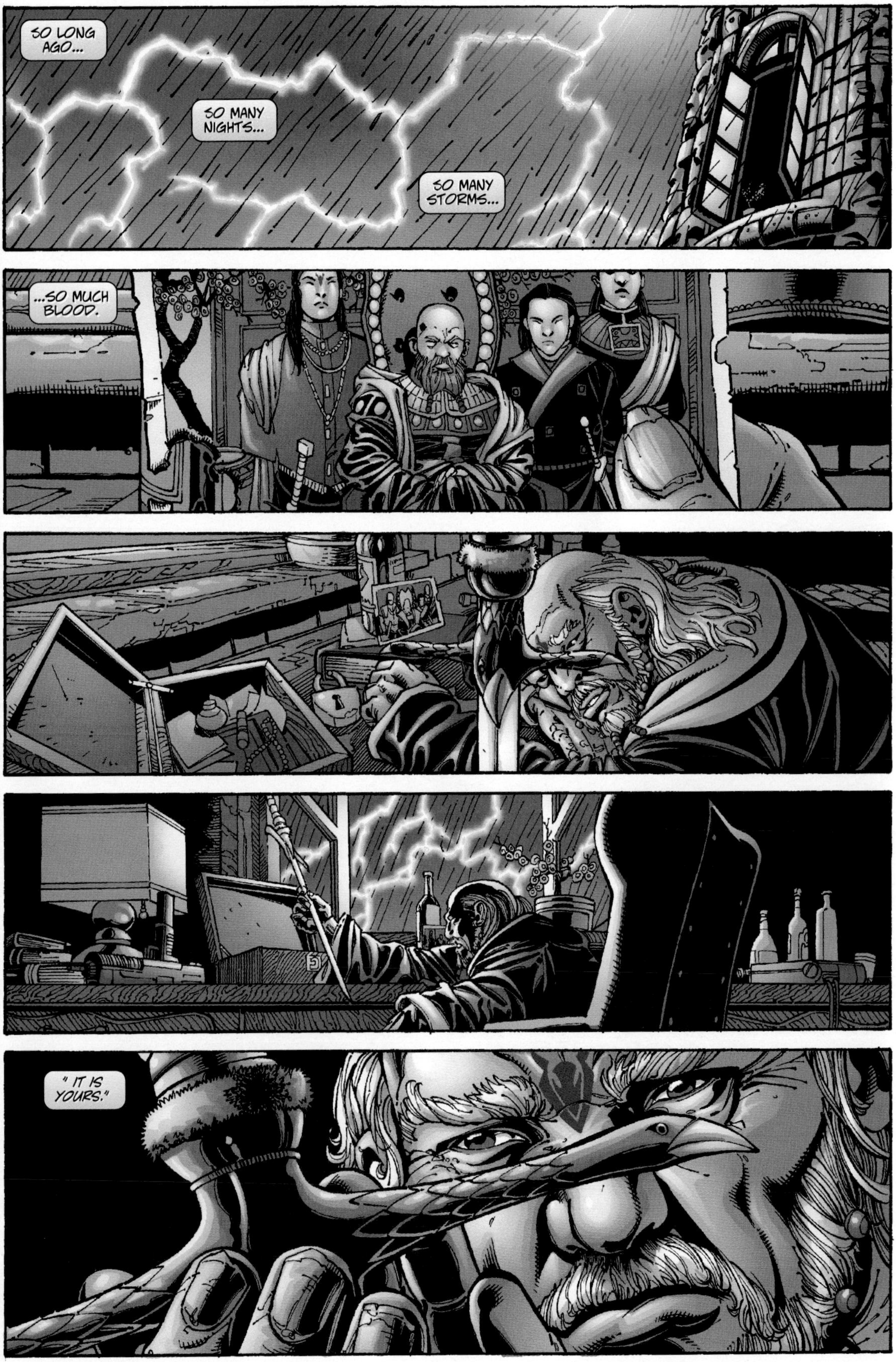
SO LONG AGO...
SO MANY NIGHTS...
SO MANY STORMS...
...SO MUCH BLOOD.
" IT IS YOURS."

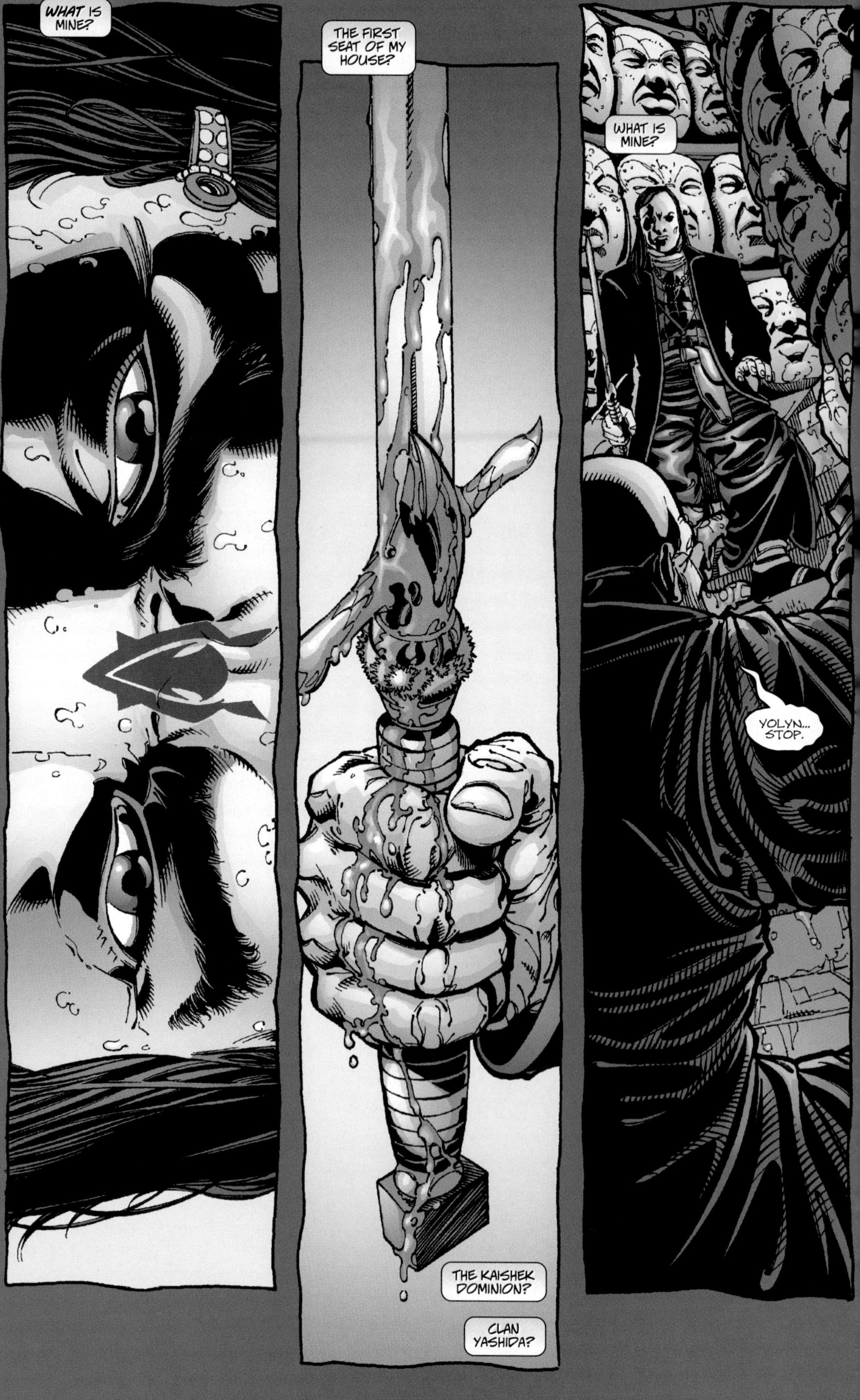
WHAT IS MINE?
THE FIRST SEAT OF MY HOUSE?
THE KAISHEK DOMINION?
CLAN YASHIDA?
WHAT IS MINE?
YOLYN... STOP.

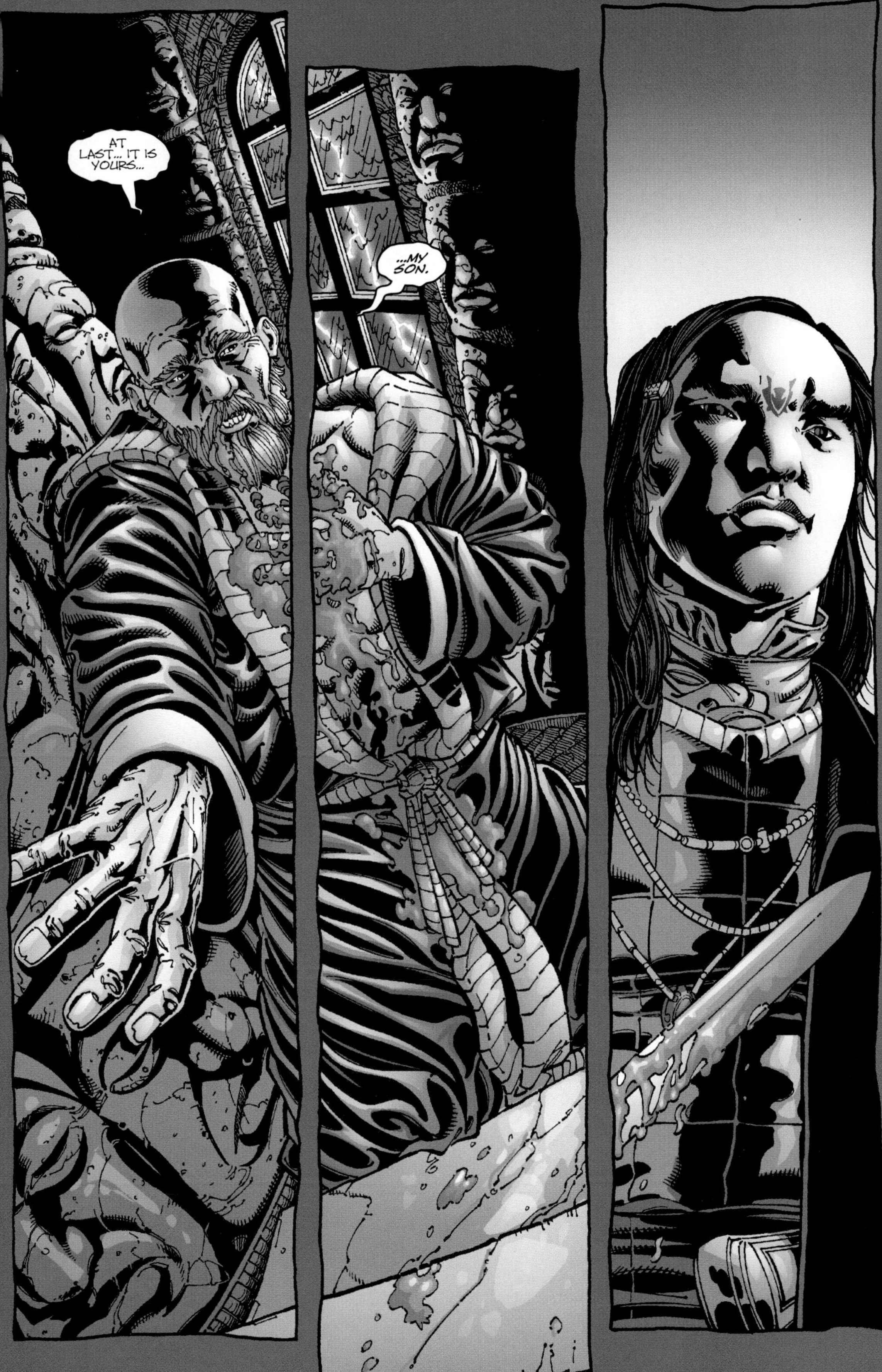
AT LAST... IT IS YOURS...
...MY SON.

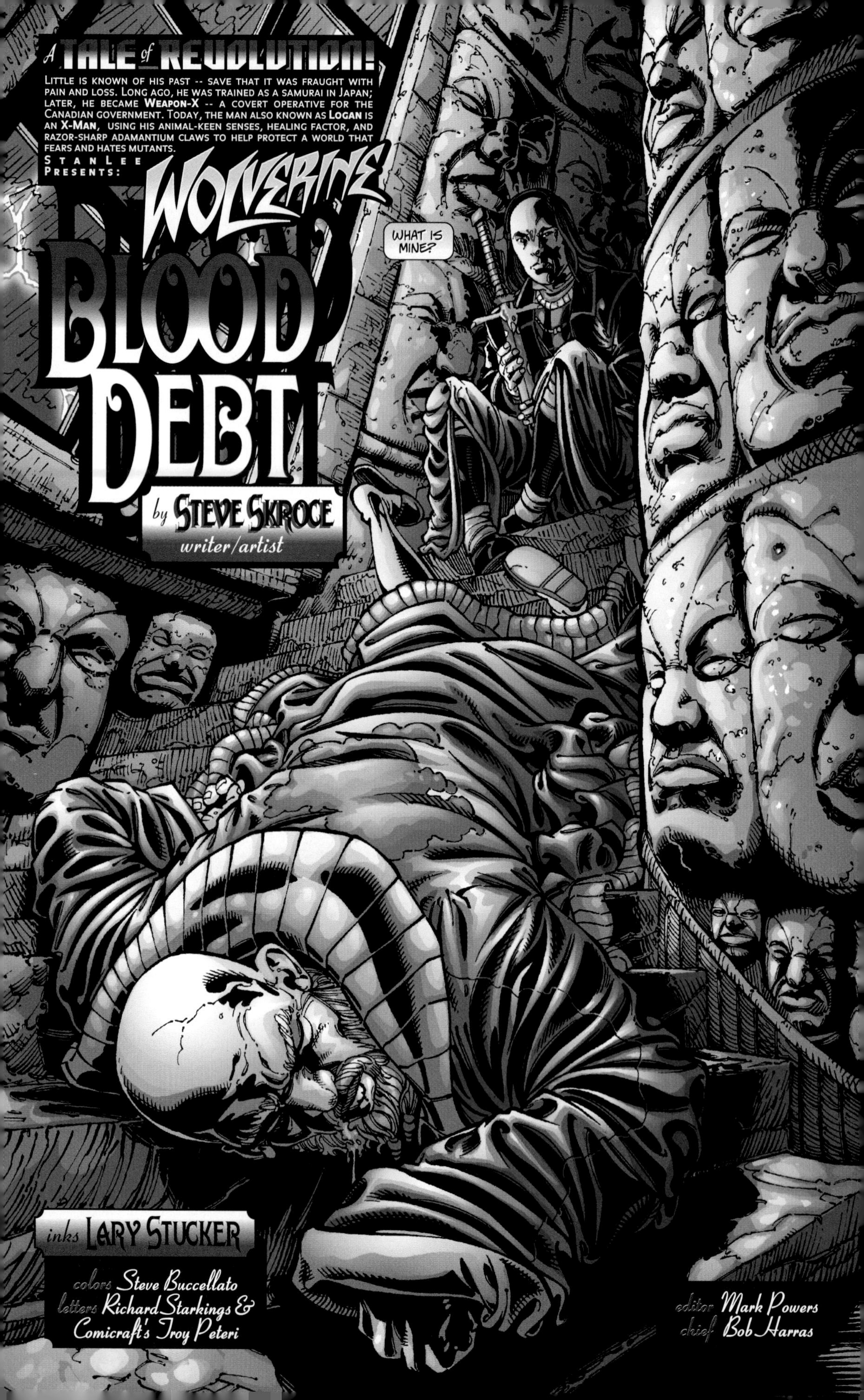
A TALE of REVOLUTION!
LITTLE IS KNOWN OF HIS PAST -- SAVE THAT IT WAS FRAUGHT WITH PAIN AND LOSS. LONG AGO, HE WAS TRAINED AS A SAMURAI IN JAPAN; LATER, HE BECAME WEAPON-X -- A COVERT OPERATIVE FOR THE CANADIAN GOVERNMENT. TODAY, THE MAN ALSO KNOWN AS LOGAN IS AN X-MAN, USING HIS ANIMAL-KEEN SENSES, HEALING FACTOR, AND RAZOR-SHARP ADAMANTIUM CLAWS TO HELP PROTECT A WORLD THAT FEARS AND HATES MUTANTS.
STAN LEE PRESENTS:
WOLVERINE
BLOOD DEBT
by STEVE SKROCE writer/artist
WHAT IS MINE?
inks LARY STUCKER
colors Steve Buccellato
letters Richard Starkings & Comicraft's Troy Peteri
editor Mark Powers
chief Bob Harras

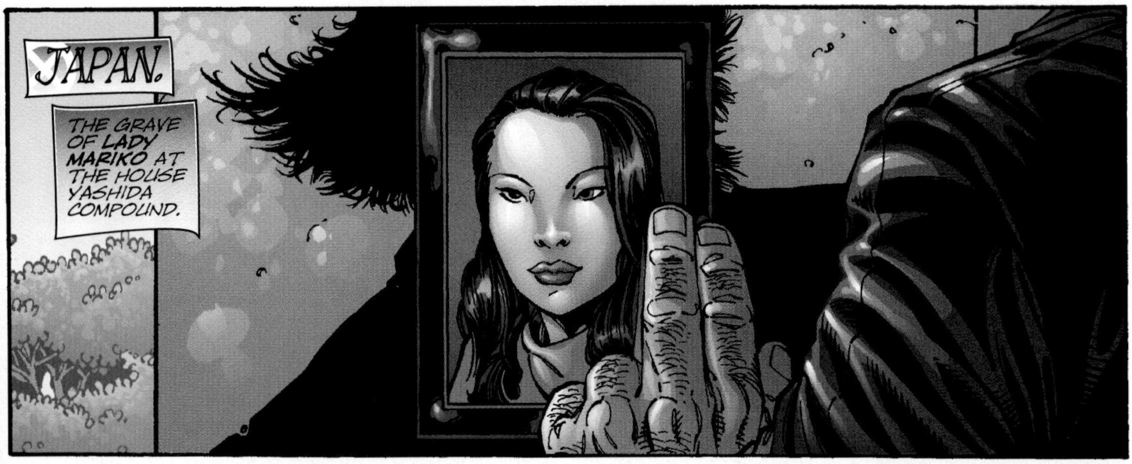
JAPAN.
THE GRAVE OF LADY MARIKO AT THE HOUSE YASHIDA COMPOUND.

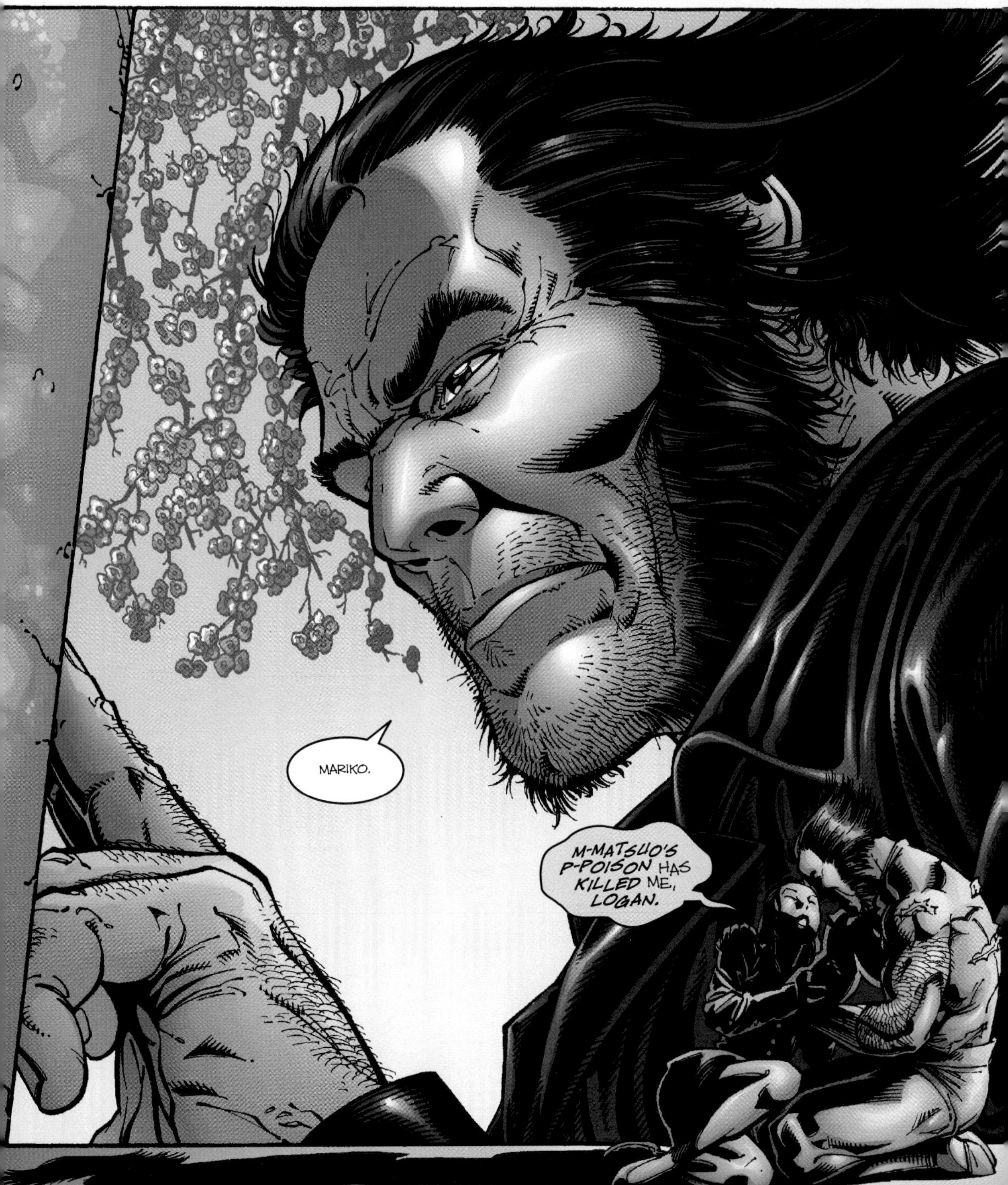
MARIKO.
M-MATSUO'S P-POISON HAS KILLED ME, LOGAN.

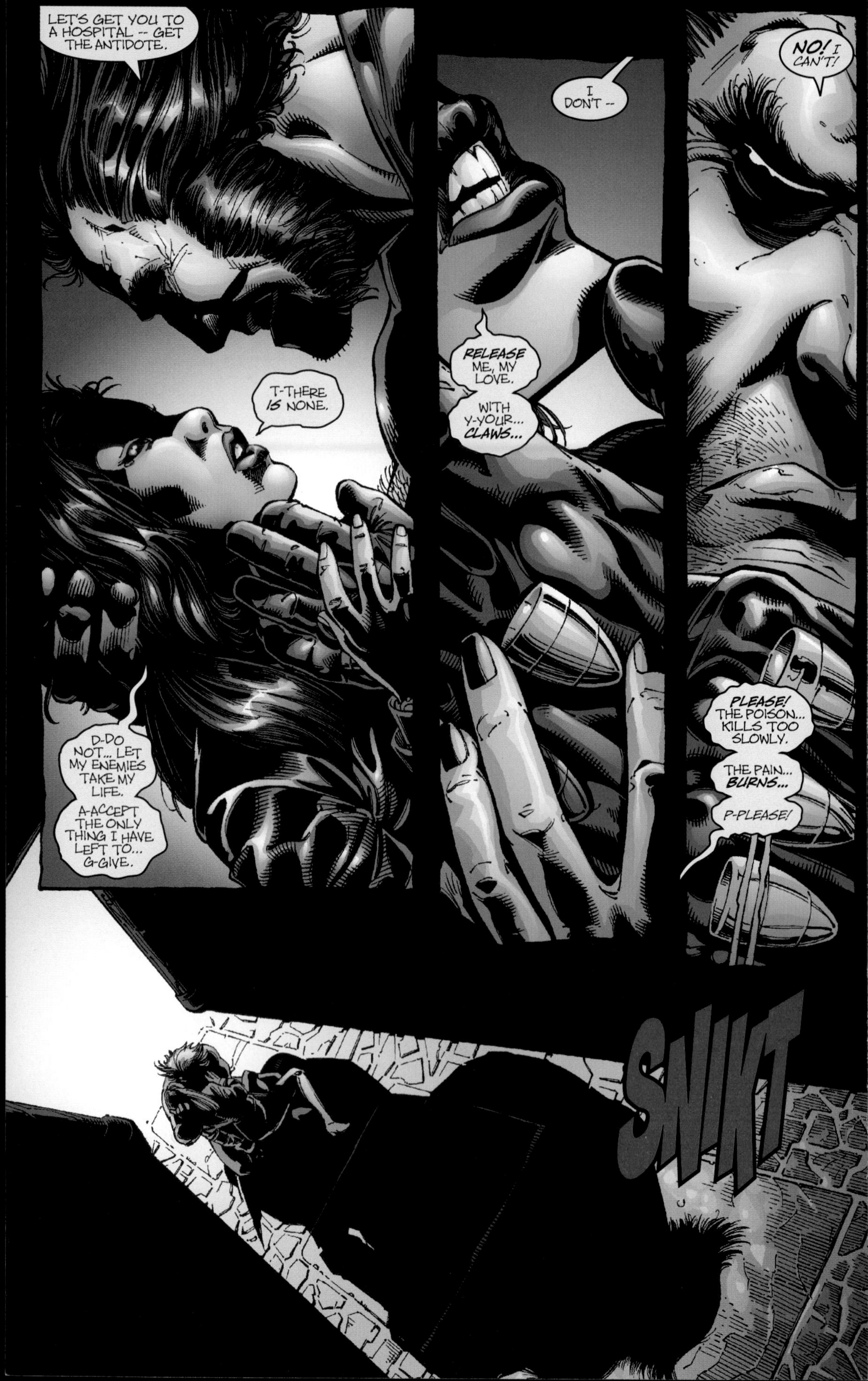
LET'S GET YOU TO A HOSPITAL -- GET THE ANTIDOTE.
T-THERE *IS* NONE.
D-DO NOT... LET MY ENEMIES TAKE MY LIFE.
A-ACCEPT THE ONLY THING I HAVE LEFT TO... G-GIVE.
I DON'T --
RELEASE ME, MY LOVE.
WITH Y-YOUR... *CLAWS...*
NO! I CAN'T!
PLEASE! THE POISON... KILLS TOO SLOWLY.
THE PAIN... *BURNS...*
P-PLEASE!
SNIKT

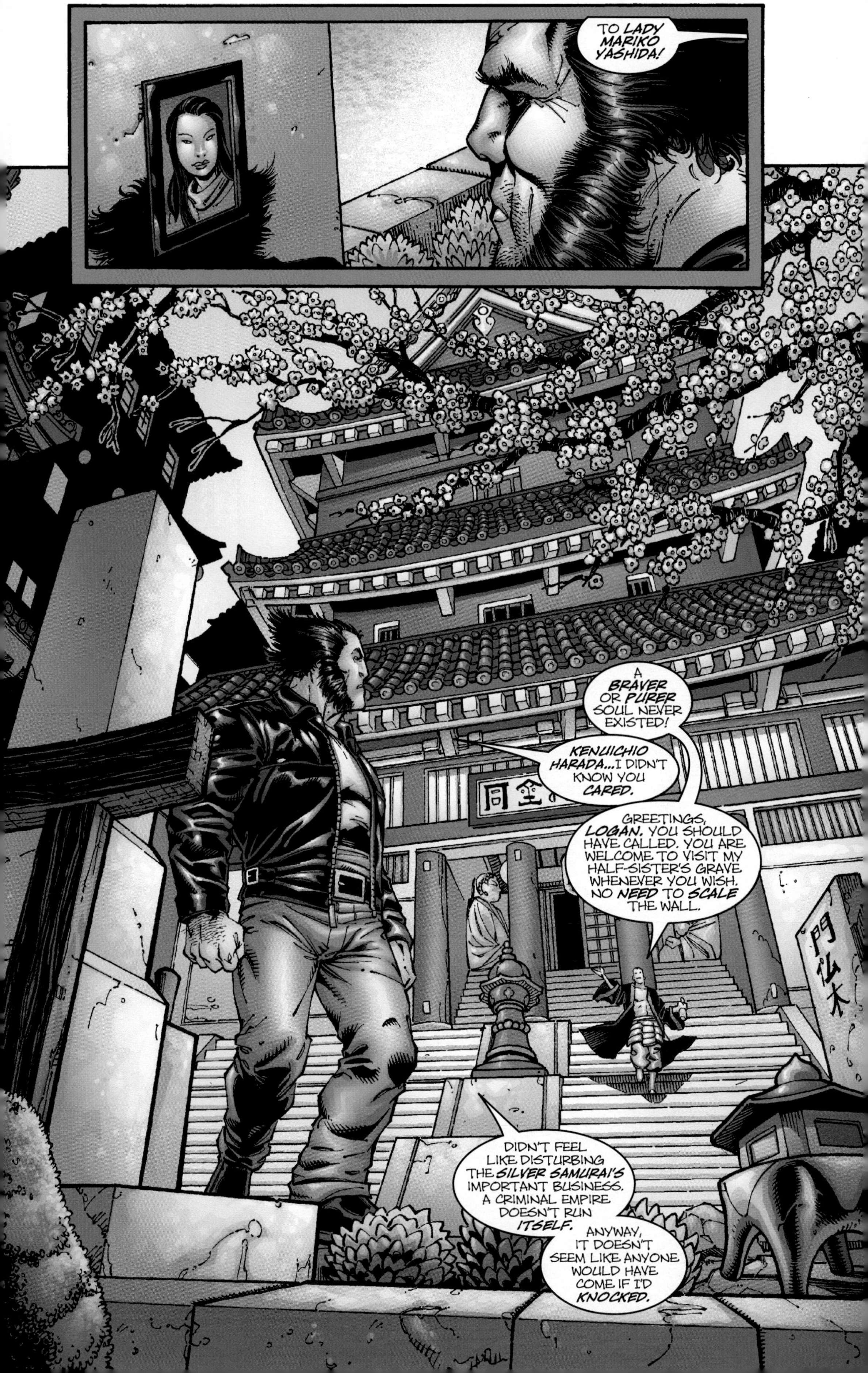
TO LADY MARIKO YASHIDA!
A BRAVER OR PURER SOUL NEVER EXISTED!
KENUICHIO HARADA...I DIDN'T KNOW YOU CARED.
GREETINGS, LOGAN. YOU SHOULD HAVE CALLED. YOU ARE WELCOME TO VISIT MY HALF-SISTER'S GRAVE WHENEVER YOU WISH. NO NEED TO SCALE THE WALL.
DIDN'T FEEL LIKE DISTURBING THE SILVER SAMURAI'S IMPORTANT BUSINESS. A CRIMINAL EMPIRE DOESN'T RUN ITSELF.
ANYWAY, IT DOESN'T SEEM LIKE ANYONE WOULD HAVE COME IF I'D KNOCKED.

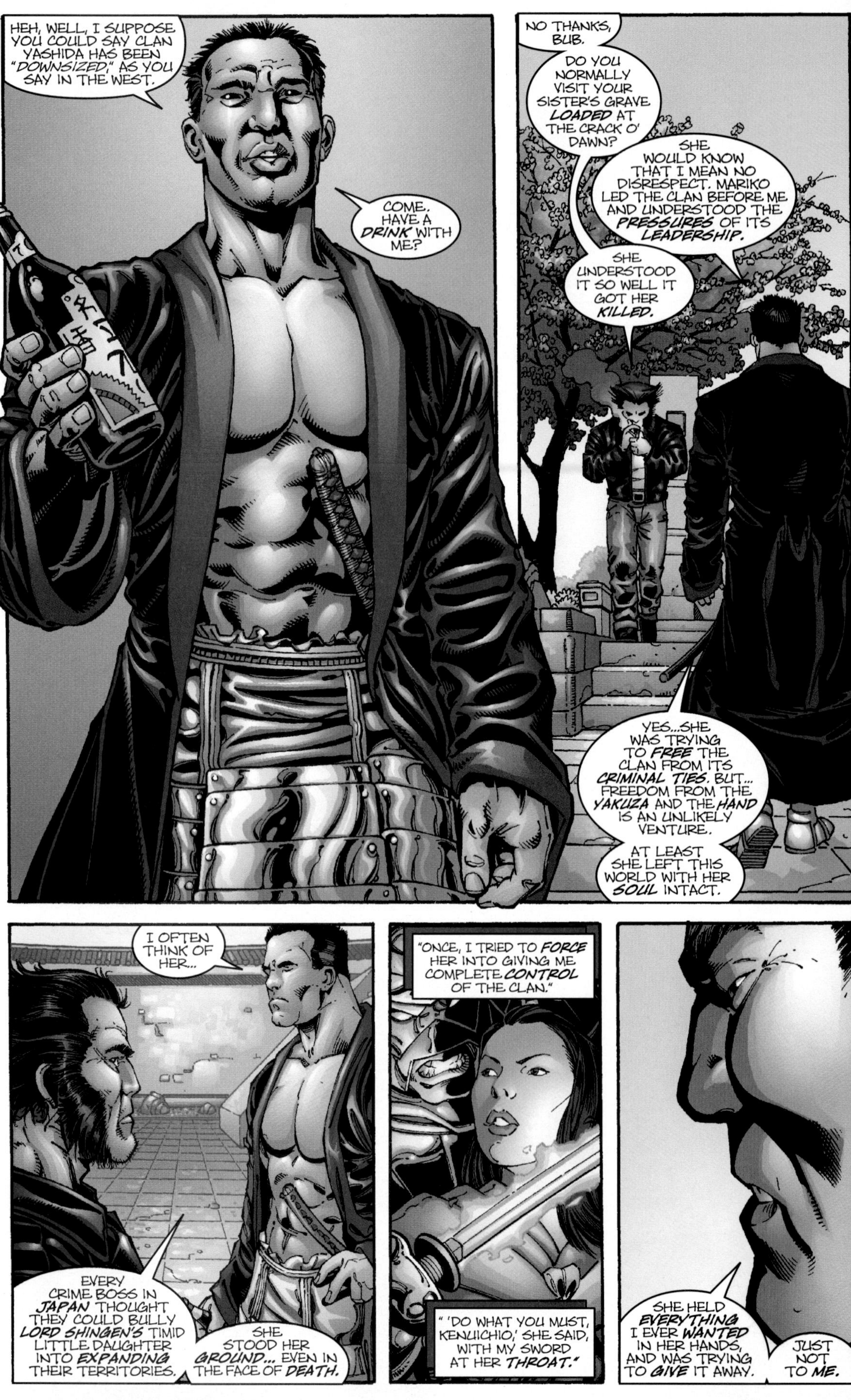
HEH, WELL, I SUPPOSE YOU COULD SAY CLAN YASHIDA HAS BEEN "DOWNSIZED," AS YOU SAY IN THE WEST.
COME. HAVE A DRINK WITH ME?
NO THANKS, BUB.
DO YOU NORMALLY VISIT YOUR SISTER'S GRAVE LOADED AT THE CRACK O' DAWN?
SHE WOULD KNOW THAT I MEAN NO DISRESPECT. MARIKO LED THE CLAN BEFORE ME AND UNDERSTOOD THE PRESSURES OF ITS LEADERSHIP.
SHE UNDERSTOOD IT SO WELL IT GOT HER KILLED.
YES...SHE WAS TRYING TO FREE THE CLAN FROM ITS CRIMINAL TIES. BUT... FREEDOM FROM THE YAKUZA AND THE HAND IS AN UNLIKELY VENTURE.
AT LEAST SHE LEFT THIS WORLD WITH HER SOUL INTACT.
I OFTEN THINK OF HER...
EVERY CRIME BOSS IN JAPAN THOUGHT THEY COULD BULLY LORD SHINGEN'S TIMID LITTLE DAUGHTER INTO EXPANDING THEIR TERRITORIES.
SHE STOOD HER GROUND... EVEN IN THE FACE OF DEATH.
"ONCE, I TRIED TO FORCE HER INTO GIVING ME COMPLETE CONTROL OF THE CLAN."
" 'DO WHAT YOU MUST, KENUICHIO,' SHE SAID, WITH MY SWORD AT HER THROAT."
SHE HELD EVERYTHING I EVER WANTED IN HER HANDS, AND WAS TRYING TO GIVE IT AWAY.
JUST NOT TO ME.

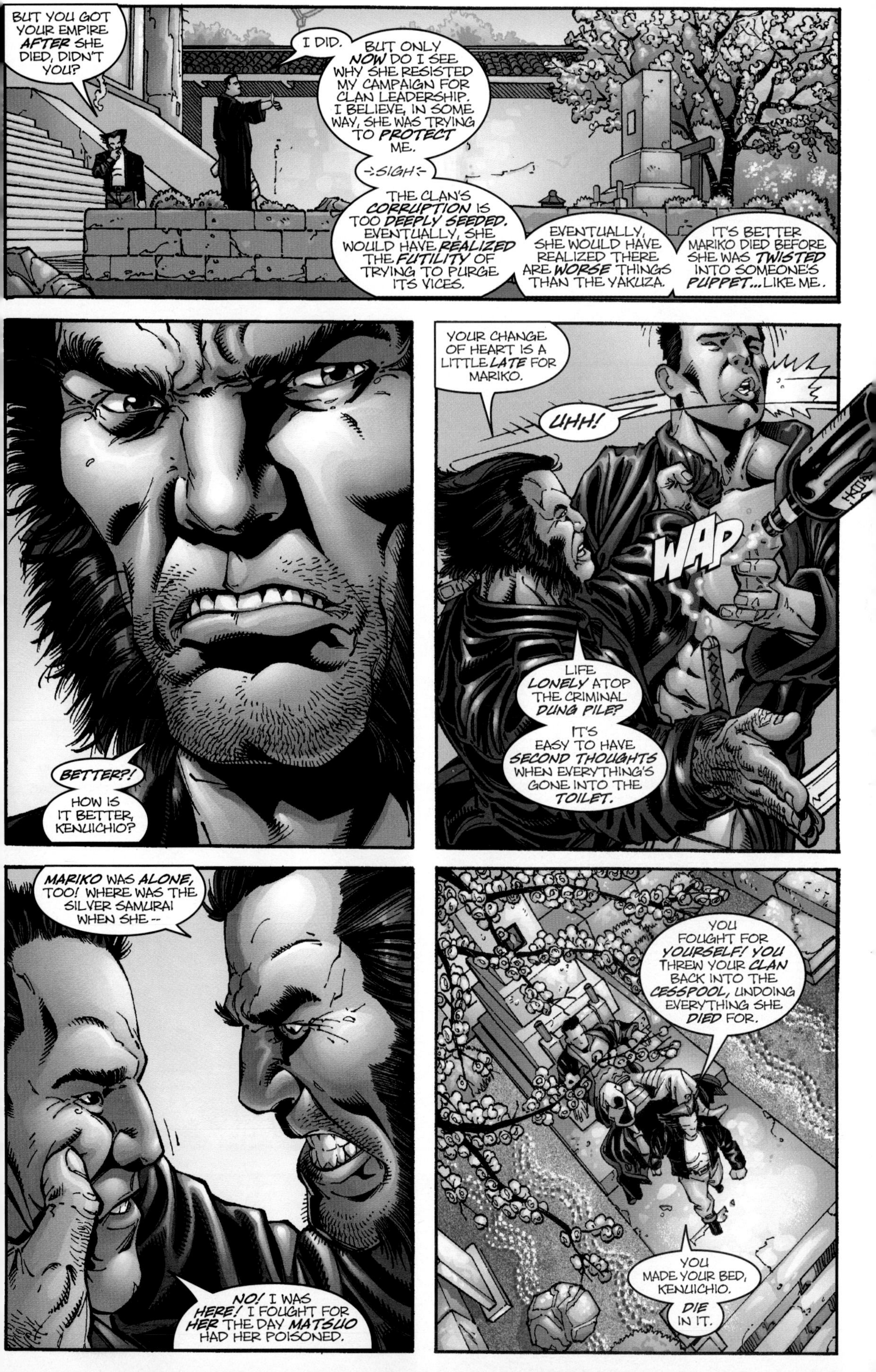

BUT YOU GOT YOUR EMPIRE AFTER SHE DIED, DIDN'T YOU?
I DID.
BUT ONLY NOW DO I SEE WHY SHE RESISTED MY CAMPAIGN FOR CLAN LEADERSHIP. I BELIEVE, IN SOME WAY, SHE WAS TRYING TO PROTECT ME.
-SIGH-
THE CLAN'S CORRUPTION IS TOO DEEPLY SEEDED. EVENTUALLY, SHE WOULD HAVE REALIZED THE FUTILITY OF TRYING TO PURGE ITS VICES.
EVENTUALLY, SHE WOULD HAVE REALIZED THERE ARE WORSE THINGS THAN THE YAKUZA.
IT'S BETTER MARIKO DIED BEFORE SHE WAS TWISTED INTO SOMEONE'S PUPPET...LIKE ME.
BETTER?!
HOW IS IT BETTER, KENUICHIO?
YOUR CHANGE OF HEART IS A LITTLE LATE FOR MARIKO.
UHH!
WAP
LIFE LONELY ATOP THE CRIMINAL DUNG PILE?
IT'S EASY TO HAVE SECOND THOUGHTS WHEN EVERYTHING'S GONE INTO THE TOILET.
MARIKO WAS ALONE, TOO! WHERE WAS THE SILVER SAMURAI WHEN SHE --
NO! I WAS HERE! I FOUGHT FOR HER THE DAY MATSUO HAD HER POISONED.
YOU FOUGHT FOR YOURSELF! YOU THREW YOUR CLAN BACK INTO THE CESSPOOL, UNDOING EVERYTHING SHE DIED FOR.
YOU MADE YOUR BED, KENUICHIO.
DIE IN IT.

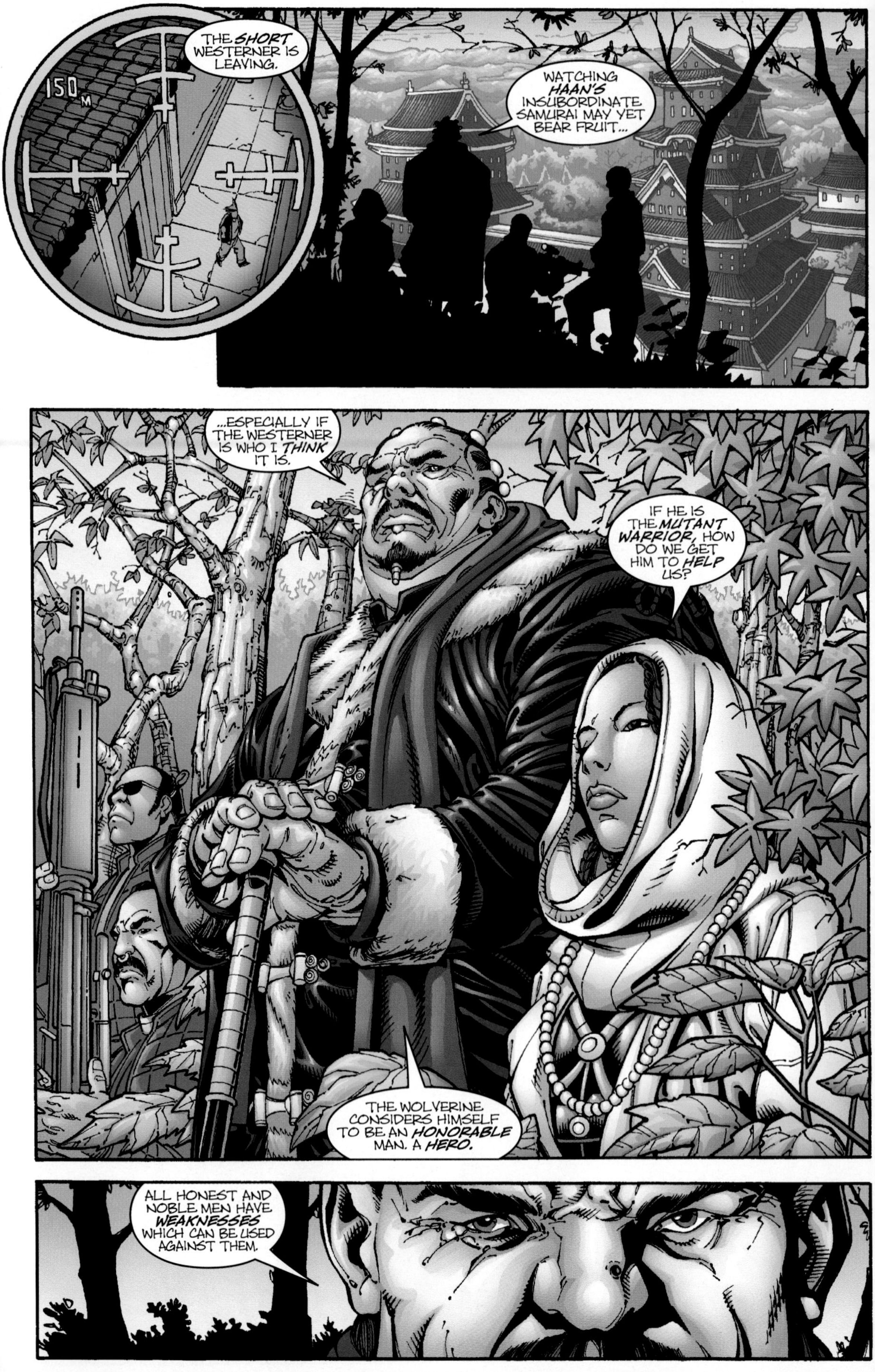
150 M
THE SHORT WESTERNER IS LEAVING.
WATCHING HAAN'S INSUBORDINATE SAMURAI MAY YET BEAR FRUIT...
...ESPECIALLY IF THE WESTERNER IS WHO I THINK IT IS.
IF HE IS THE MUTANT WARRIOR, HOW DO WE GET HIM TO HELP US?
THE WOLVERINE CONSIDERS HIMSELF TO BE AN HONORABLE MAN. A HERO.
ALL HONEST AND NOBLE MEN HAVE WEAKNESSES WHICH CAN BE USED AGAINST THEM.

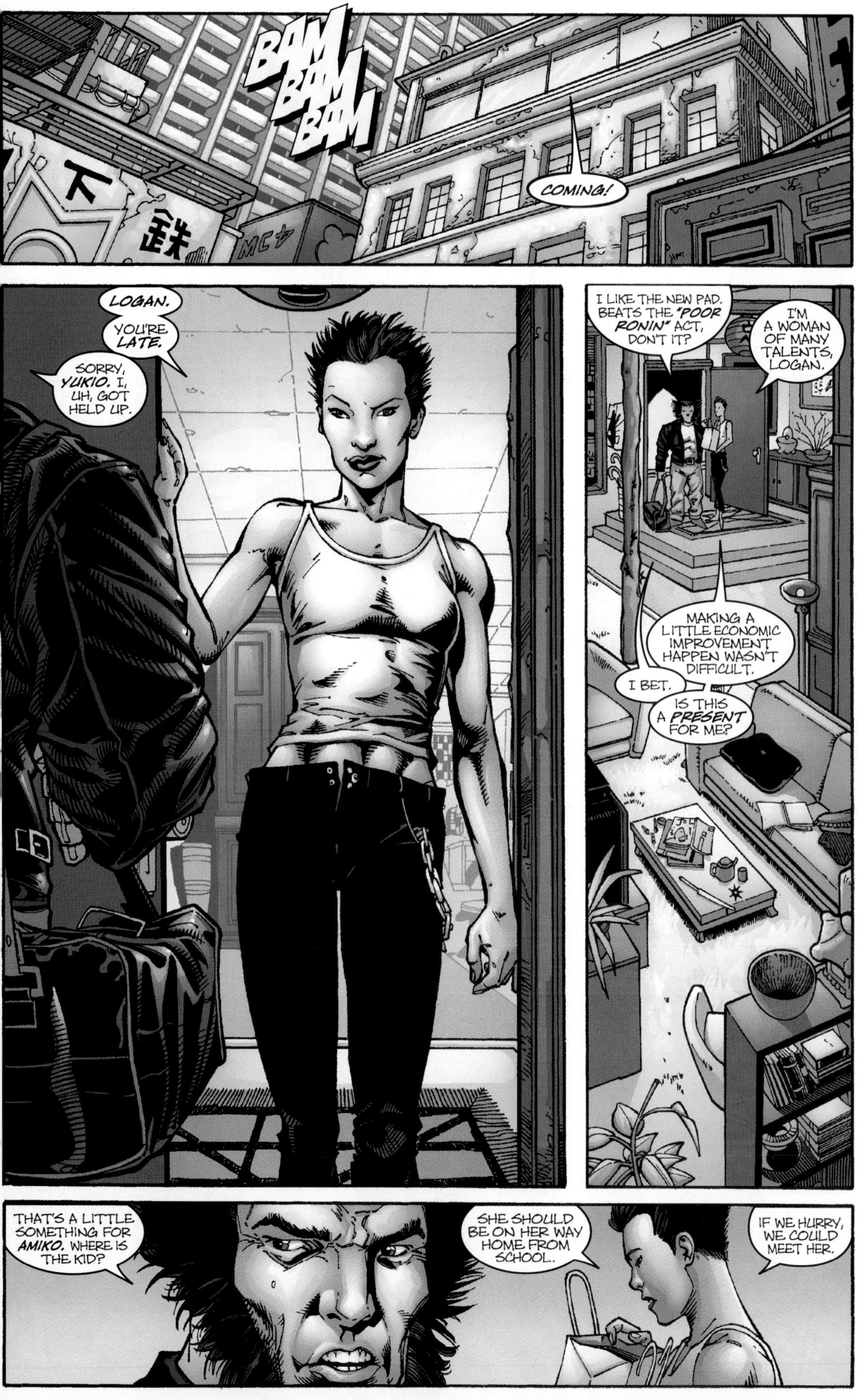
BAM BAM BAM
COMING!
LOGAN.
YOU'RE LATE.
SORRY, YUKIO. I, UH, GOT HELD UP.
I LIKE THE NEW PAD. BEATS THE "POOR RONIN" ACT, DON'T IT?
I'M A WOMAN OF MANY TALENTS, LOGAN.
MAKING A LITTLE ECONOMIC IMPROVEMENT HAPPEN WASN'T DIFFICULT.
I BET.
IS THIS A PRESENT FOR ME?
THAT'S A LITTLE SOMETHING FOR AMIKO. WHERE IS THE KID?
SHE SHOULD BE ON HER WAY HOME FROM SCHOOL.
IF WE HURRY, WE COULD MEET HER.

...LIFE IS GOOD, LOGAN. *BETTER* THAN I'D GUESSED IT WOULD BE AFTER YOU GAVE ME AMIKO TO LOOK AFTER.

WHO WOULD'VE THOUGHT THAT I HAVE MATERNAL INSTINCT AS WELL AS *KILLER* INSTINCT?

HEH.

YOU WON'T BELIEVE HOW MUCH AMIKO'S *CHANGED.* SHE'S REALLY COME OUT OF HER SHELL, LOTS OF FRIENDS. A FEW PROBLEMS WITH SOME BULLIES, BUT THAT WORKED ITSELF OUT.

GOOD... CAN'T WAIT TO SEE HER, I'VE BEEN AWAY TOO *LONG.*

JUST BE PREPARED FOR A LITTLE PREADOLESCENT ATTITUDE.

YEAH?

CAN YOU *BLAME* HER?

AFTER HER MOTHER DIED, SHE PUT YOU ON A PEDESTAL. YOU PROMISED TO WATCH OVER HER. I THINK YOUR LONG ABSENCES --

-- HAVE *HURT* HER. I WANTED TO SEE HER, BUT MY RESPONSIBILITIES TO THE *X-MEN* ALWAYS PULL ME AWAY.

"WE'RE JUST PULLIN' THROUGH SOME BAD TIMES.

"I...WASN'T MYSELF.

"*APOCALYPSE* TRANSFORMED ME INTO HIS *HORSEMAN OF DEATH,* BONDED ADAMANTIUM TO MY SKELETON TO MAKE ME UNSTOPPABLE AND UNBREAKABLE.

"I MANAGED TO SHATTER APOCALYPSE'S HOLD ON ME, BUT NOT BEFORE *CYCLOPS* GAVE HIS *LIFE* TO STOP HIM.

IT'S BEEN SIX MONTHS, YUKIO, BUT THE HURT -- AN' THE *GUILT* -- WON'T GO AWAY.

SUMMERS AN' I, WE NEVER SAW EYE TO EYE. BUT I *RESPECTED* HIM.

NOW HE'S GONE...AN' I'M NOT SURE IF I SHOULDN'T SHARE SOME O' THE *BLAME.*

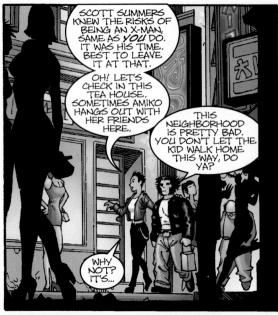

SCOTT SUMMERS KNEW THE RISKS OF BEING AN X-MAN, SAME AS *YOU* DO. IT WAS HIS TIME. BEST TO LEAVE IT AT THAT.

OH! LET'S CHECK IN THIS TEA HOUSE. SOMETIMES AMIKO HANGS OUT WITH HER FRIENDS HERE.

THIS NEIGHBORHOOD IS PRETTY BAD. YOU DON'T LET THE KID WALK HOME THIS WAY, DO YA?

WHY NOT? IT'S...

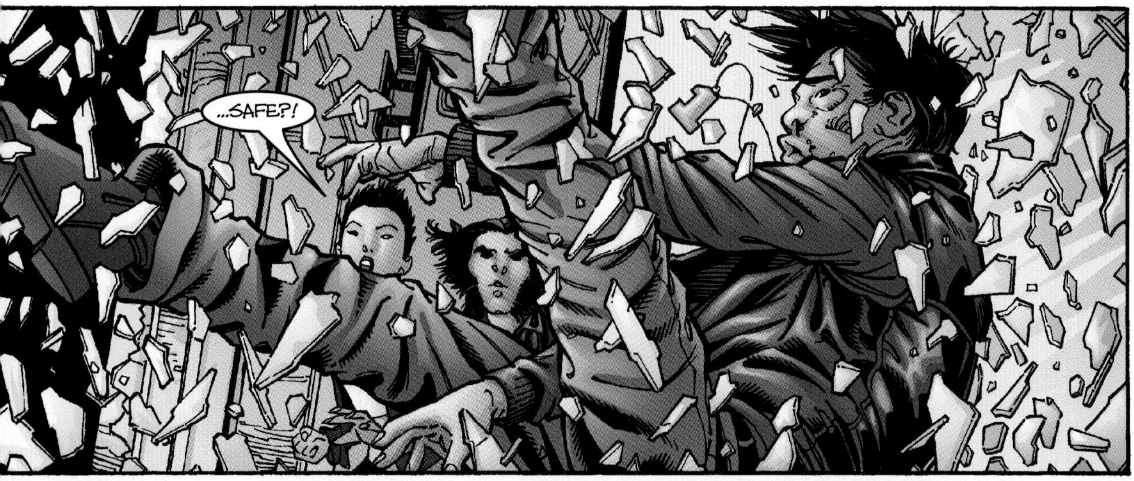
...SAFE?!

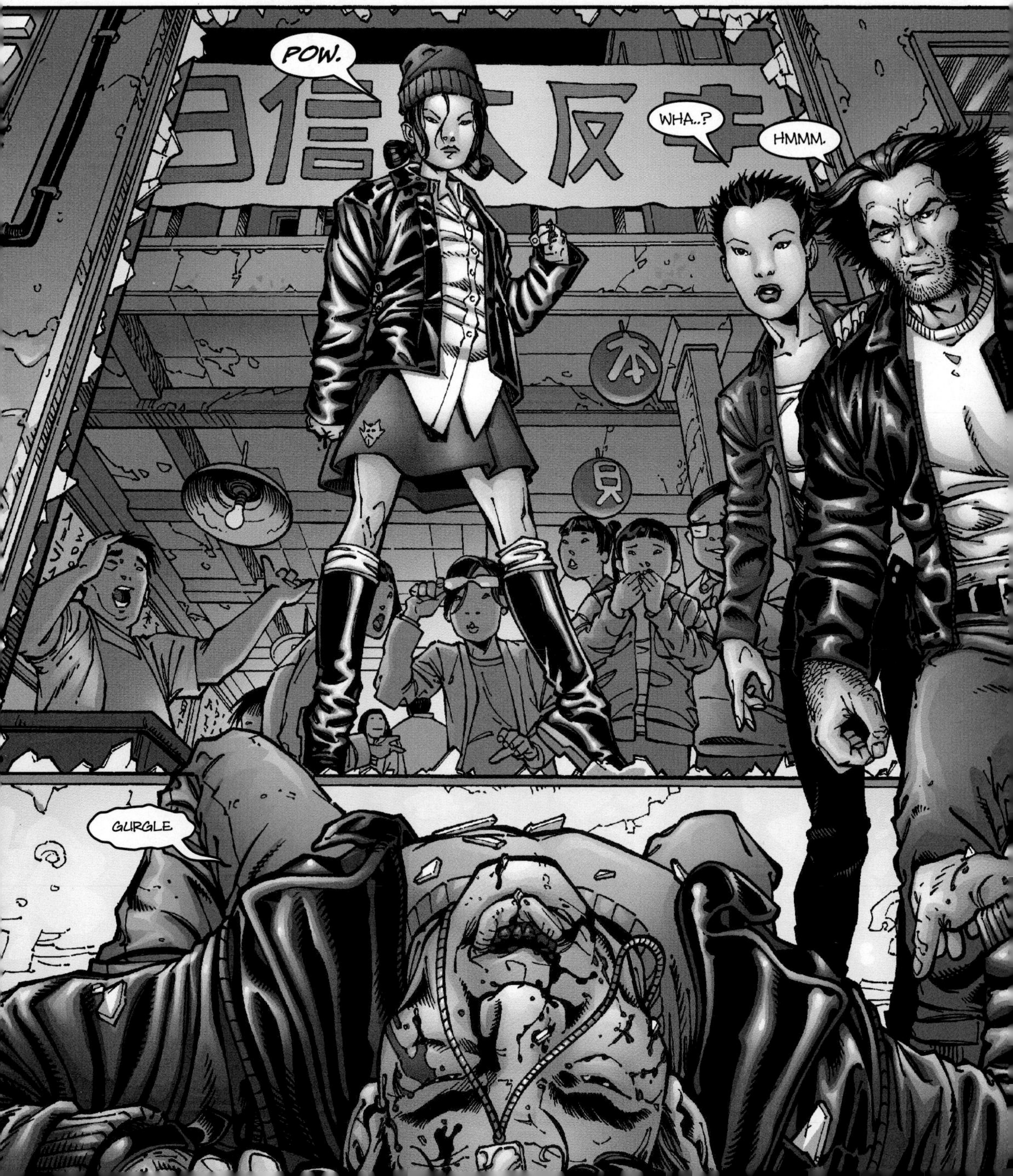
POW.
WHA..?
HMMM.
GURGLE

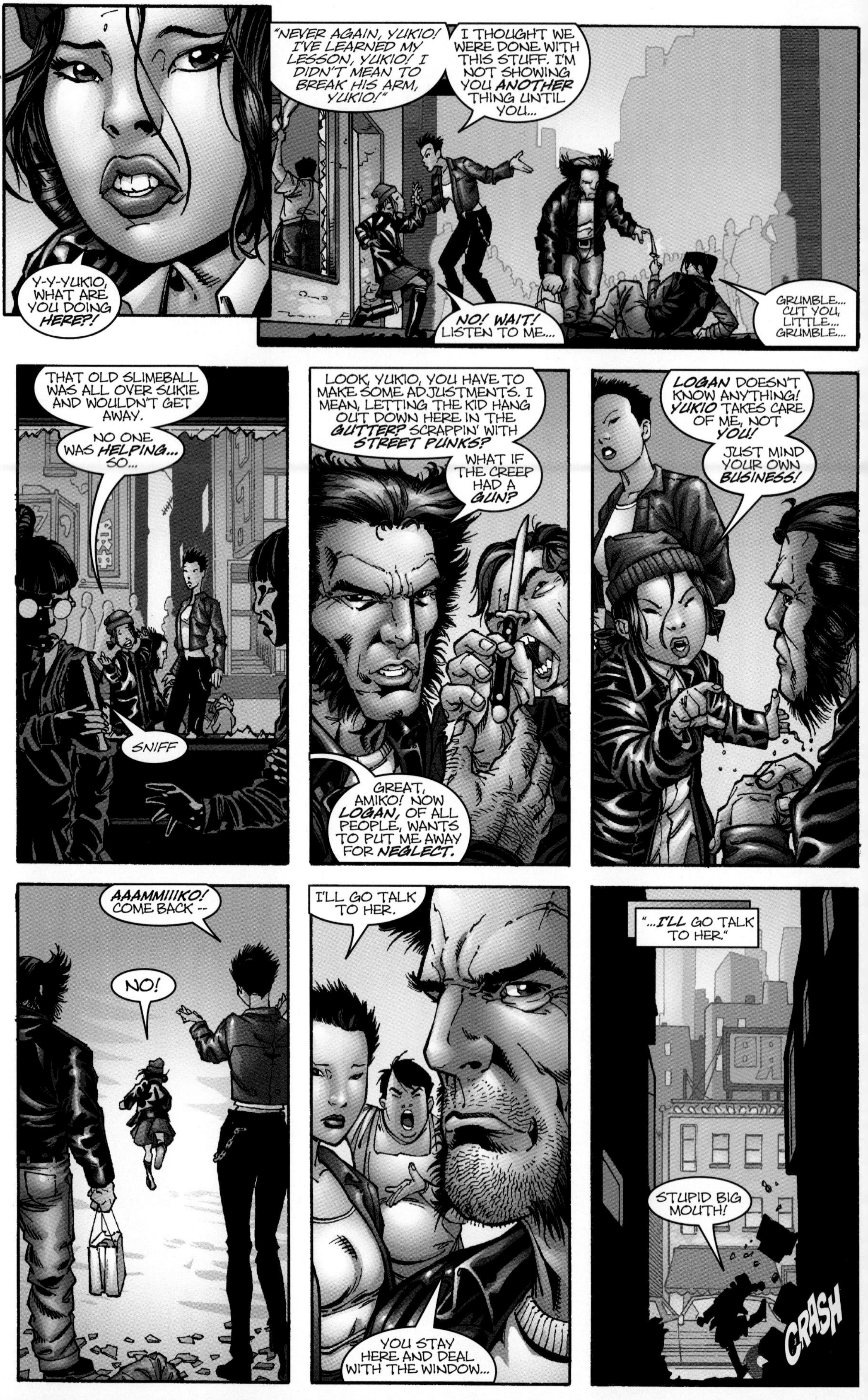
Y-Y-YUKIO, WHAT ARE YOU DOING HERE?!
"NEVER AGAIN, YUKIO! I'VE LEARNED MY LESSON, YUKIO! I DIDN'T MEAN TO BREAK HIS ARM, YUKIO!"
I THOUGHT WE WERE DONE WITH THIS STUFF. I'M NOT SHOWING YOU ANOTHER THING UNTIL YOU...
NO! WAIT! LISTEN TO ME...
GRUMBLE... CUT YOU, LITTLE... GRUMBLE...
THAT OLD SLIMEBALL WAS ALL OVER SUKIE AND WOULDN'T GET AWAY.
NO ONE WAS HELPING... SO...
SNIFF
LOOK, YUKIO, YOU HAVE TO MAKE SOME ADJUSTMENTS. I MEAN, LETTING THE KID HANG OUT DOWN HERE IN THE GUTTER? SCRAPPIN' WITH STREET PUNKS?
WHAT IF THE CREEP HAD A GUN?
GREAT, AMIKO! NOW LOGAN, OF ALL PEOPLE, WANTS TO PUT ME AWAY FOR NEGLECT.
LOGAN DOESN'T KNOW ANYTHING! YUKIO TAKES CARE OF ME, NOT YOU!
JUST MIND YOUR OWN BUSINESS!
AAAMMIIIKO! COME BACK --
NO!
I'LL GO TALK TO HER.
YOU STAY HERE AND DEAL WITH THE WINDOW...
"...I'LL GO TALK TO HER."
STUPID BIG MOUTH!
CRASH

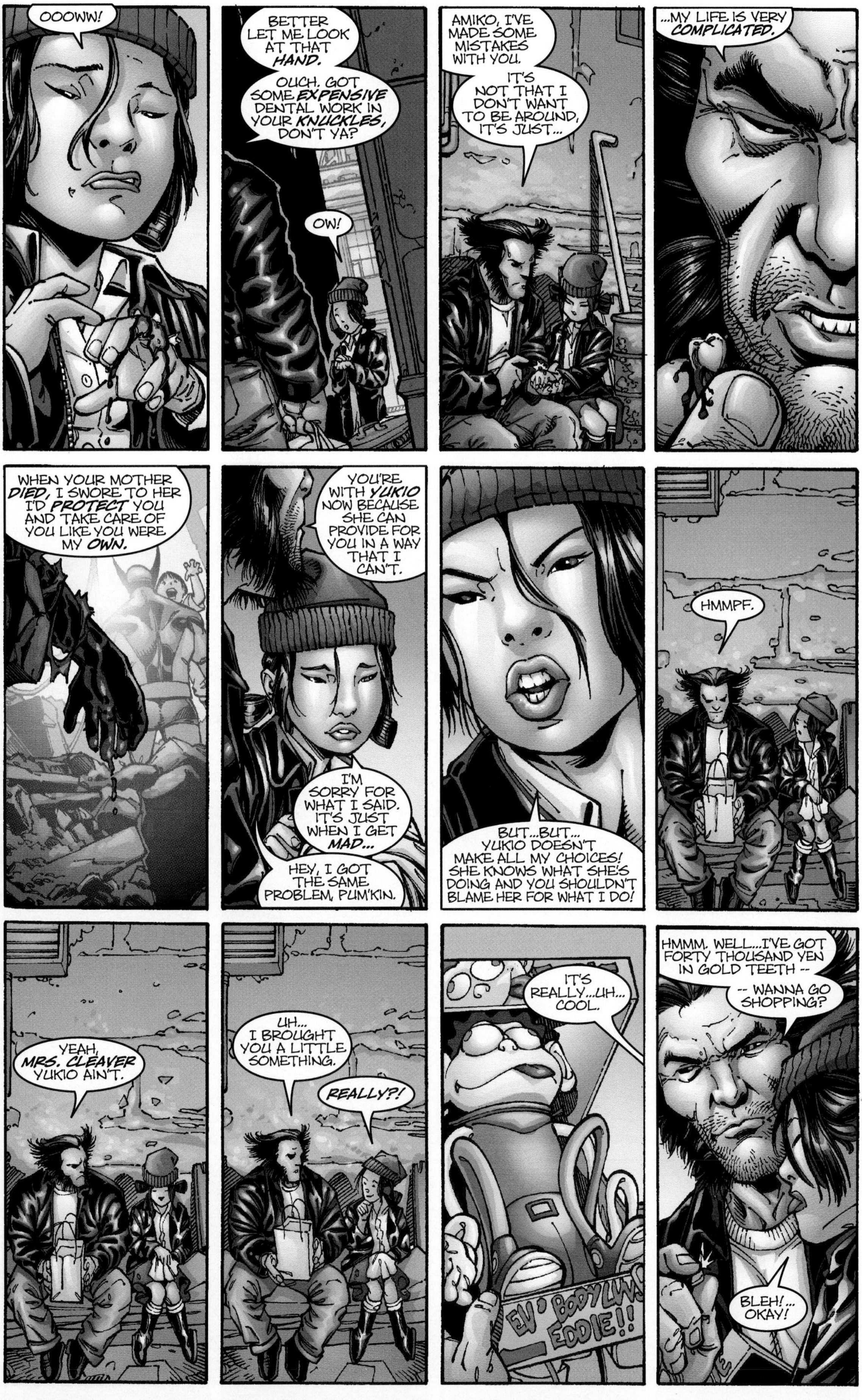
OOOWW!
BETTER LET ME LOOK AT THAT HAND.
OUCH. GOT SOME EXPENSIVE DENTAL WORK IN YOUR KNUCKLES, DON'T YA?
OW!
AMIKO, I'VE MADE SOME MISTAKES WITH YOU.
IT'S NOT THAT I DON'T WANT TO BE AROUND, IT'S JUST...
...MY LIFE IS VERY COMPLICATED.
WHEN YOUR MOTHER DIED, I SWORE TO HER I'D PROTECT YOU AND TAKE CARE OF YOU LIKE YOU WERE MY OWN.
YOU'RE WITH YUKIO NOW BECAUSE SHE CAN PROVIDE FOR YOU IN A WAY THAT I CAN'T.
I'M SORRY FOR WHAT I SAID. IT'S JUST WHEN I GET MAD...
HEY, I GOT THE SAME PROBLEM, PUM'KIN.
BUT...BUT... YUKIO DOESN'T MAKE ALL MY CHOICES! SHE KNOWS WHAT SHE'S DOING AND YOU SHOULDN'T BLAME HER FOR WHAT I DO!
HMMPF.
YEAH, MRS. CLEAVER YUKIO AIN'T.
UH... I BROUGHT YOU A LITTLE SOMETHING.
REALLY?!
IT'S REALLY...UH... COOL.
EV' BODY LUVS EDDIE!!
HMMM. WELL...I'VE GOT FORTY THOUSAND YEN IN GOLD TEETH --
-- WANNA GO SHOPPING?
BLEH!... OKAY!

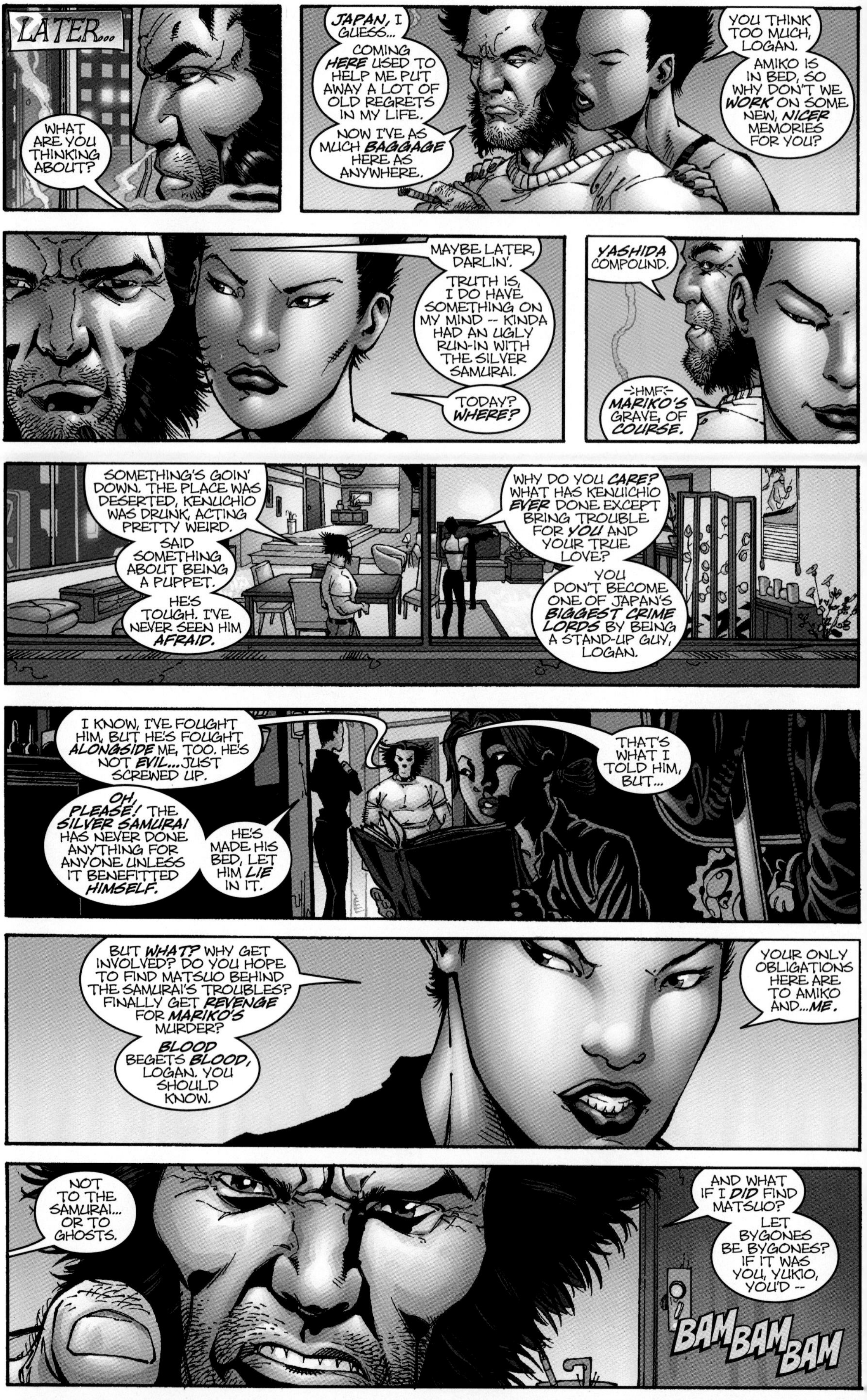
LATER...
WHAT ARE YOU THINKING ABOUT?
JAPAN, I GUESS... COMING HERE USED TO HELP ME PUT AWAY A LOT OF OLD REGRETS IN MY LIFE.
NOW I'VE AS MUCH BAGGAGE HERE AS ANYWHERE.
YOU THINK TOO MUCH, LOGAN.
AMIKO IS IN BED, SO WHY DON'T WE WORK ON SOME NEW, NICER MEMORIES FOR YOU?
MAYBE LATER, DARLIN'.
TRUTH IS, I DO HAVE SOMETHING ON MY MIND -- KINDA HAD AN UGLY RUN-IN WITH THE SILVER SAMURAI.
TODAY? WHERE?
YASHIDA COMPOUND.
-HMF- MARIKO'S GRAVE, OF COURSE.
SOMETHING'S GOIN' DOWN. THE PLACE WAS DESERTED, KENUCHIO WAS DRUNK, ACTING PRETTY WEIRD.
SAID SOMETHING ABOUT BEING A PUPPET.
HE'S TOUGH. I'VE NEVER SEEN HIM AFRAID.
WHY DO YOU CARE? WHAT HAS KENUICHIO EVER DONE EXCEPT BRING TROUBLE FOR YOU AND YOUR TRUE LOVE?
YOU DON'T BECOME ONE OF JAPAN'S BIGGEST CRIME LORDS BY BEING A STAND-UP GUY, LOGAN.
I KNOW, I'VE FOUGHT HIM, BUT HE'S FOUGHT ALONGSIDE ME, TOO. HE'S NOT EVIL... JUST SCREWED UP.
OH, PLEASE! THE SILVER SAMURAI HAS NEVER DONE ANYTHING FOR ANYONE UNLESS IT BENEFITTED HIMSELF.
HE'S MADE HIS BED, LET HIM LIE IN IT.
THAT'S WHAT I TOLD HIM, BUT...
BUT WHAT? WHY GET INVOLVED? DO YOU HOPE TO FIND MATSUO BEHIND THE SAMURAI'S TROUBLES? FINALLY GET REVENGE FOR MARIKO'S MURDER?
BLOOD BEGETS BLOOD, LOGAN. YOU SHOULD KNOW.
YOUR ONLY OBLIGATIONS HERE ARE TO AMIKO AND...ME.
NOT TO THE SAMURAI... OR TO GHOSTS.
AND WHAT IF I DID FIND MATSUO?
LET BYGONES BE BYGONES? IF IT WAS YOU, YUKIO, YOU'D --
BAM BAM BAM

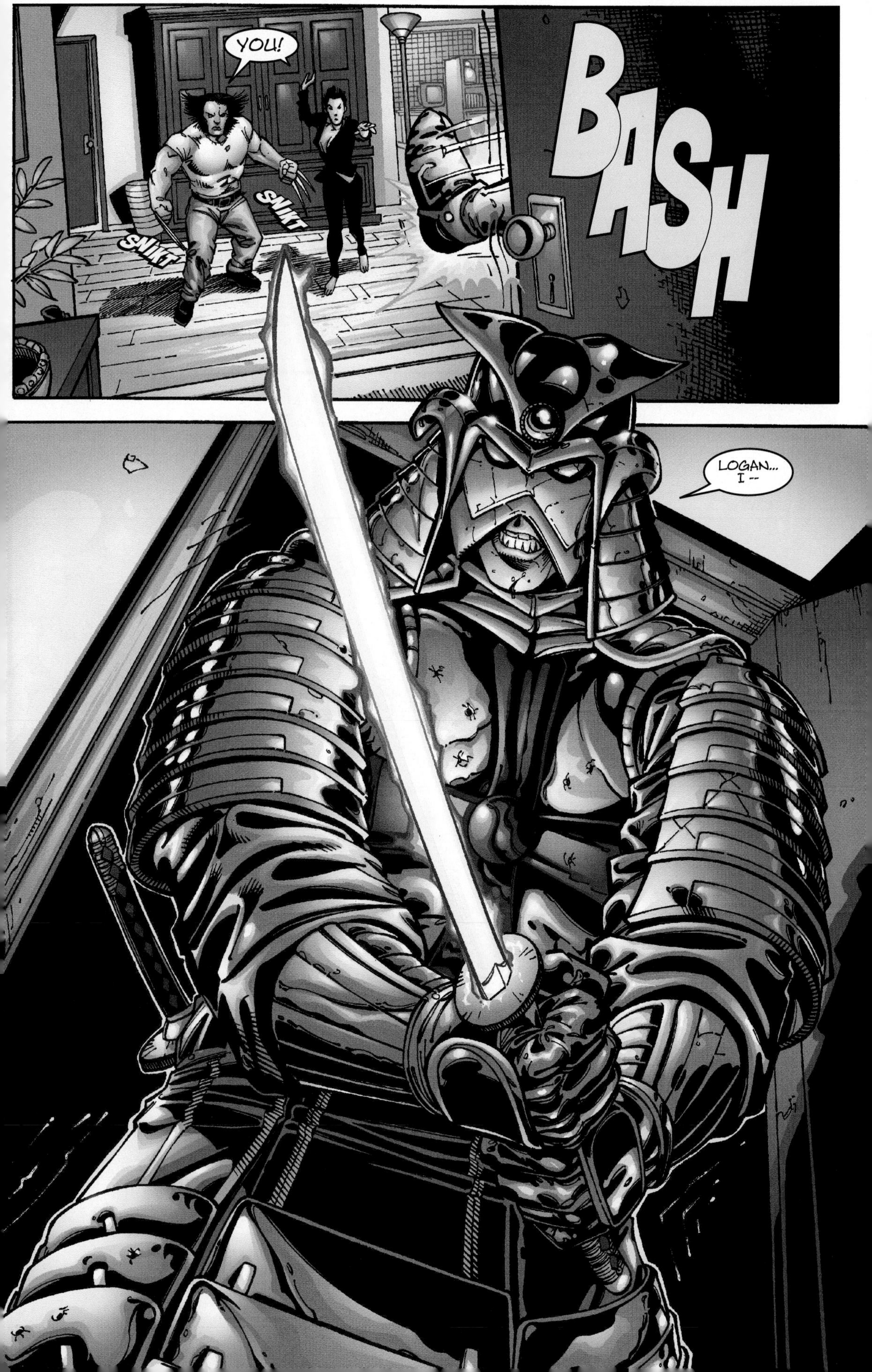
YOU!
SNIKT
SNIKT
BASH
LOGAN... I --

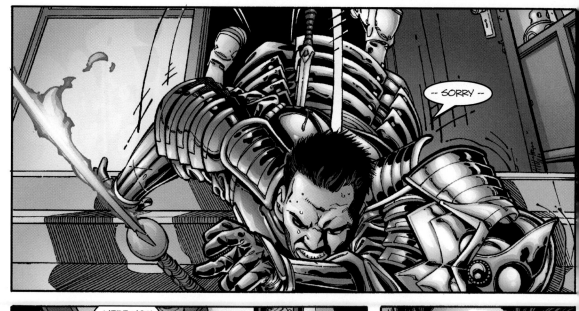

-- SORRY --

WERE YOU FOLLOWED?

N-NO, I WAS CAREFUL.

THE WOUND ISN'T VERY *DEEP* -- YOUR ARMOR STOPPED MOST OF IT.

YOU'RE A *WIMP,* KENUICHIO. *AMIKO!* GET THE FIRST AID KIT.

-- NOWHERE ELSE TO *GO*...

DON'T WORRY, KENUICHIO, LOGAN WAS *DYING* TO SEE YOU...

HIS NAME IS *HAAN KAISHEK* -- THE NEW LEADER OF THE *OLDEST* AND MOST *POWERFUL* CLAN EVER TO COME OUT OF OUTER *MONGOLIA.*

THE KAISHEK'S CRIMINAL DOMINION EXTENDS THROUGHOUT *ASIA, EASTERN EUROPE* AND NOW, THANKS TO ME...*JAPAN.*

SHINGEN DEFENDED CLAN YASHIDA'S TERRITORIES FROM HAAN'S FATHER FOR YEARS... I PROVED TO BE MUCH EASIER TO OVERTHROW.

HAAN *SPARED* ME SO I COULD HELP EASE IN HIS CONTROL OF THE CLAN'S INTERESTS.

THE IDEA OF HAVING *LORD SHINGEN'S* MUTANT SON FOR A HENCHMAN AMUSED HIM.

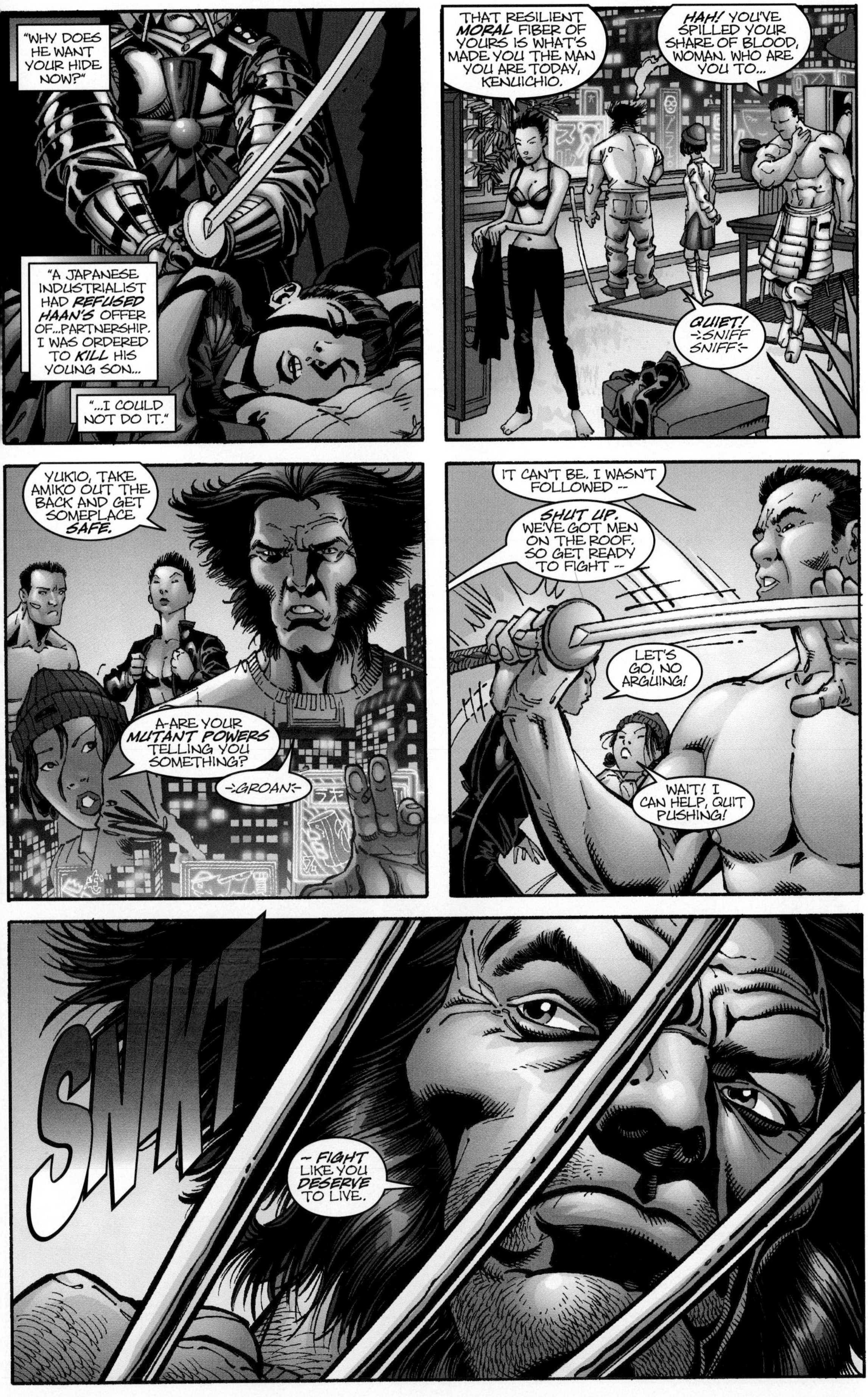
"WHY DOES HE WANT YOUR HIDE NOW?"
"A JAPANESE INDUSTRIALIST HAD REFUSED HAAN'S OFFER OF...PARTNERSHIP. I WAS ORDERED TO KILL HIS YOUNG SON...
"...I COULD NOT DO IT."
THAT RESILIENT MORAL FIBER OF YOURS IS WHAT'S MADE YOU THE MAN YOU ARE TODAY, KENUICHIO.
HAH! YOU'VE SPILLED YOUR SHARE OF BLOOD, WOMAN. WHO ARE YOU TO...
QUIET! -SNIFF SNIFF-
YUKIO, TAKE AMIKO OUT THE BACK AND GET SOMEPLACE SAFE.
A-ARE YOUR MUTANT POWERS TELLING YOU SOMETHING?
-GROAN-
IT CAN'T BE. I WASN'T FOLLOWED --
SHUT UP. WE'VE GOT MEN ON THE ROOF, SO GET READY TO FIGHT --
LET'S GO, NO ARGUING!
WAIT! I CAN HELP, QUIT PUSHING!
SNIKT
-- FIGHT LIKE YOU DESERVE TO LIVE.

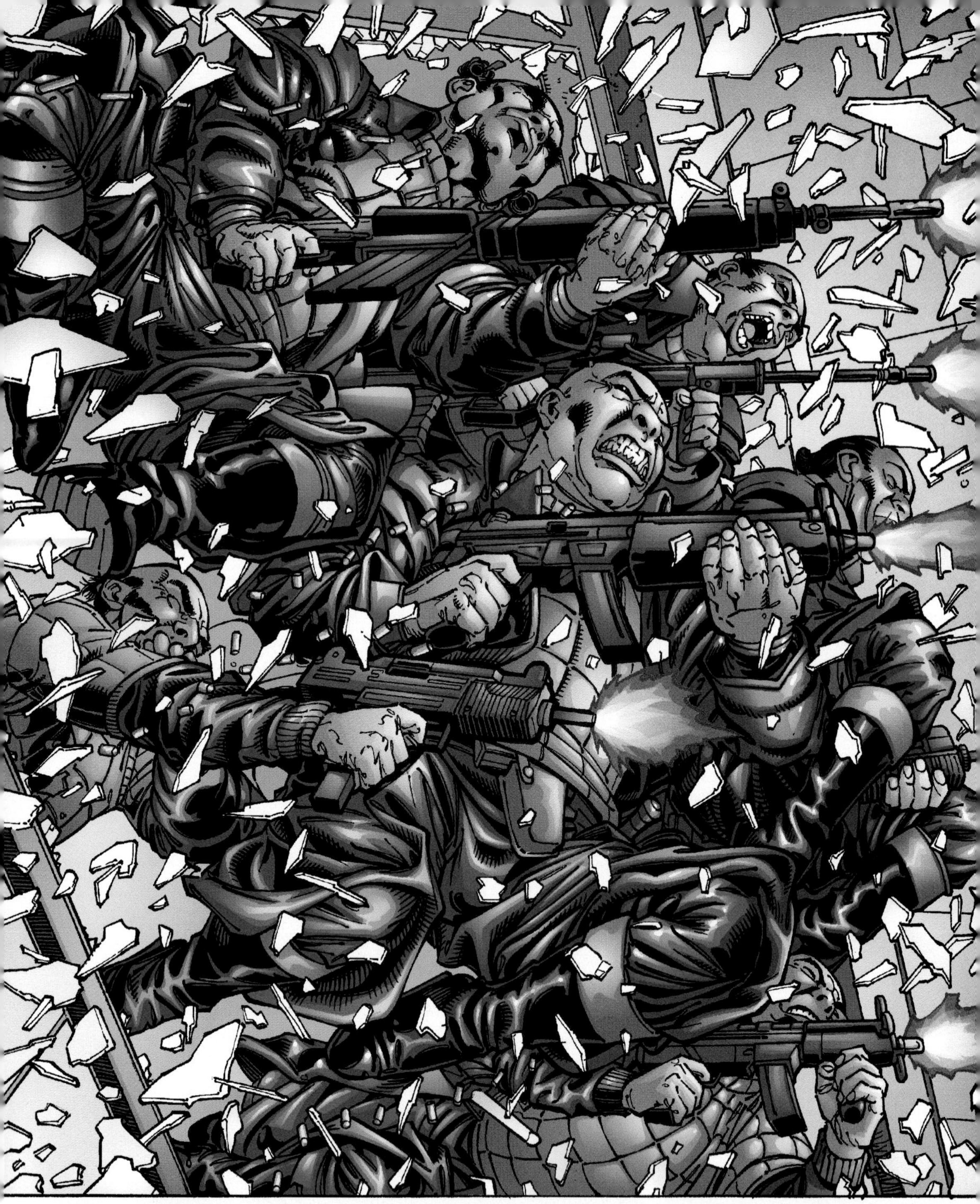

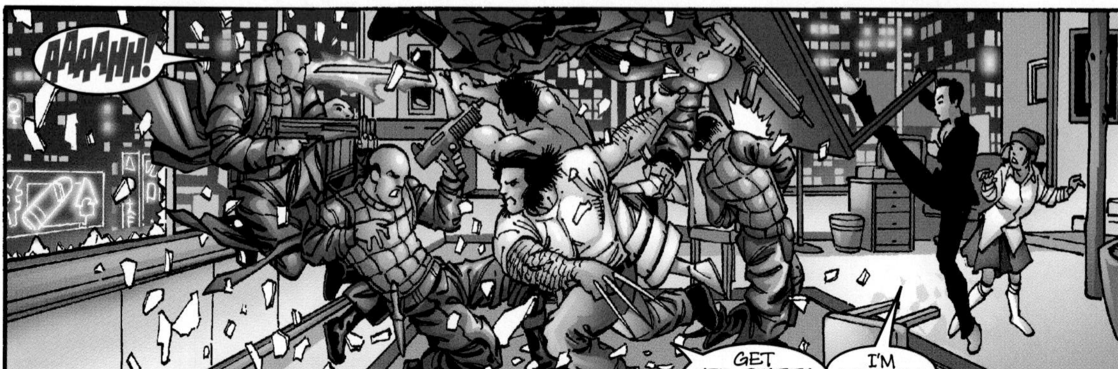
AAAAHH!
GET HER OUTTA HERE, YUKIO!
I'M TRYING!

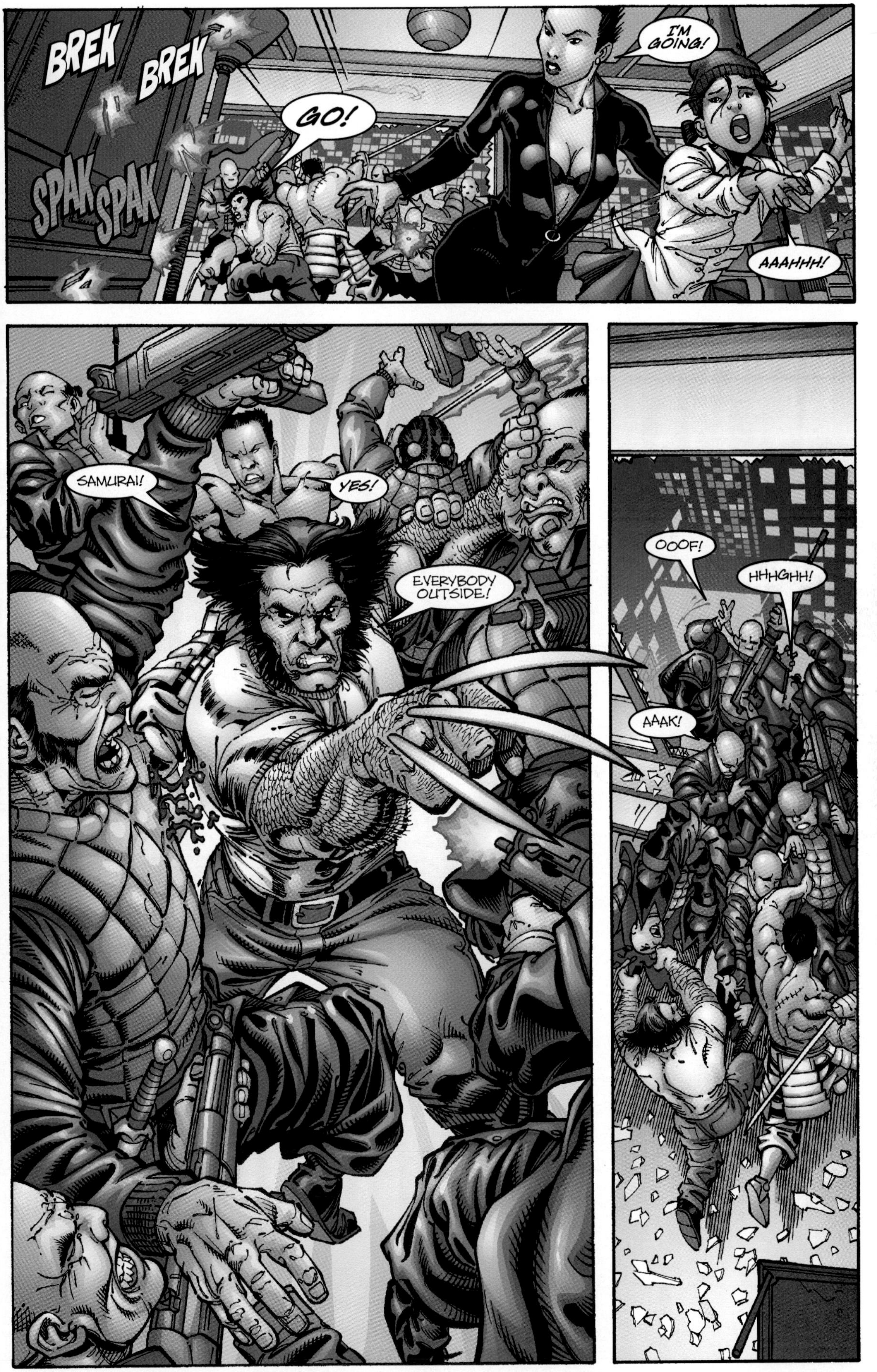
BREK
BREK
SPAK SPAK
GO!
I'M GOING!
AAAHHH!
SAMURAI!
YES!
EVERYBODY OUTSIDE!
OOOF!
HHHGHH!
AAAK!

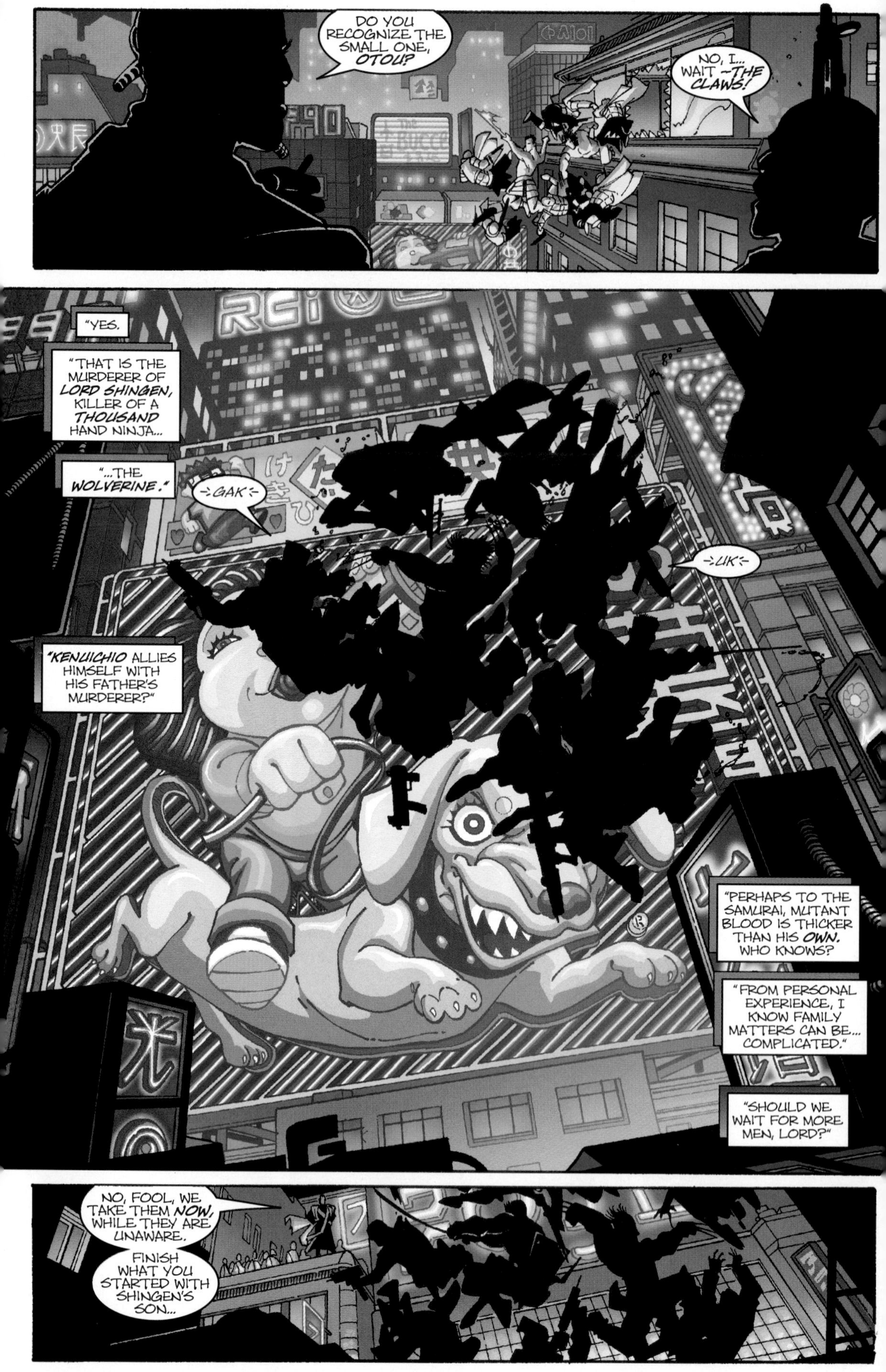
DO YOU RECOGNIZE THE SMALL ONE, OTOU?
NO, I... WAIT --THE CLAWS!
"YES.
"THAT IS THE MURDERER OF LORD SHINGEN, KILLER OF A THOUSAND HAND NINJA...
"...THE WOLVERINE."
GAK
UK
"KENUICHIO ALLIES HIMSELF WITH HIS FATHER'S MURDERER?"
"PERHAPS TO THE SAMURAI, MUTANT BLOOD IS THICKER THAN HIS OWN. WHO KNOWS?
"FROM PERSONAL EXPERIENCE, I KNOW FAMILY MATTERS CAN BE... COMPLICATED."
"SHOULD WE WAIT FOR MORE MEN, LORD?"
NO, FOOL, WE TAKE THEM NOW, WHILE THEY ARE UNAWARE.
FINISH WHAT YOU STARTED WITH SHINGEN'S SON...

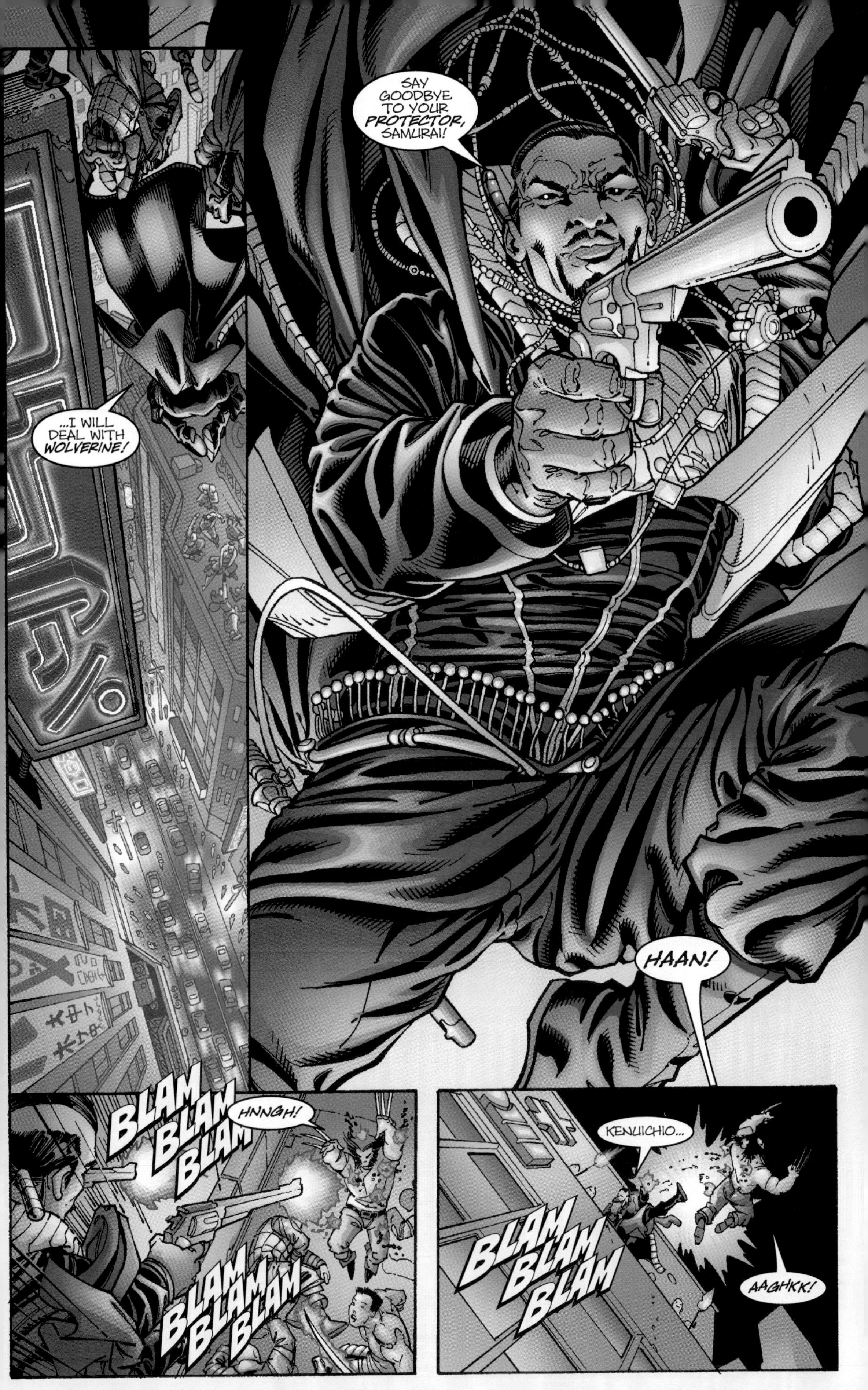
SAY GOODBYE TO YOUR PROTECTOR, SAMURAI!
...I WILL DEAL WITH WOLVERINE!
HAAN!
BLAM BLAM BLAM
HNNGH!
BLAM BLAM BLAM
KENUICHIO...
BLAM BLAM BLAM
AAGHKK!

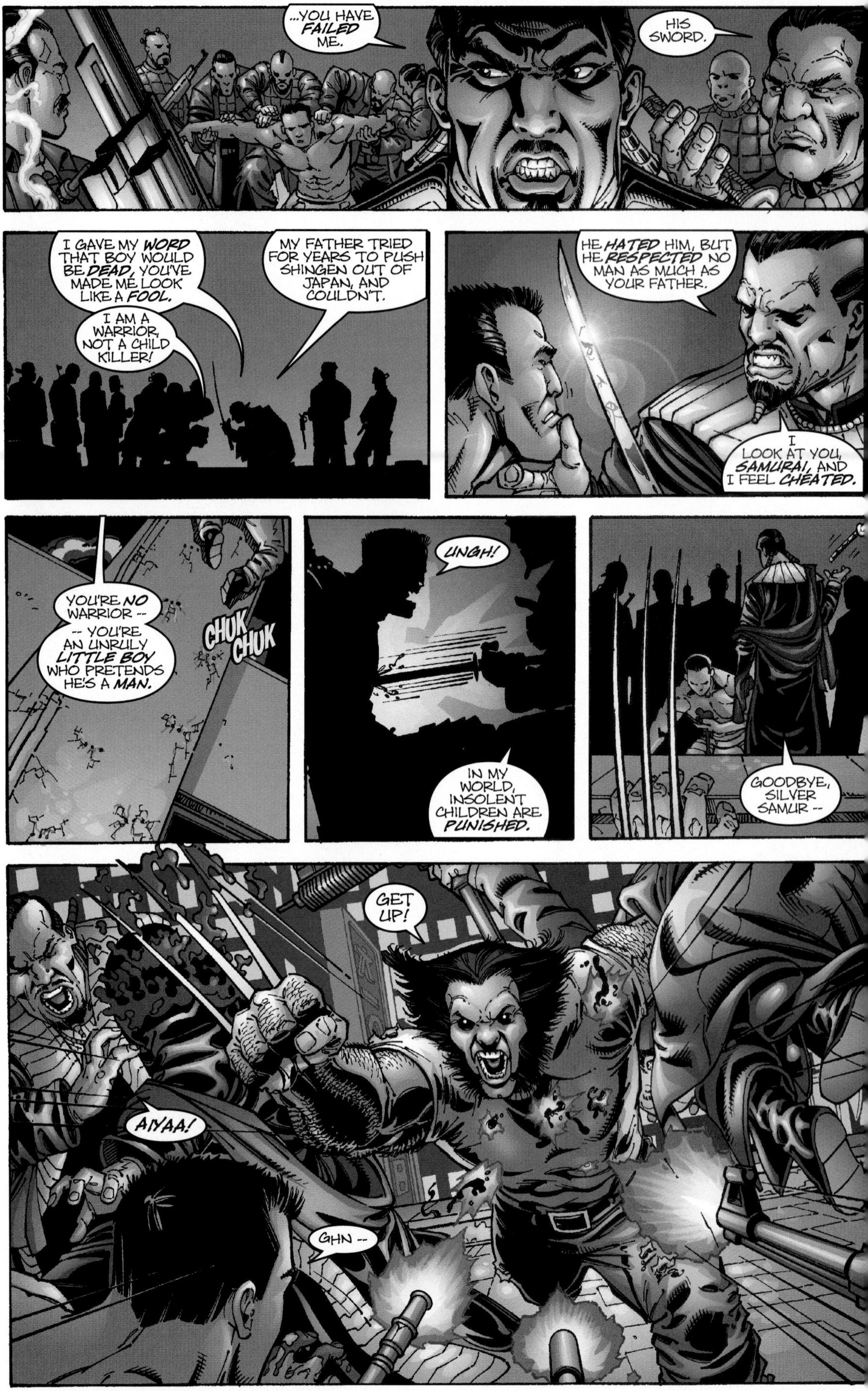
...YOU HAVE FAILED ME.
HIS SWORD.
I GAVE MY WORD THAT BOY WOULD BE DEAD, YOU'VE MADE ME LOOK LIKE A FOOL.
I AM A WARRIOR, NOT A CHILD KILLER!
MY FATHER TRIED FOR YEARS TO PUSH SHINGEN OUT OF JAPAN, AND COULDN'T.
HE HATED HIM, BUT HE RESPECTED NO MAN AS MUCH AS YOUR FATHER.
I LOOK AT YOU, SAMURAI, AND I FEEL CHEATED.
YOU'RE NO WARRIOR --
-- YOU'RE AN UNRULY LITTLE BOY WHO PRETENDS HE'S A MAN.
CHUK CHUK
UNGH!
IN MY WORLD, INSOLENT CHILDREN ARE PUNISHED.
GOODBYE, SILVER SAMUR --
GET UP!
AIYAA!
GHN --

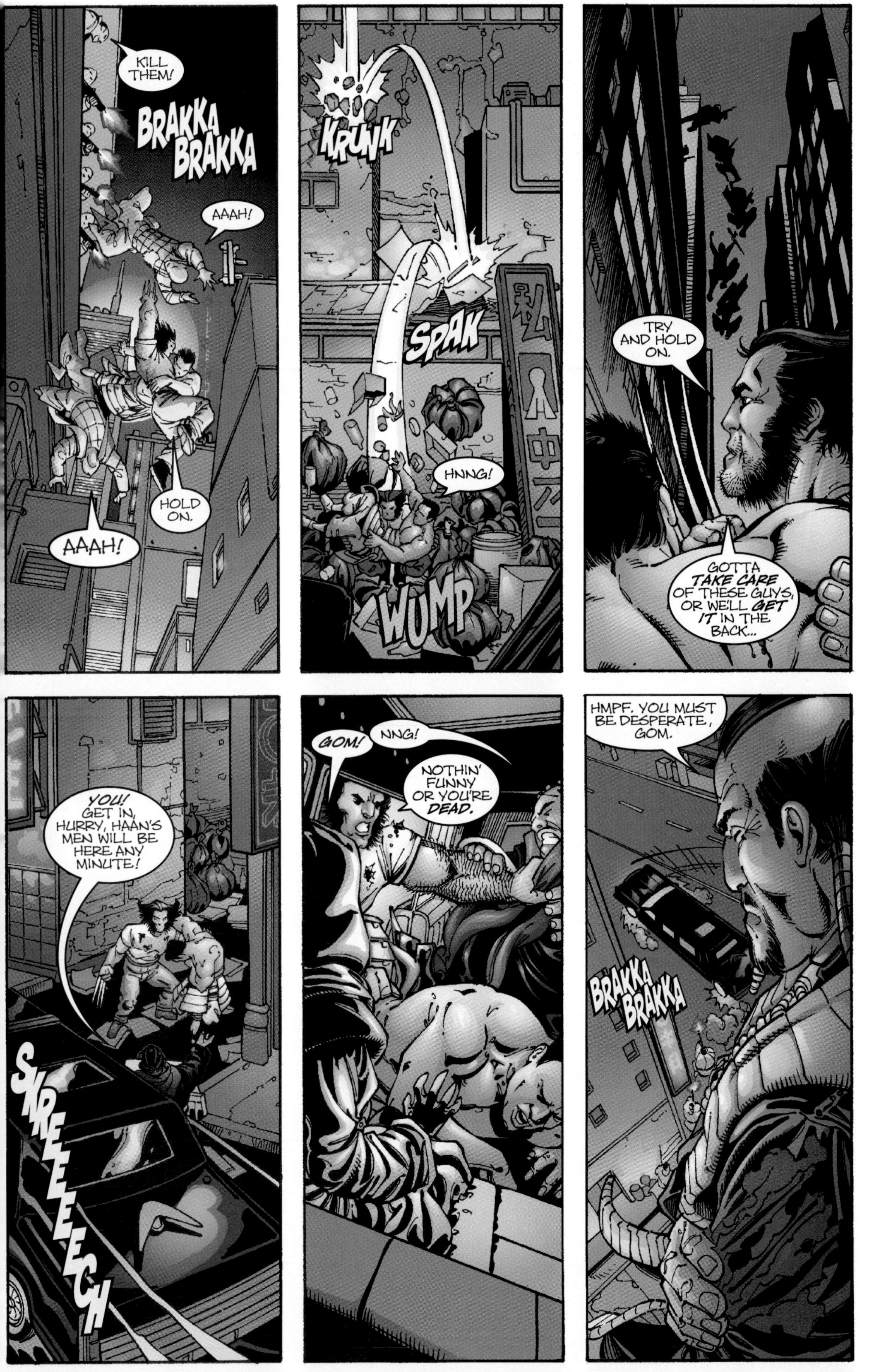
KILL THEM!
BRAKKA BRAKKA
AAAH!
HOLD ON.
AAAH!
KRUNK
SPAK
HNNG!
WUMP
TRY AND HOLD ON.
GOTTA TAKE CARE OF THESE GUYS, OR WE'LL GET IT IN THE BACK...
YOU! GET IN, HURRY, HAAN'S MEN WILL BE HERE ANY MINUTE!
SKREEEEECH
GOM!
NNG!
NOTHIN' FUNNY OR YOU'RE DEAD.
HMPF. YOU MUST BE DESPERATE, GOM.
BRAKKA BRAKKA

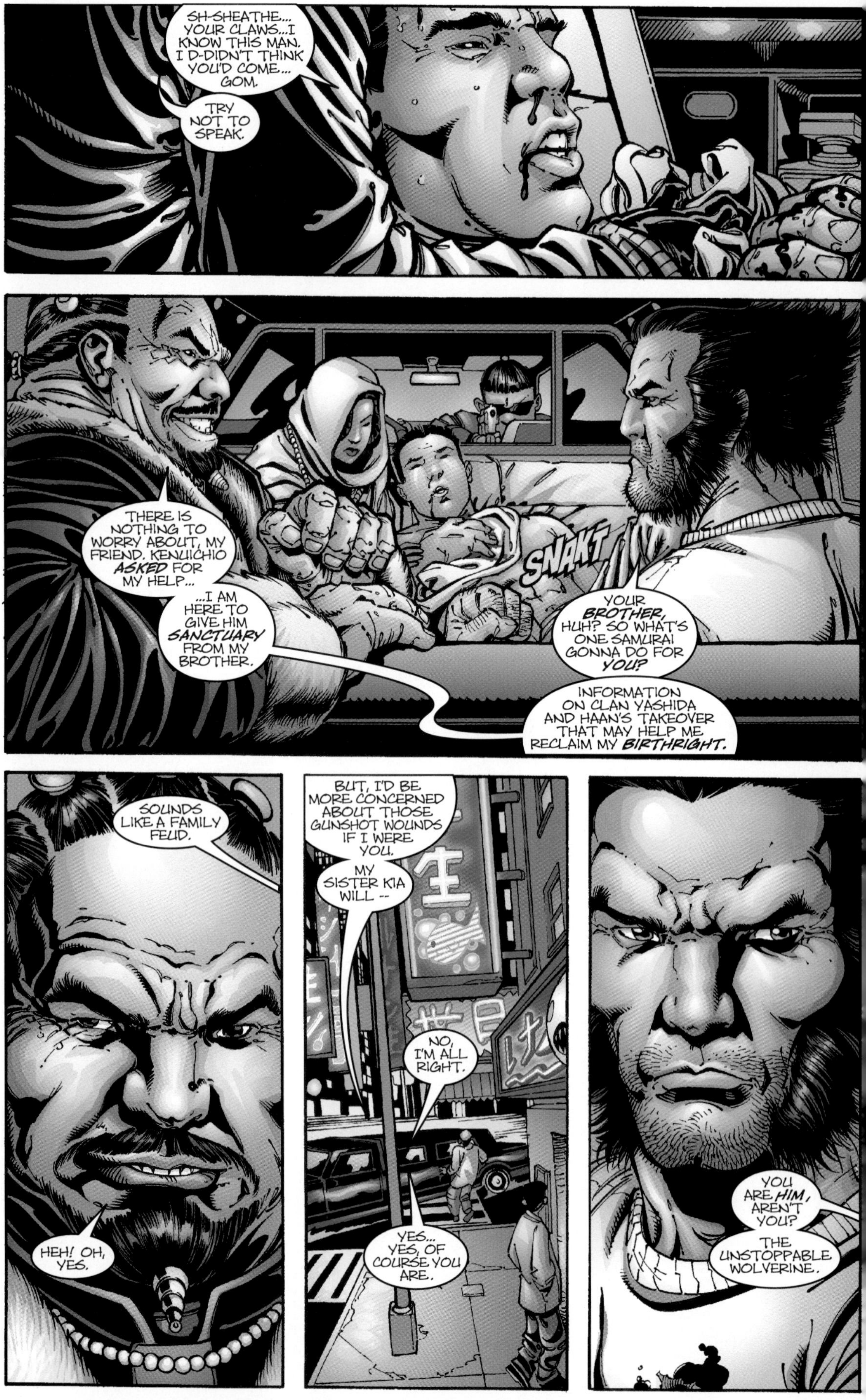
SH-SHEATHE... YOUR CLAWS...I KNOW THIS MAN. I D-DIDN'T THINK YOU'D COME... GOM.
TRY NOT TO SPEAK.
THERE IS NOTHING TO WORRY ABOUT, MY FRIEND. KENUICHIO ASKED FOR MY HELP...
...I AM HERE TO GIVE HIM SANCTUARY FROM MY BROTHER.
SNAKT
YOUR BROTHER, HUH? SO WHAT'S ONE SAMURAI GONNA DO FOR YOU?
INFORMATION ON CLAN YASHIDA AND HAAN'S TAKEOVER THAT MAY HELP ME RECLAIM MY BIRTHRIGHT.
SOUNDS LIKE A FAMILY FEUD.
HEH! OH, YES.
BUT, I'D BE MORE CONCERNED ABOUT THOSE GUNSHOT WOUNDS IF I WERE YOU.
MY SISTER KIA WILL --
NO, I'M ALL RIGHT.
YES... YES, OF COURSE YOU ARE.
YOU ARE HIM, AREN'T YOU?
THE UNSTOPPABLE WOLVERINE.

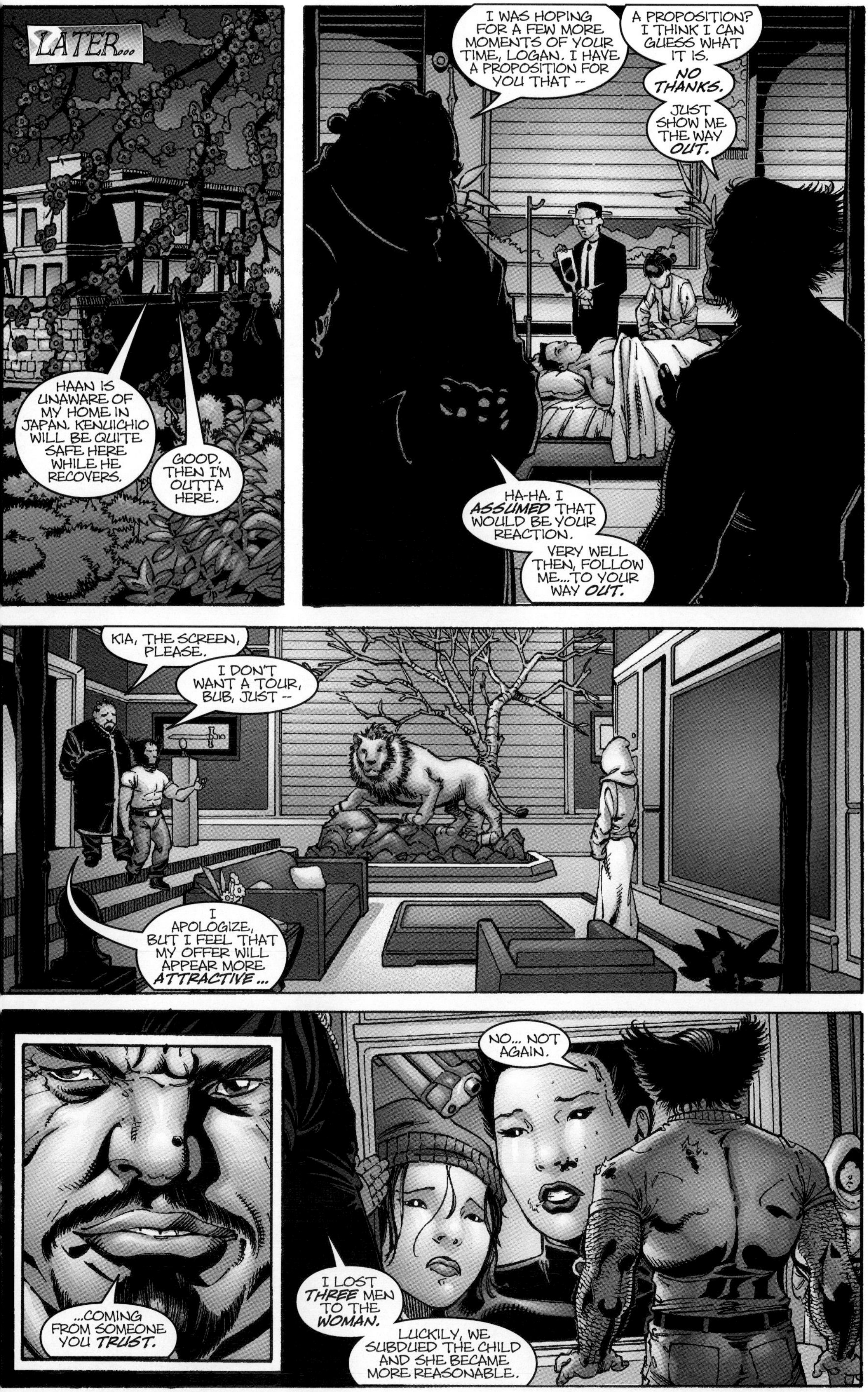
LATER...
HAAN IS UNAWARE OF MY HOME IN JAPAN. KENUICHIO WILL BE QUITE SAFE HERE WHILE HE RECOVERS.
GOOD. THEN I'M OUTTA HERE.
I WAS HOPING FOR A FEW MORE MOMENTS OF YOUR TIME, LOGAN. I HAVE A PROPOSITION FOR YOU THAT --
A PROPOSITION? I THINK I CAN GUESS WHAT IT IS. NO THANKS.
JUST SHOW ME THE WAY OUT.
HA-HA. I ASSUMED THAT WOULD BE YOUR REACTION.
VERY WELL THEN, FOLLOW ME...TO YOUR WAY OUT.
KIA, THE SCREEN, PLEASE.
I DON'T WANT A TOUR, BUB, JUST --
I APOLOGIZE, BUT I FEEL THAT MY OFFER WILL APPEAR MORE ATTRACTIVE ...
...COMING FROM SOMEONE YOU TRUST.
NO... NOT AGAIN.
I LOST THREE MEN TO THE WOMAN.
LUCKILY, WE SUBDUED THE CHILD AND SHE BECAME MORE REASONABLE.

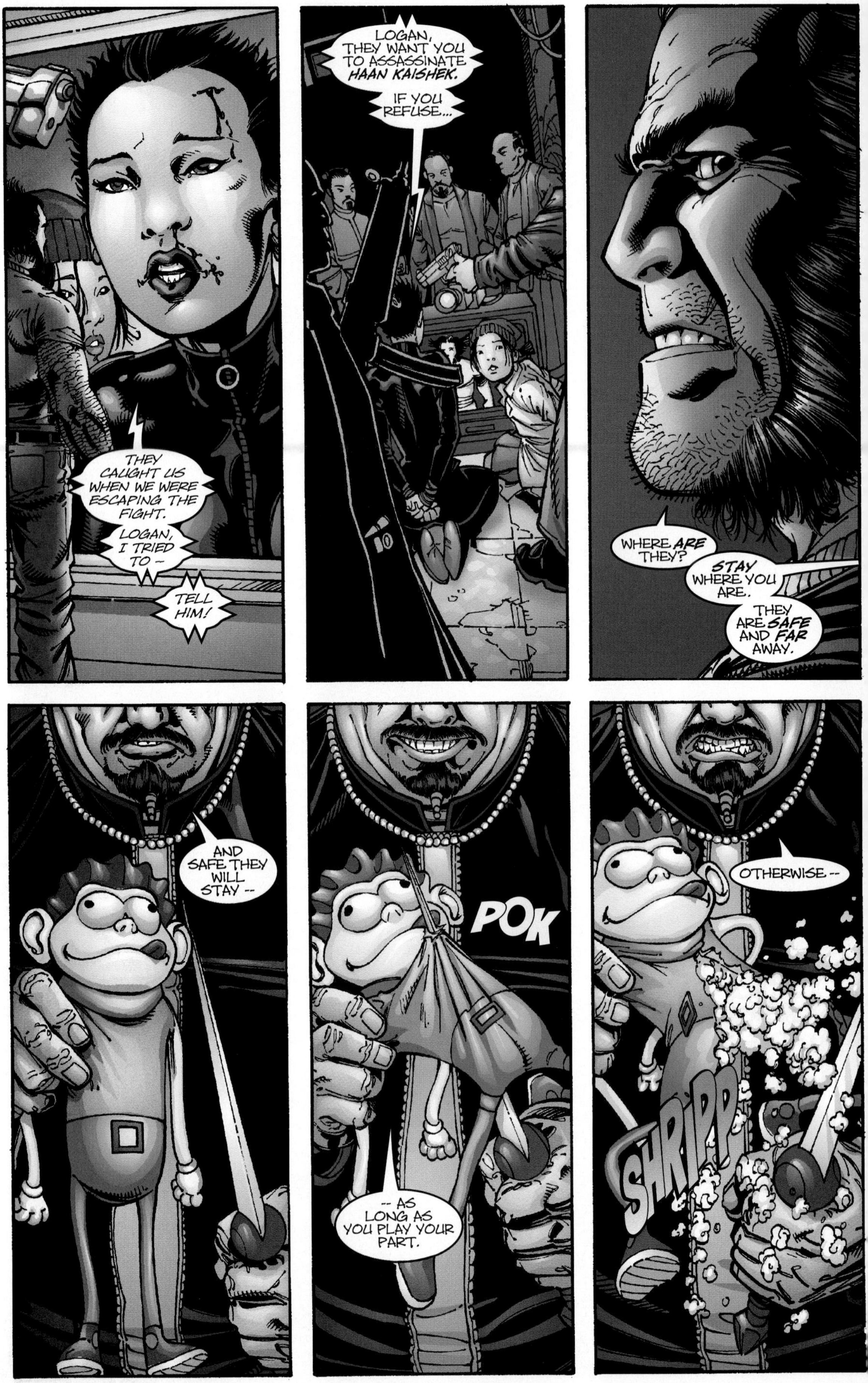

THEY CAUGHT US WHEN WE WERE ESCAPING THE FIGHT.
LOGAN, I TRIED TO --
TELL HIM!
LOGAN, THEY WANT YOU TO ASSASSINATE HAAN KAISHEK.
IF YOU REFUSE...
WHERE ARE THEY?
STAY WHERE YOU ARE.
THEY ARE SAFE AND FAR AWAY.
AND SAFE THEY WILL STAY --
POK
-- AS LONG AS YOU PLAY YOUR PART.
OTHERWISE --
SHRIPP

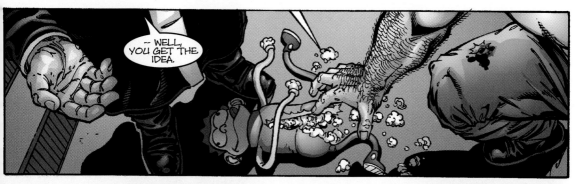

-- WELL, YOU GET THE IDEA.

HAAN'S TOKYO PENTHOUSE IS A *FORTRESS*, BUT WITH YOUR *CLAWS*...EASILY ACCESSIBLE.

THEY WILL NOT BE PREPARED FOR SOMEONE LIKE YOU.

NO! DON'T --

HGLUGH!

WHERE ARE THEY?!

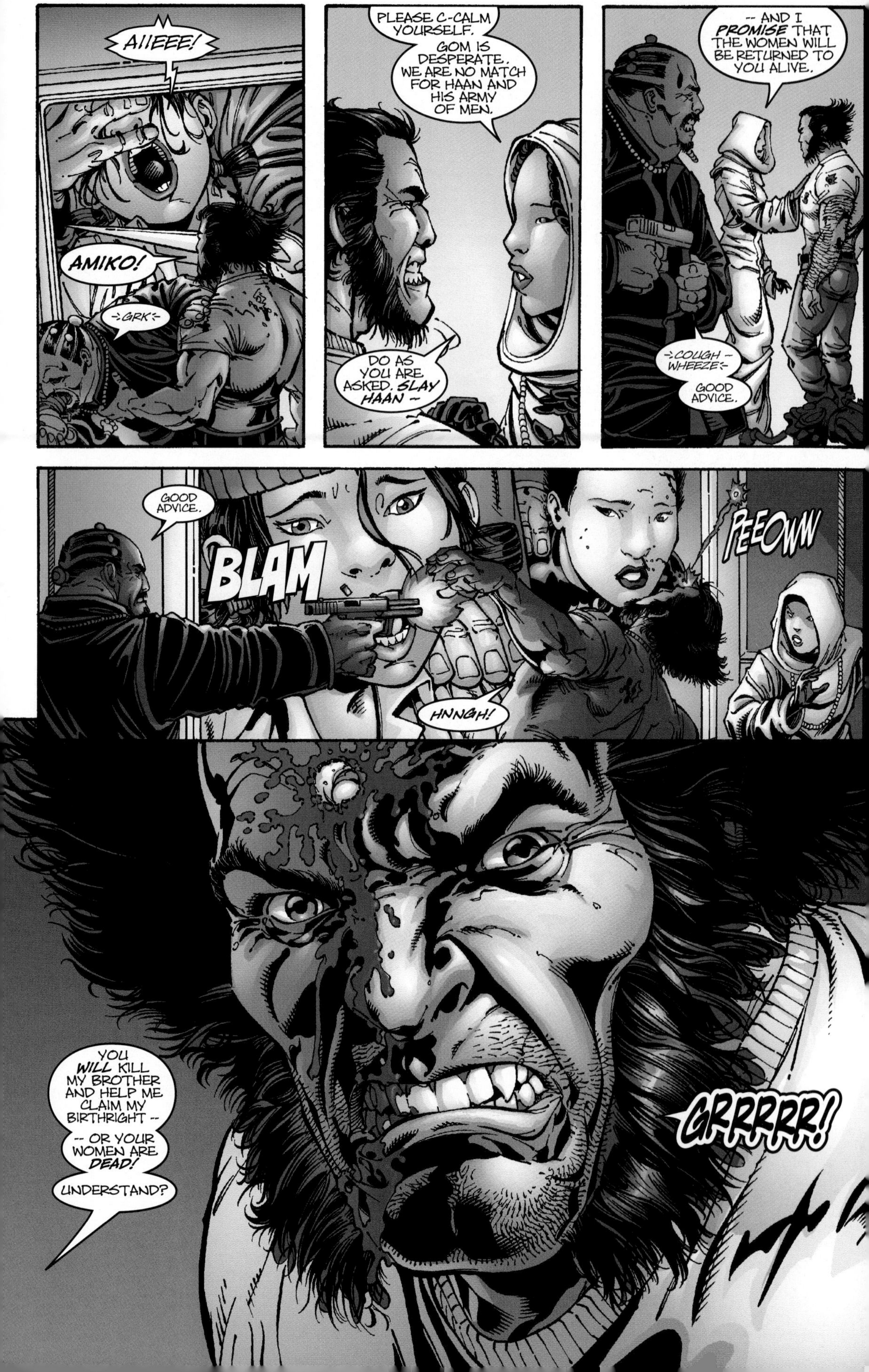
AIIEEE!
AMIKO!
-GRK-
PLEASE C-CALM YOURSELF.
GOM IS DESPERATE. WE ARE NO MATCH FOR HAAN AND HIS ARMY OF MEN.
DO AS YOU ARE ASKED. SLAY HAAN --
-- AND I PROMISE THAT THE WOMEN WILL BE RETURNED TO YOU ALIVE.
-COUGH- WHEEZE-
GOOD ADVICE.
GOOD ADVICE.
BLAM
PEEOWW
HNNGH!
YOU WILL KILL MY BROTHER AND HELP ME CLAIM MY BIRTHRIGHT --
-- OR YOUR WOMEN ARE DEAD!
UNDERSTAND?
GRRRRR!

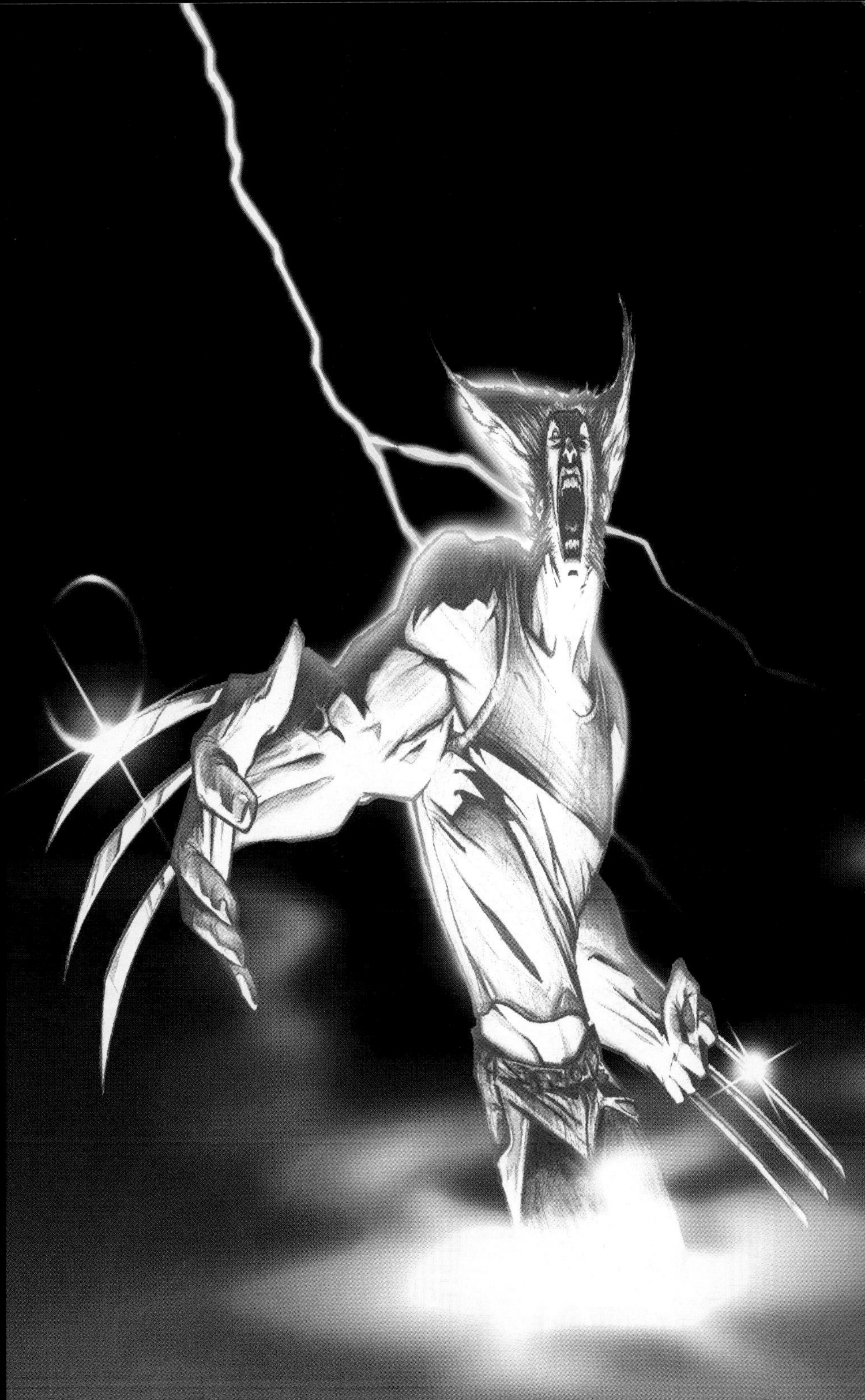

ALTERNATE COVER
by Adam Pollina

CHAPTER TWO

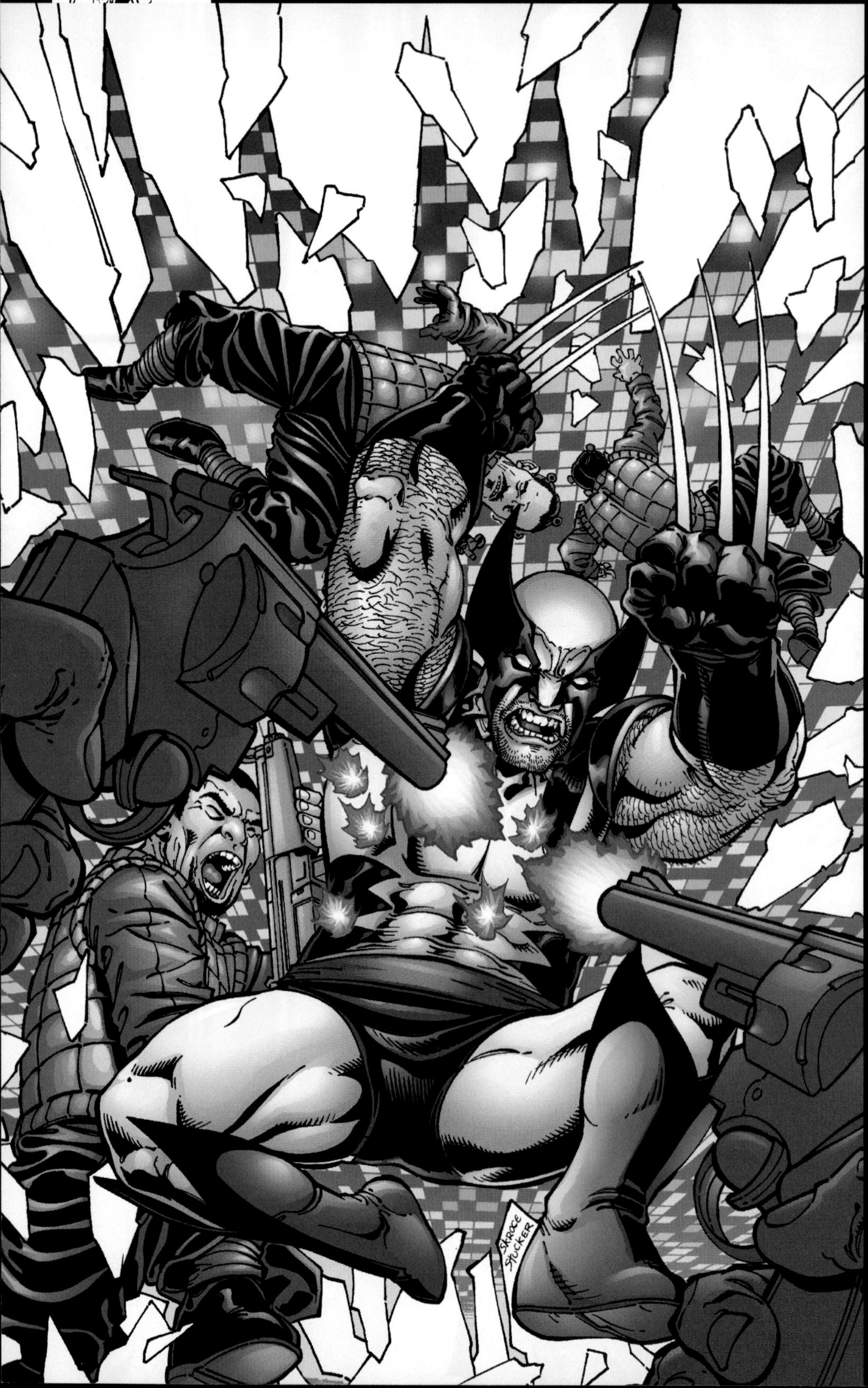
SKROCE STUCKER

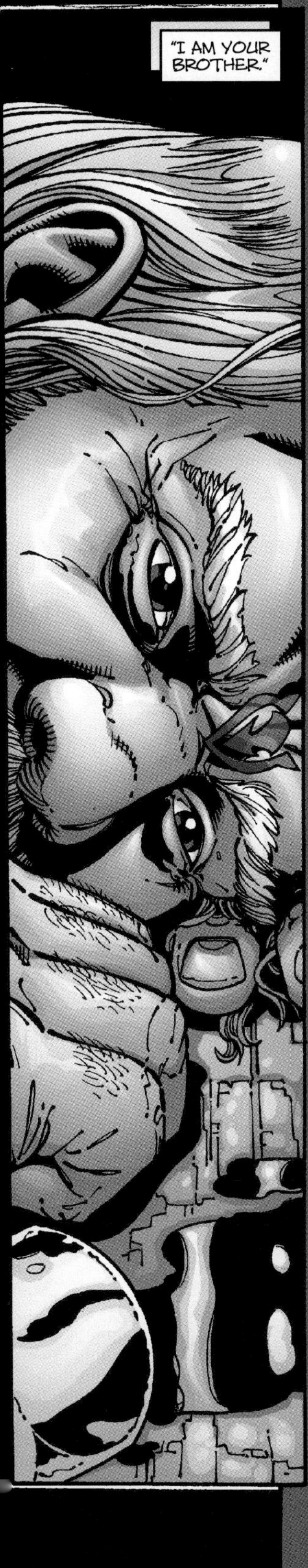
"I AM YOUR BROTHER."

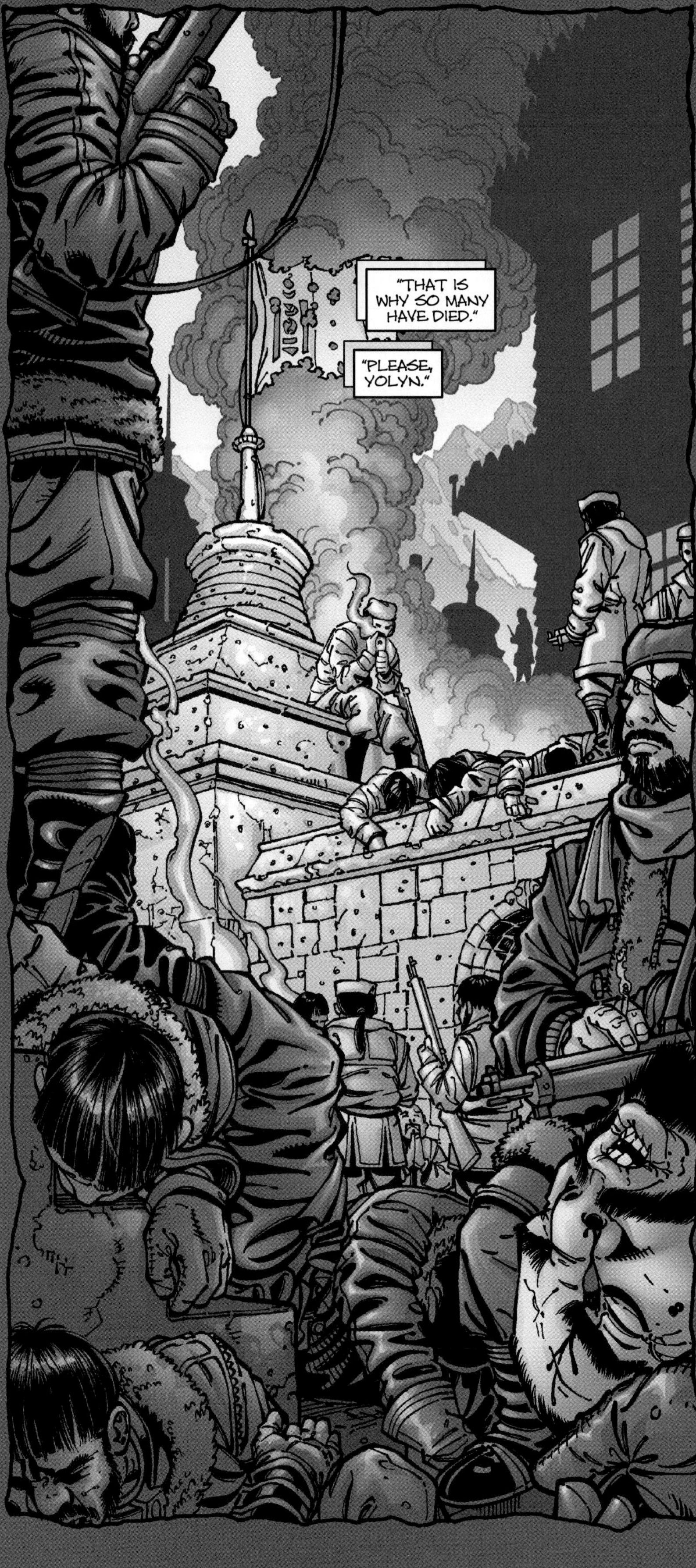
"THAT IS WHY SO MANY HAVE DIED."
"PLEASE, YOLYN."

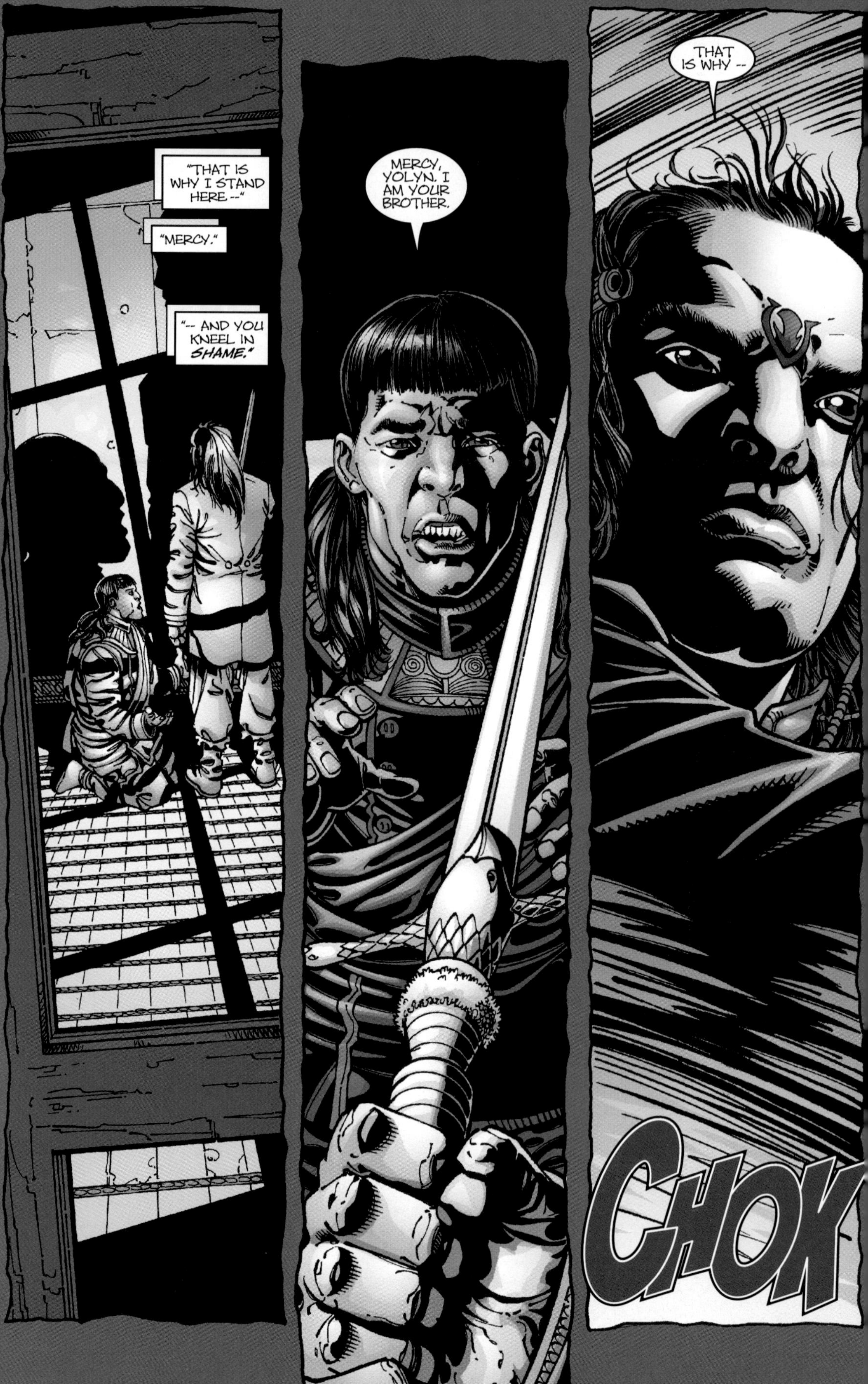
"THAT IS WHY I STAND HERE --"
"MERCY."
"-- AND YOU KNEEL IN SHAME."
MERCY, YOLYN. I AM YOUR BROTHER.
THAT IS WHY --
CHOK

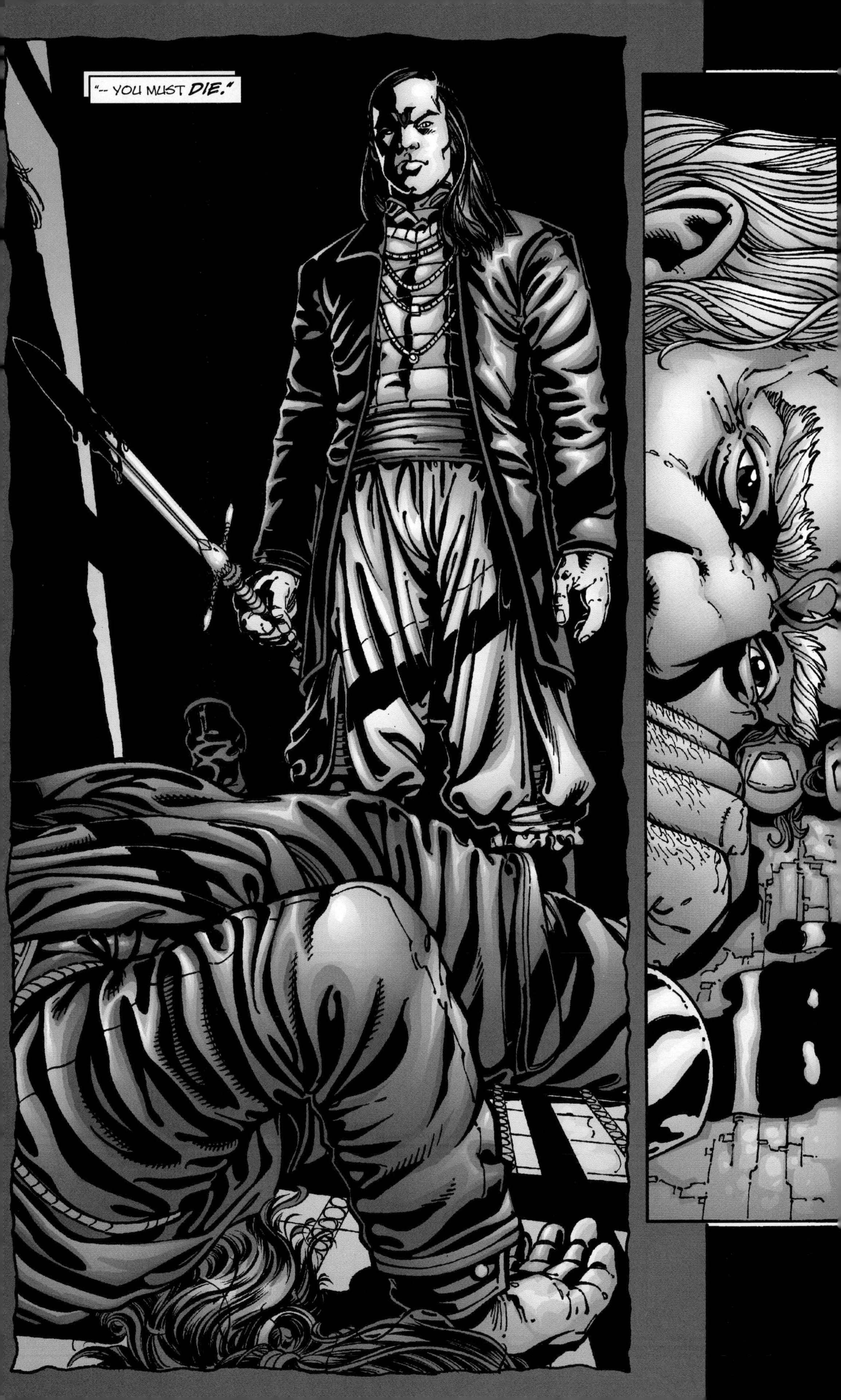
"-- YOU MUST DIE."

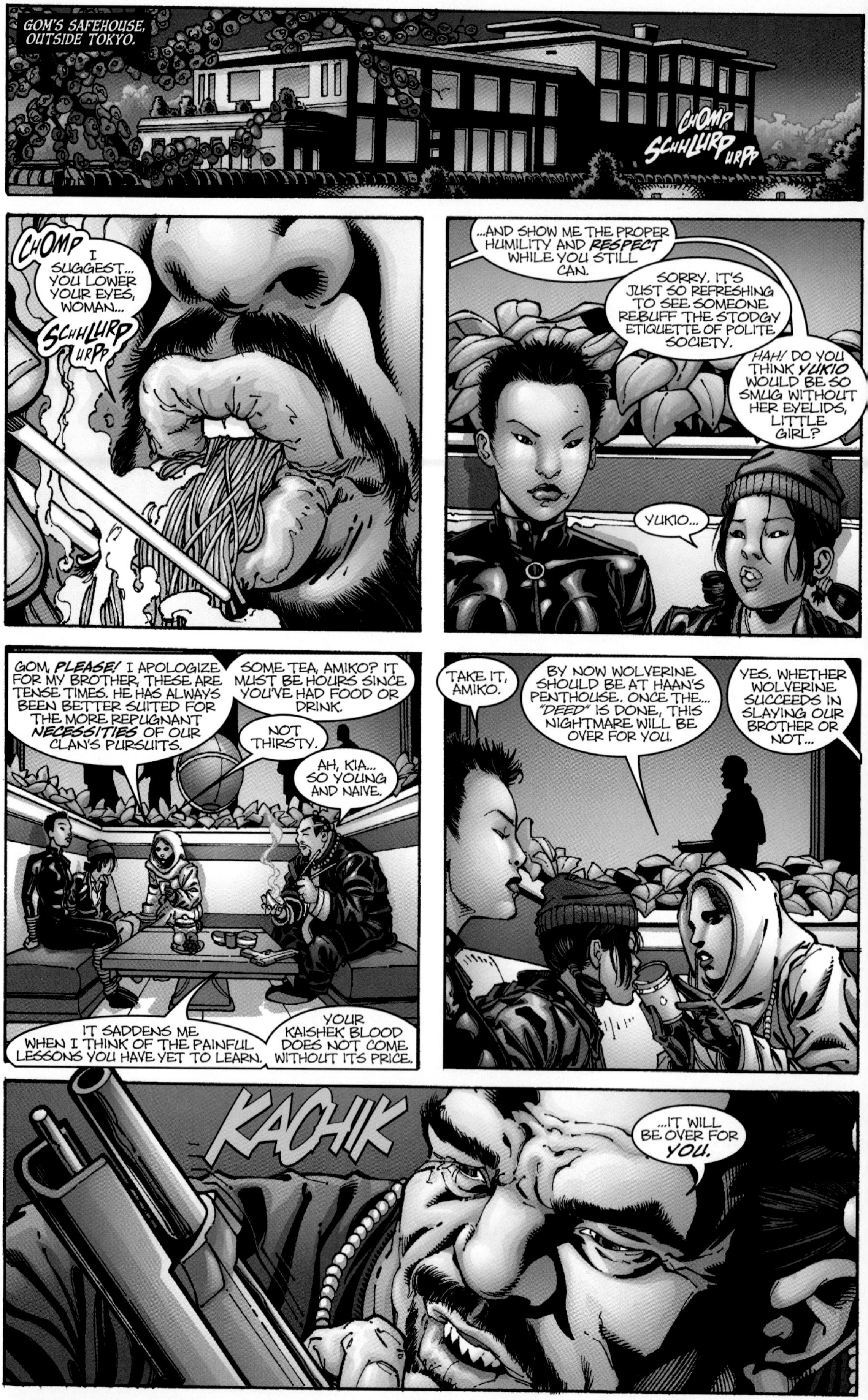
GOM'S SAFEHOUSE, OUTSIDE TOKYO.
CHOMP
SCHHLURP URPP
CHOMP
I SUGGEST... YOU LOWER YOUR EYES, WOMAN...
SCHHLURP URPP
...AND SHOW ME THE PROPER HUMILITY AND RESPECT WHILE YOU STILL CAN.
SORRY. IT'S JUST SO REFRESHING TO SEE SOMEONE REBUFF THE STODGY ETIQUETTE OF POLITE SOCIETY.
HAH! DO YOU THINK YUKIO WOULD BE SO SMUG WITHOUT HER EYELIDS, LITTLE GIRL?
YUKIO...
GOM, PLEASE! I APOLOGIZE FOR MY BROTHER. THESE ARE TENSE TIMES. HE HAS ALWAYS BEEN BETTER SUITED FOR THE MORE REPUGNANT NECESSITIES OF OUR CLAN'S PURSUITS.
SOME TEA, AMIKO? IT MUST BE HOURS SINCE YOU'VE HAD FOOD OR DRINK.
NOT THIRSTY.
AH, KIA... SO YOUNG AND NAIVE.
IT SADDENS ME WHEN I THINK OF THE PAINFUL LESSONS YOU HAVE YET TO LEARN.
YOUR KAISHEK BLOOD DOES NOT COME WITHOUT ITS PRICE.
TAKE IT, AMIKO.
BY NOW WOLVERINE SHOULD BE AT HAAN'S PENTHOUSE. ONCE THE... "DEED" IS DONE, THIS NIGHTMARE WILL BE OVER FOR YOU.
YES. WHETHER WOLVERINE SUCCEEDS IN SLAYING OUR BROTHER OR NOT...
KACHIK
...IT WILL BE OVER FOR YOU.

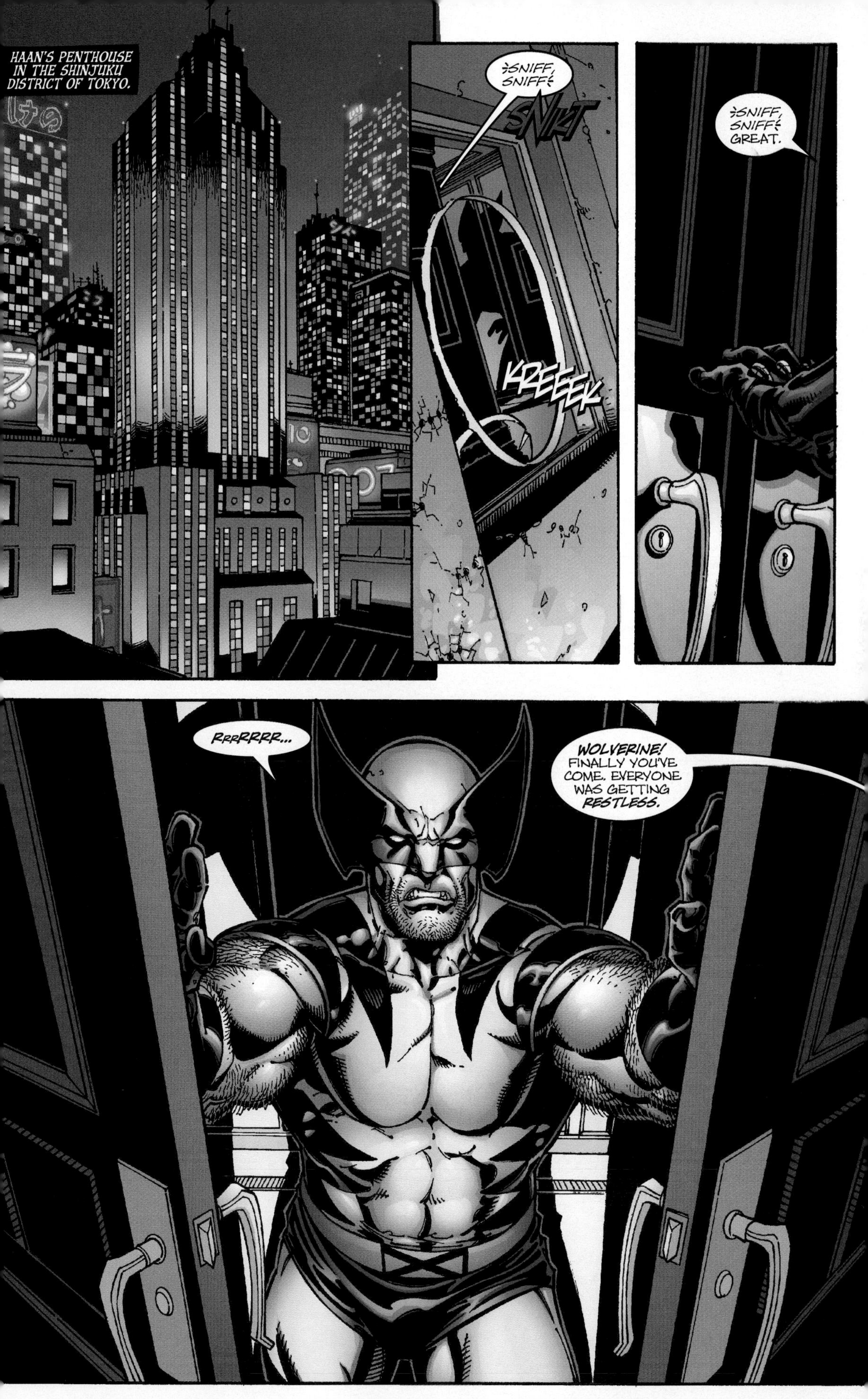
HAAN'S PENTHOUSE IN THE SHINJUKU DISTRICT OF TOKYO.
SNIFF, SNIFF
SNIKT
KREEEEK
SNIFF, SNIFF GREAT.
RRRRRRR...
WOLVERINE! FINALLY YOU'VE COME. EVERYONE WAS GETTING RESTLESS.

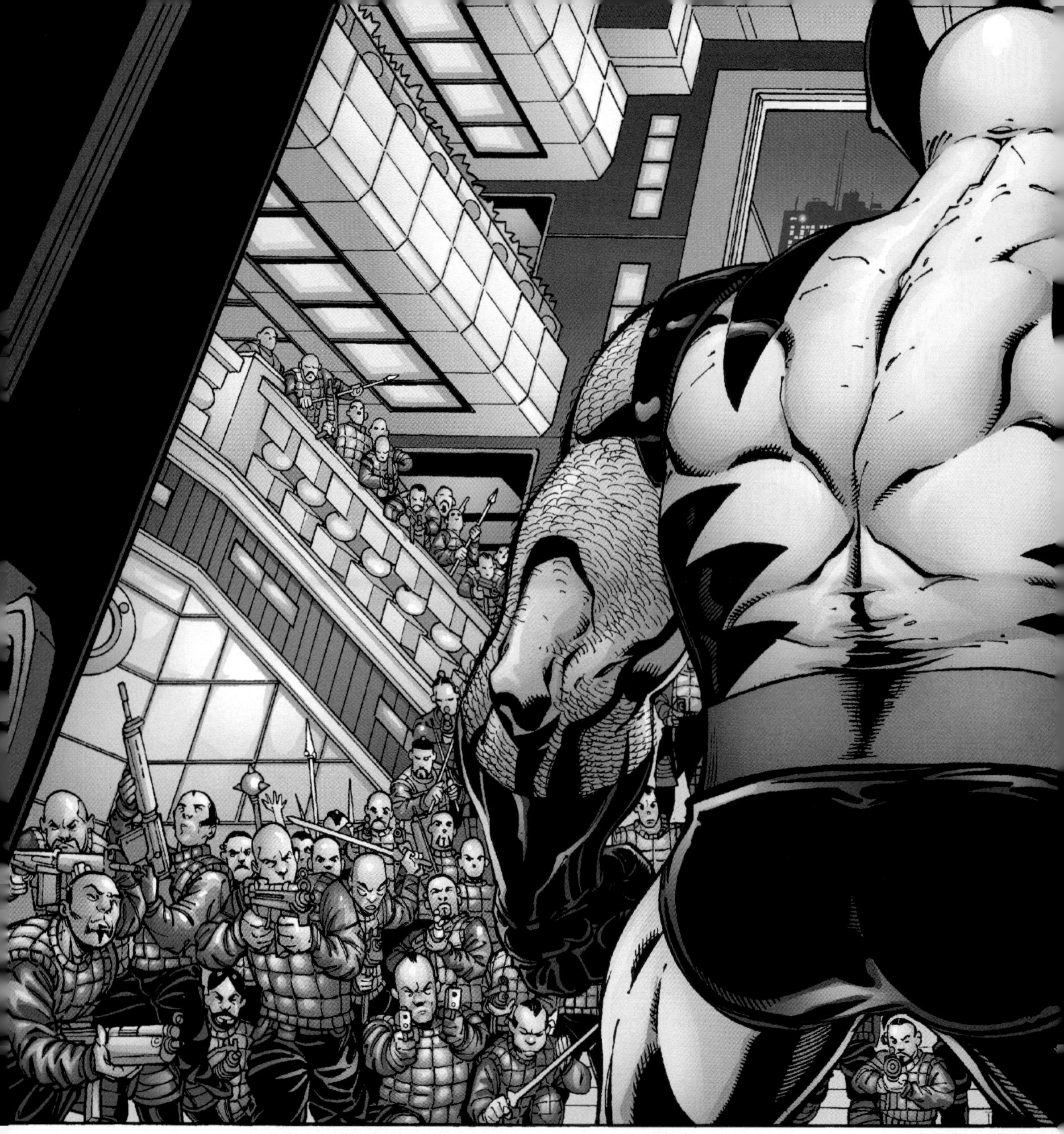

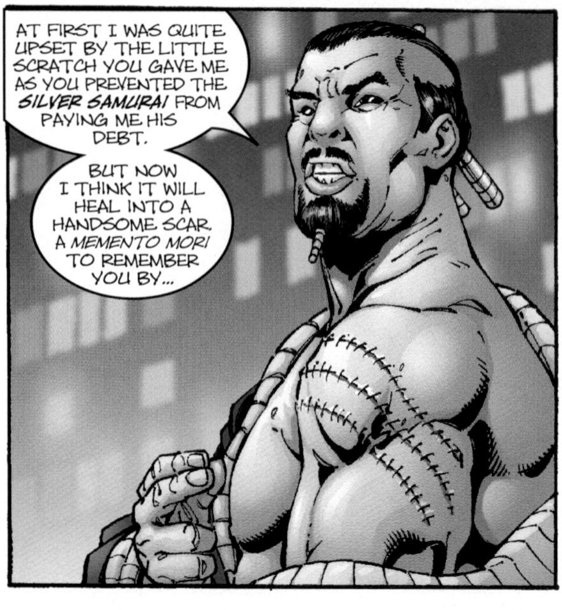
AT FIRST I WAS QUITE UPSET BY THE LITTLE SCRATCH YOU GAVE ME AS YOU PREVENTED THE SILVER SAMURAI FROM PAYING ME HIS DEBT.
BUT NOW I THINK IT WILL HEAL INTO A HANDSOME SCAR. A MEMENTO MORI TO REMEMBER YOU BY...

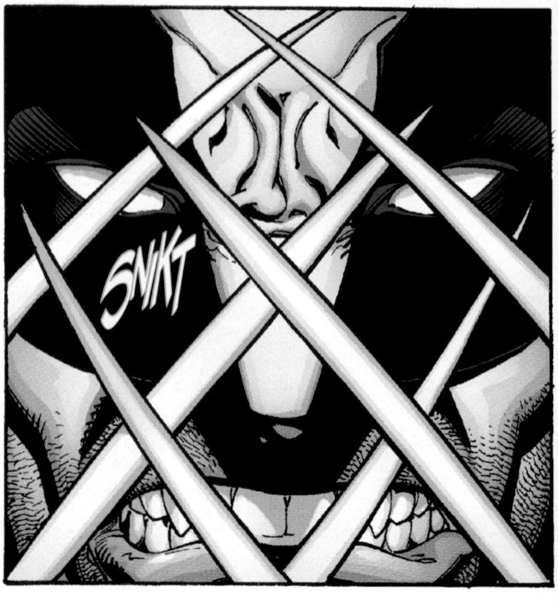
SNIKT

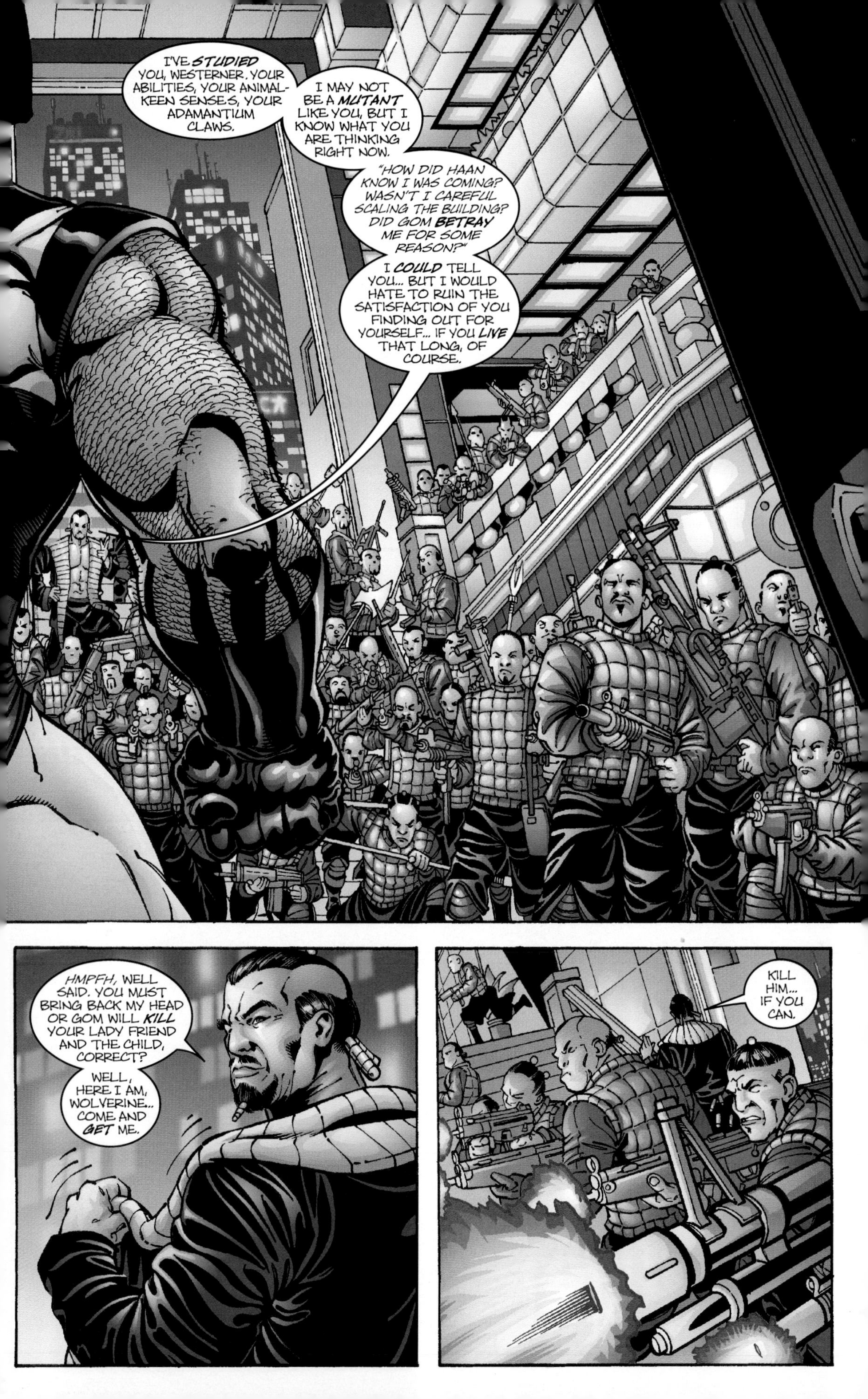
I'VE STUDIED YOU, WESTERNER. YOUR ABILITIES, YOUR ANIMAL-KEEN SENSES, YOUR ADAMANTIUM CLAWS.
I MAY NOT BE A MUTANT LIKE YOU, BUT I KNOW WHAT YOU ARE THINKING RIGHT NOW.
"HOW DID HAAN KNOW I WAS COMING? WASN'T I CAREFUL SCALING THE BUILDING? DID GOM BETRAY ME FOR SOME REASON?"
I COULD TELL YOU... BUT I WOULD HATE TO RUIN THE SATISFACTION OF YOU FINDING OUT FOR YOURSELF... IF YOU LIVE THAT LONG, OF COURSE.
HMPFH, WELL SAID. YOU MUST BRING BACK MY HEAD OR GOM WILL KILL YOUR LADY FRIEND AND THE CHILD, CORRECT?
WELL, HERE I AM, WOLVERINE... COME AND GET ME.
KILL HIM... IF YOU CAN.

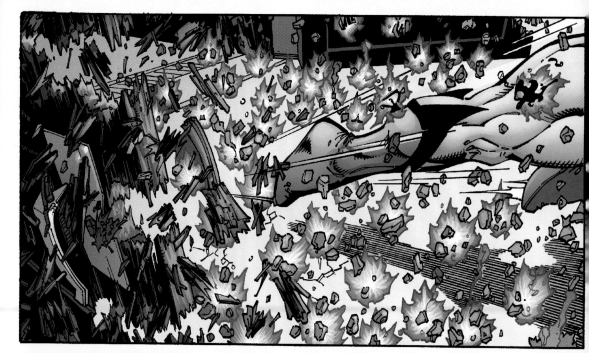

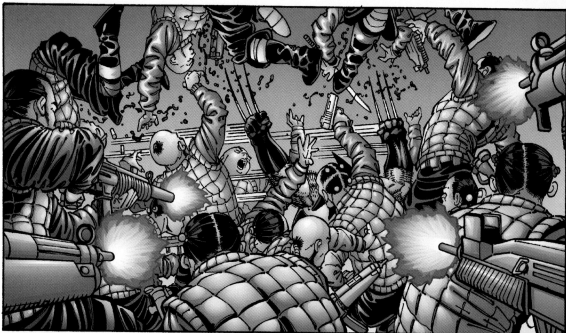

IS EVERYONE IN PLACE, OTOU?

READY AND AWAITING YOUR ORDERS... AND UPSTAIRS?

AS EXPECTED...

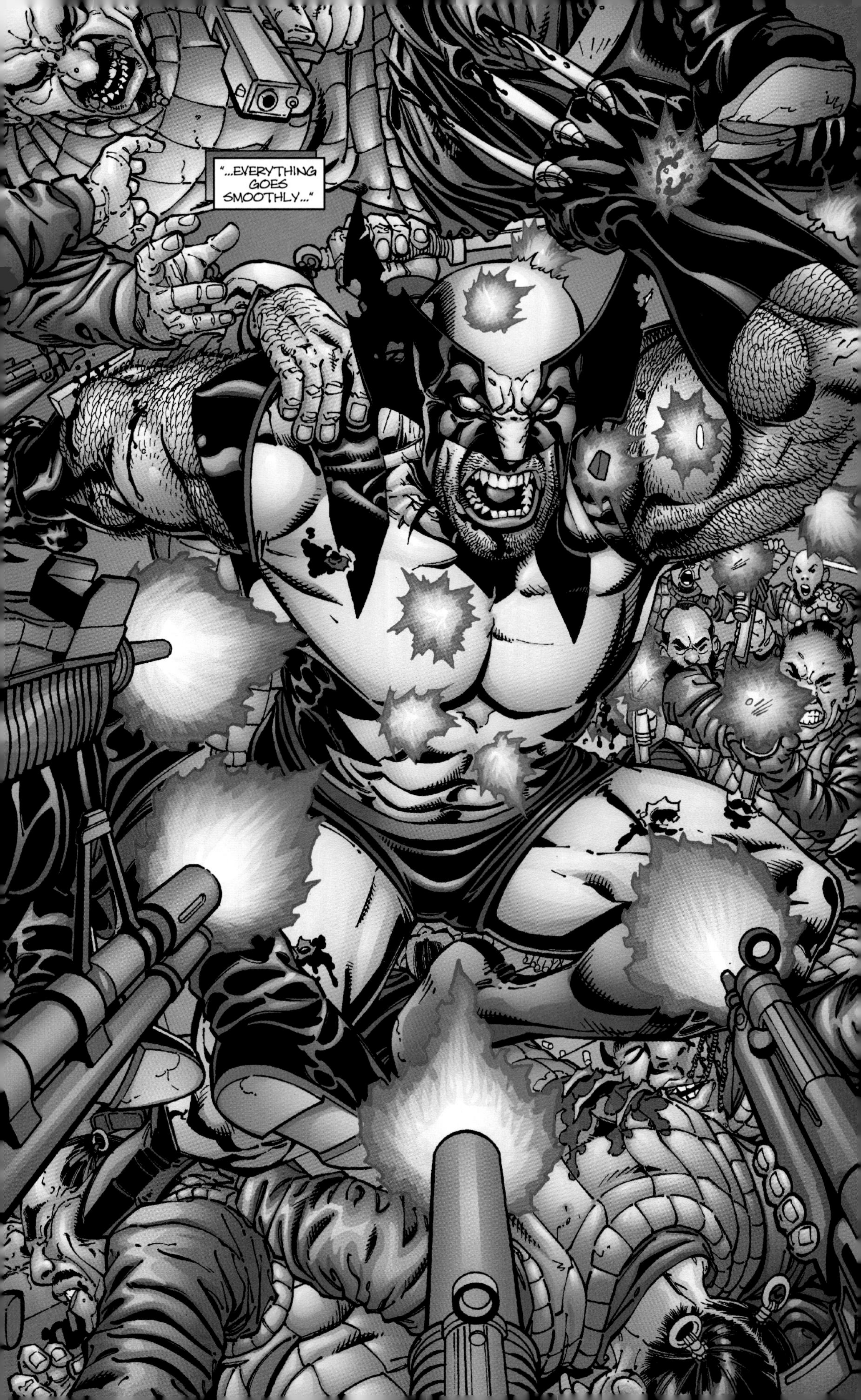
"...EVERYTHING GOES SMOOTHLY..."

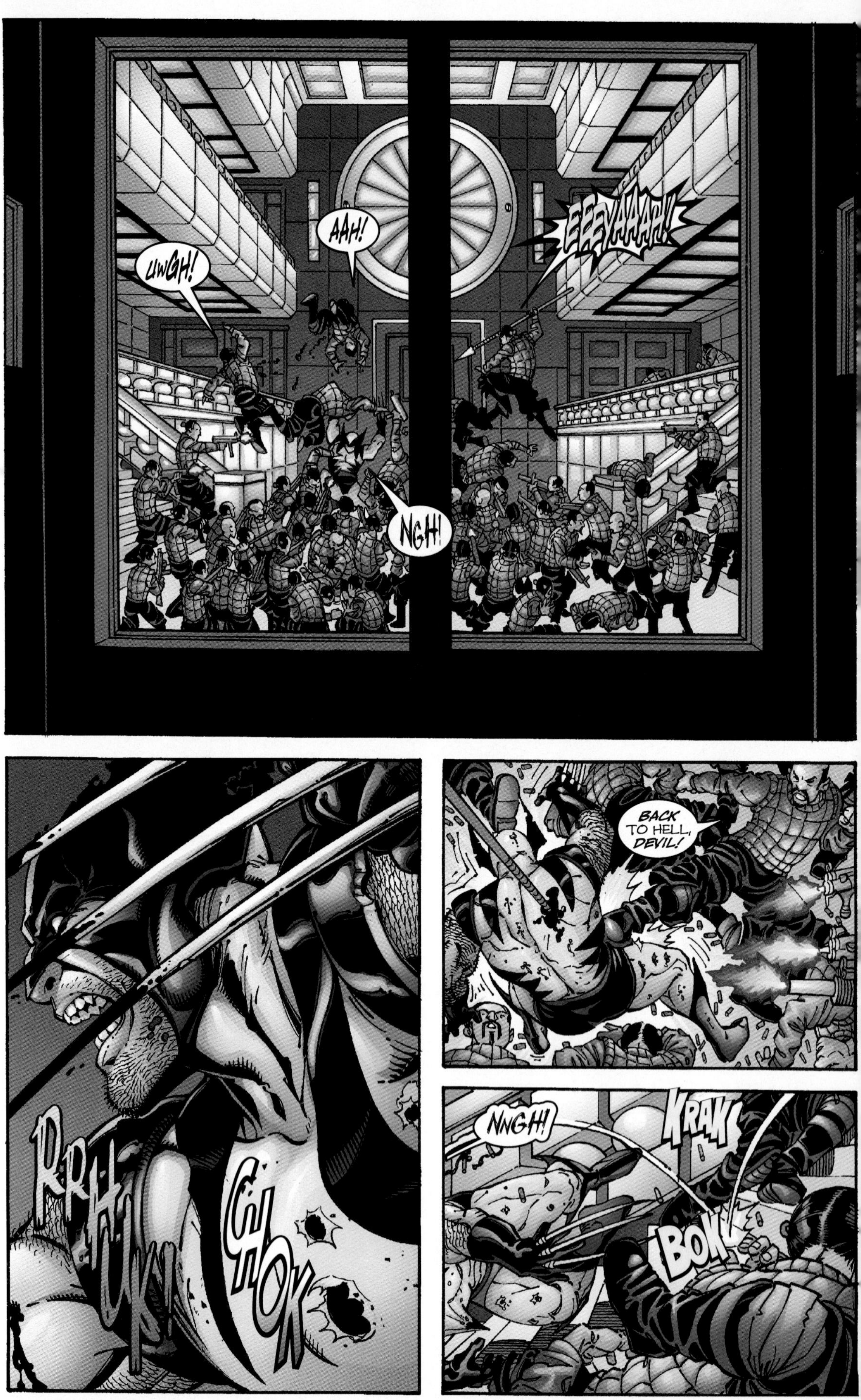

UWGH!
AAH!
EEEYAAAAH!
NGH!
RRHUK!
CHOK
BACK TO HELL, DEVIL!
NNGH!
KRAK
BOK

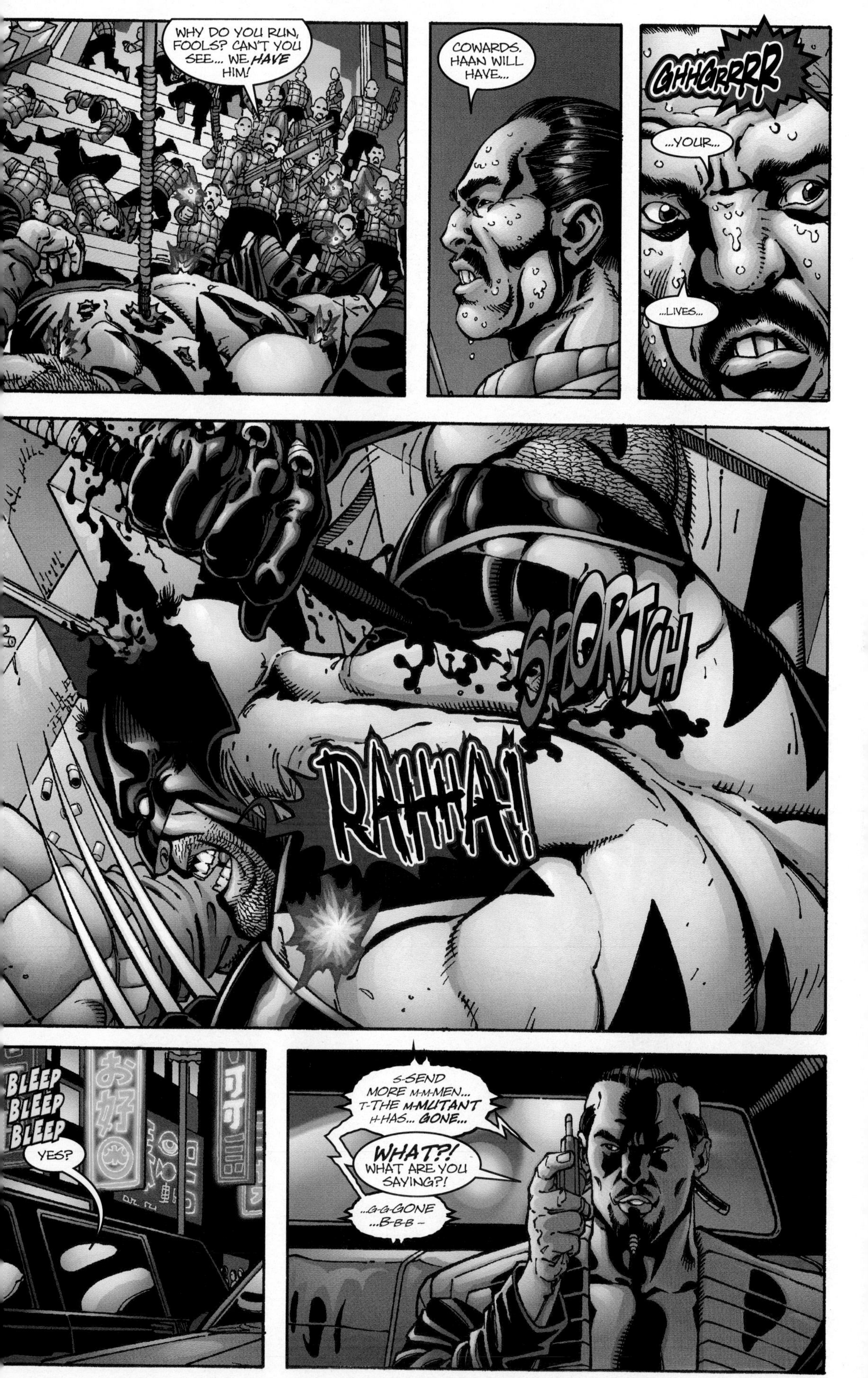
WHY DO YOU RUN, FOOLS? CAN'T YOU SEE... WE HAVE HIM!
COWARDS. HAAN WILL HAVE...
GAHHGRRRR
...YOUR...
...LIVES...
SPORTCH
RAHHA!
BLEEP BLEEP BLEEP
YES?
S-SEND MORE M-M-MEN... T-THE M-MUTANT H-HAS... GONE...
WHAT?! WHAT ARE YOU SAYING?!
...G-G-GONE ...B-B-B –

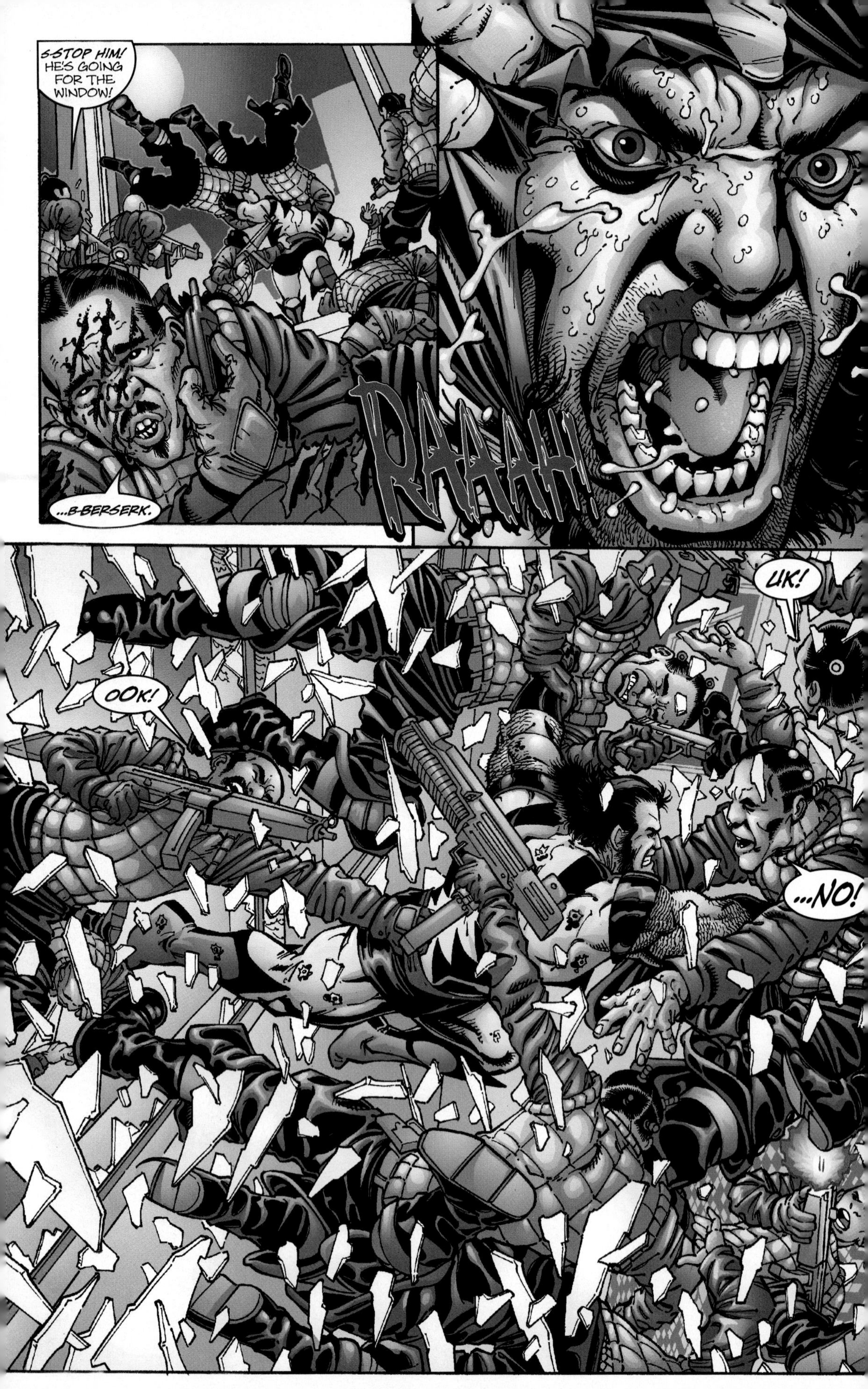
S-STOP HIM! HE'S GOING FOR THE WINDOW!
...B-BERSERK.
RAAAH!
UK!
OOK!
...NO!

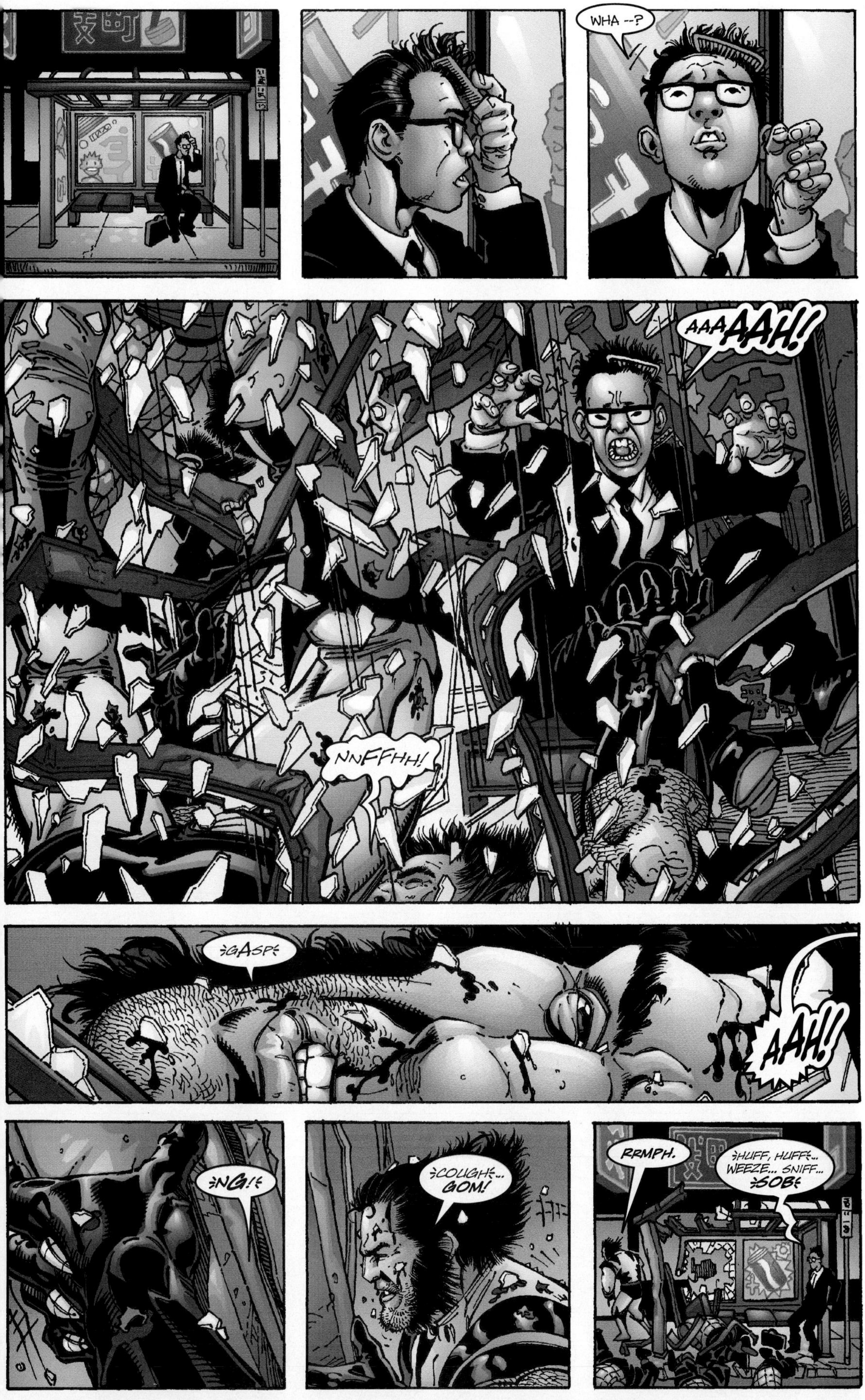
WHA --?
AAAAAH!
NNFFHH!
GASP
AAH!!
NG!
COUGH...
GOM!
RRMPH.
HUFF, HUFF...
WEEZE... SNIFF...
SOB

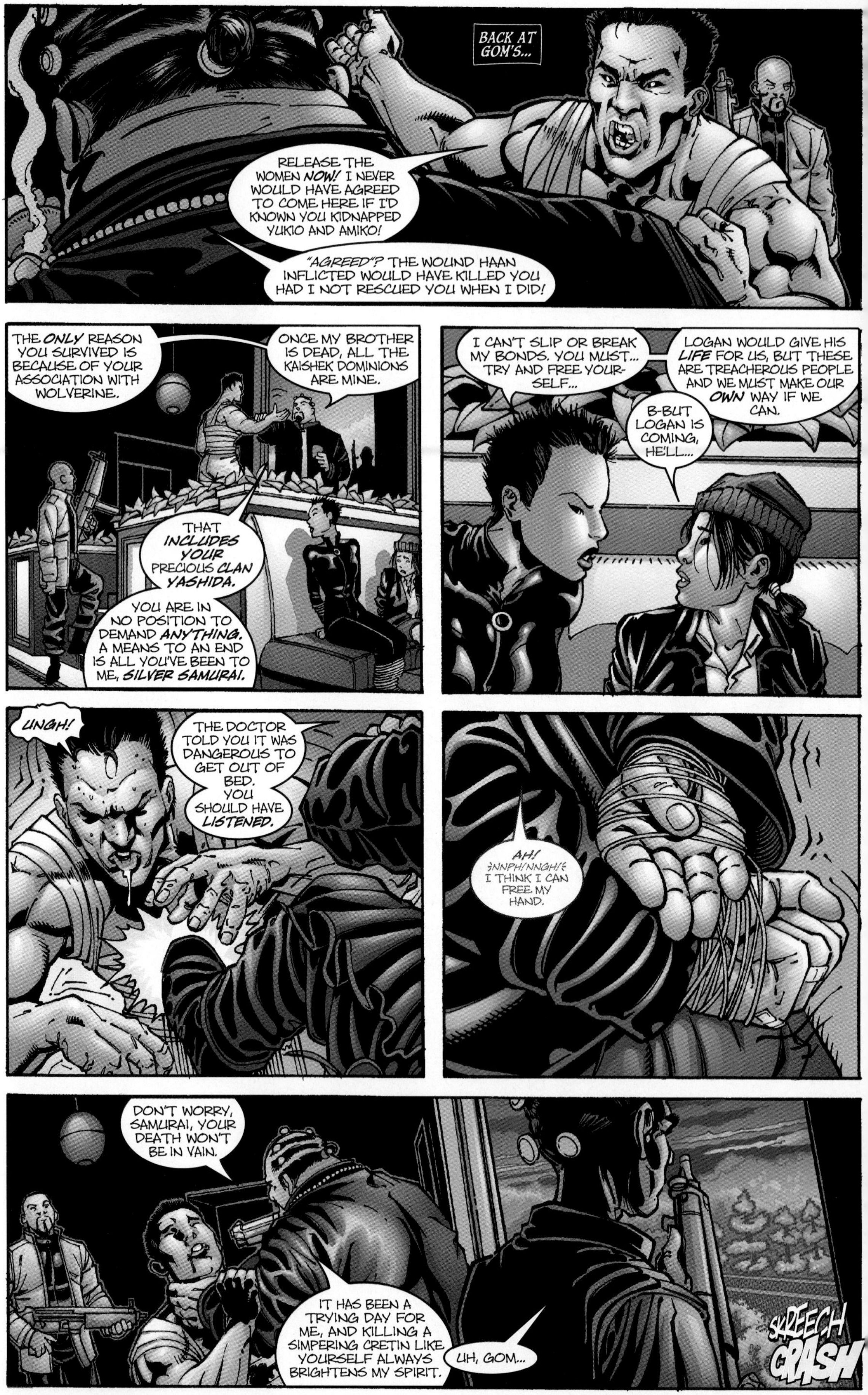
BACK AT GOM'S...
RELEASE THE WOMEN NOW! I NEVER WOULD HAVE AGREED TO COME HERE IF I'D KNOWN YOU KIDNAPPED YUKIO AND AMIKO!
"AGREED"? THE WOUND HAAN INFLICTED WOULD HAVE KILLED YOU HAD I NOT RESCUED YOU WHEN I DID!
THE ONLY REASON YOU SURVIVED IS BECAUSE OF YOUR ASSOCIATION WITH WOLVERINE.
ONCE MY BROTHER IS DEAD, ALL THE KAISHEK DOMINIONS ARE MINE.
THAT INCLUDES YOUR PRECIOUS CLAN YASHIDA.
YOU ARE IN NO POSITION TO DEMAND ANYTHING. A MEANS TO AN END IS ALL YOU'VE BEEN TO ME, SILVER SAMURAI.
I CAN'T SLIP OR BREAK MY BONDS. YOU MUST... TRY AND FREE YOURSELF...
LOGAN WOULD GIVE HIS LIFE FOR US, BUT THESE ARE TREACHEROUS PEOPLE AND WE MUST MAKE OUR OWN WAY IF WE CAN.
B-BUT LOGAN IS COMING, HE'LL...
UNGH!
THE DOCTOR TOLD YOU IT WAS DANGEROUS TO GET OUT OF BED. YOU SHOULD HAVE LISTENED.
AH! NNPH! NNGH! I THINK I CAN FREE MY HAND.
DON'T WORRY, SAMURAI, YOUR DEATH WON'T BE IN VAIN.
IT HAS BEEN A TRYING DAY FOR ME, AND KILLING A SIMPERING CRETIN LIKE YOURSELF ALWAYS BRIGHTENS MY SPIRIT.
UH, GOM...
SKREECH
CRASH

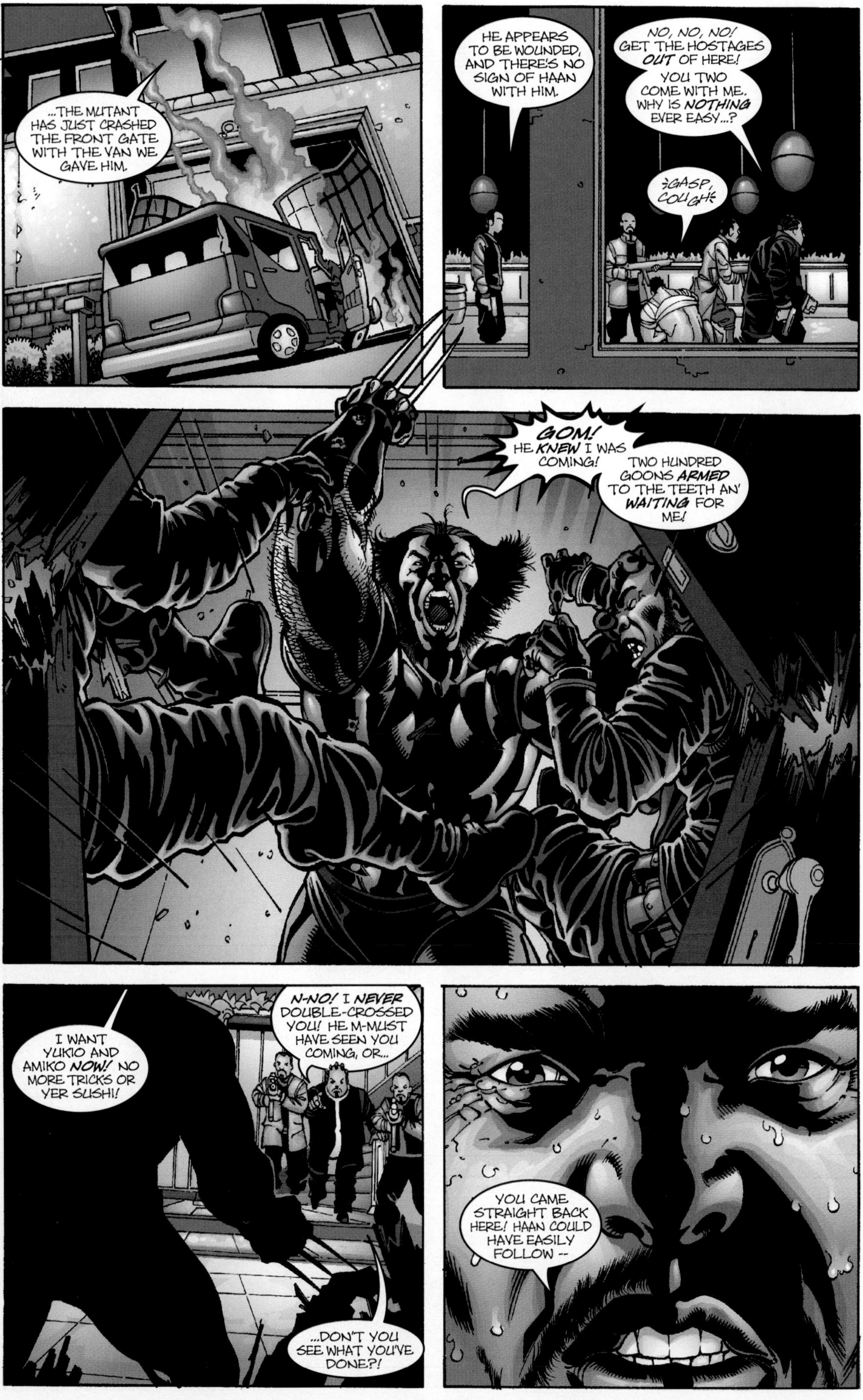
...THE MUTANT HAS JUST CRASHED THE FRONT GATE WITH THE VAN WE GAVE HIM.
HE APPEARS TO BE WOUNDED, AND THERE'S NO SIGN OF HAAN WITH HIM.
NO, NO, NO! GET THE HOSTAGES OUT OF HERE!
YOU TWO COME WITH ME. WHY IS NOTHING EVER EASY...?
GASP, COUGH
GOM! HE KNEW I WAS COMING!
TWO HUNDRED GOONS ARMED TO THE TEETH AN' WAITING FOR ME!
I WANT YUKIO AND AMIKO NOW! NO MORE TRICKS OR YER SUSHI!
N-NO! I NEVER DOUBLE-CROSSED YOU! HE M-MUST HAVE SEEN YOU COMING, OR...
...DON'T YOU SEE WHAT YOU'VE DONE?!
YOU CAME STRAIGHT BACK HERE! HAAN COULD HAVE EASILY FOLLOW --

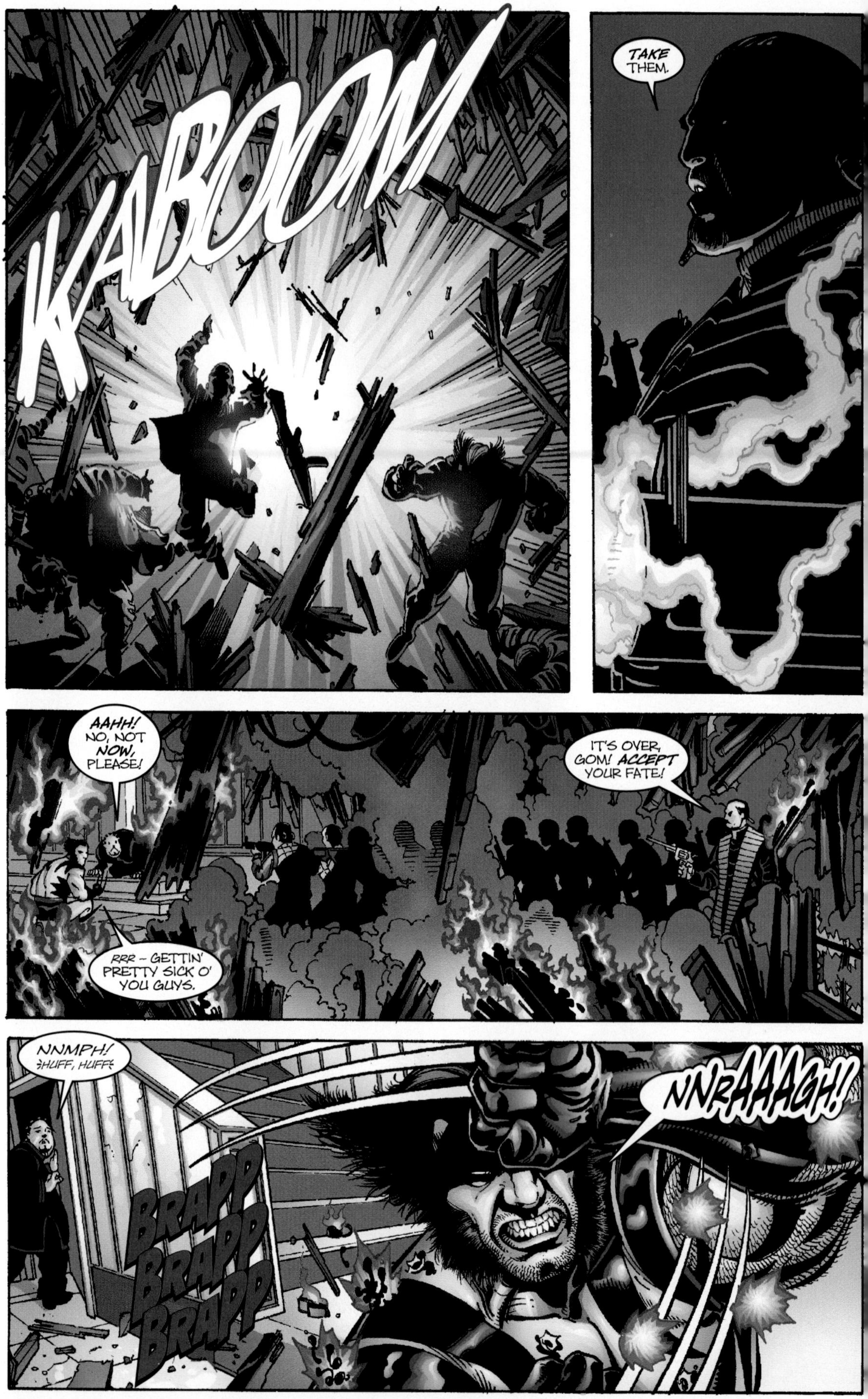
KABOOM
TAKE THEM.
AAHH! NO, NOT NOW, PLEASE!
IT'S OVER, GOM! ACCEPT YOUR FATE!
RRR -- GETTIN' PRETTY SICK O' YOU GUYS.
NNMPH! HUFF, HUFF
NNRAAAAGH!
BRAPP BRAPP BRAPP

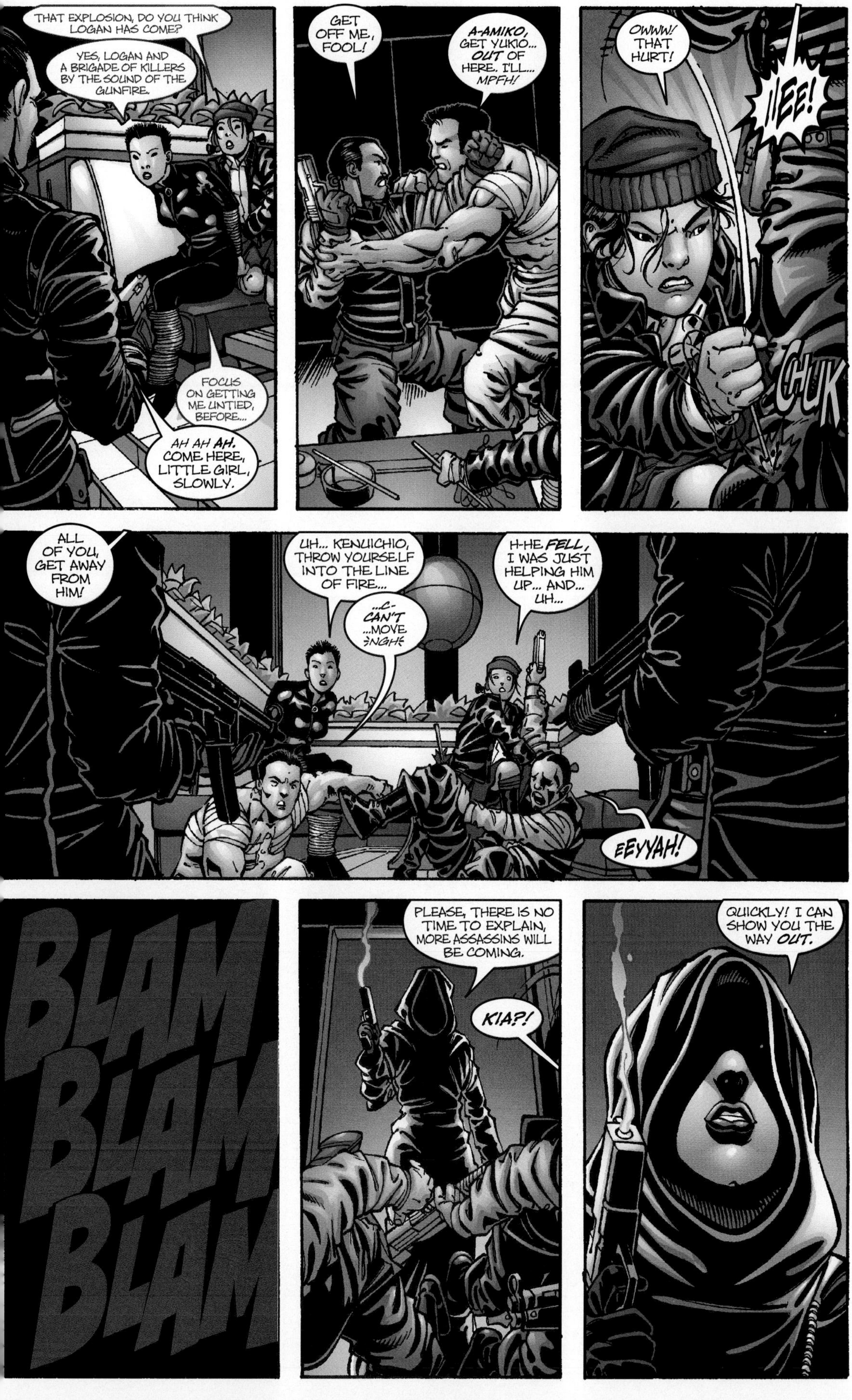
THAT EXPLOSION, DO YOU THINK LOGAN HAS COME?
YES, LOGAN AND A BRIGADE OF KILLERS BY THE SOUND OF THE GUNFIRE.
FOCUS ON GETTING ME UNTIED, BEFORE...
AH AH AH. COME HERE, LITTLE GIRL, SLOWLY.
GET OFF ME, FOOL!
A-AMIKO, GET YUKIO... OUT OF HERE. I'LL... MPFH!
OWWW! THAT HURT!
IIEE!
CHUK
ALL OF YOU, GET AWAY FROM HIM!
UH... KENUICHIO, THROW YOURSELF INTO THE LINE OF FIRE...
...C-CAN'T ...MOVE NGH
H-HE FELL, I WAS JUST HELPING HIM UP... AND... UH...
EEYYAH!
BLAM BLAM BLAM
PLEASE, THERE IS NO TIME TO EXPLAIN, MORE ASSASSINS WILL BE COMING.
KIA?!
QUICKLY! I CAN SHOW YOU THE WAY OUT.

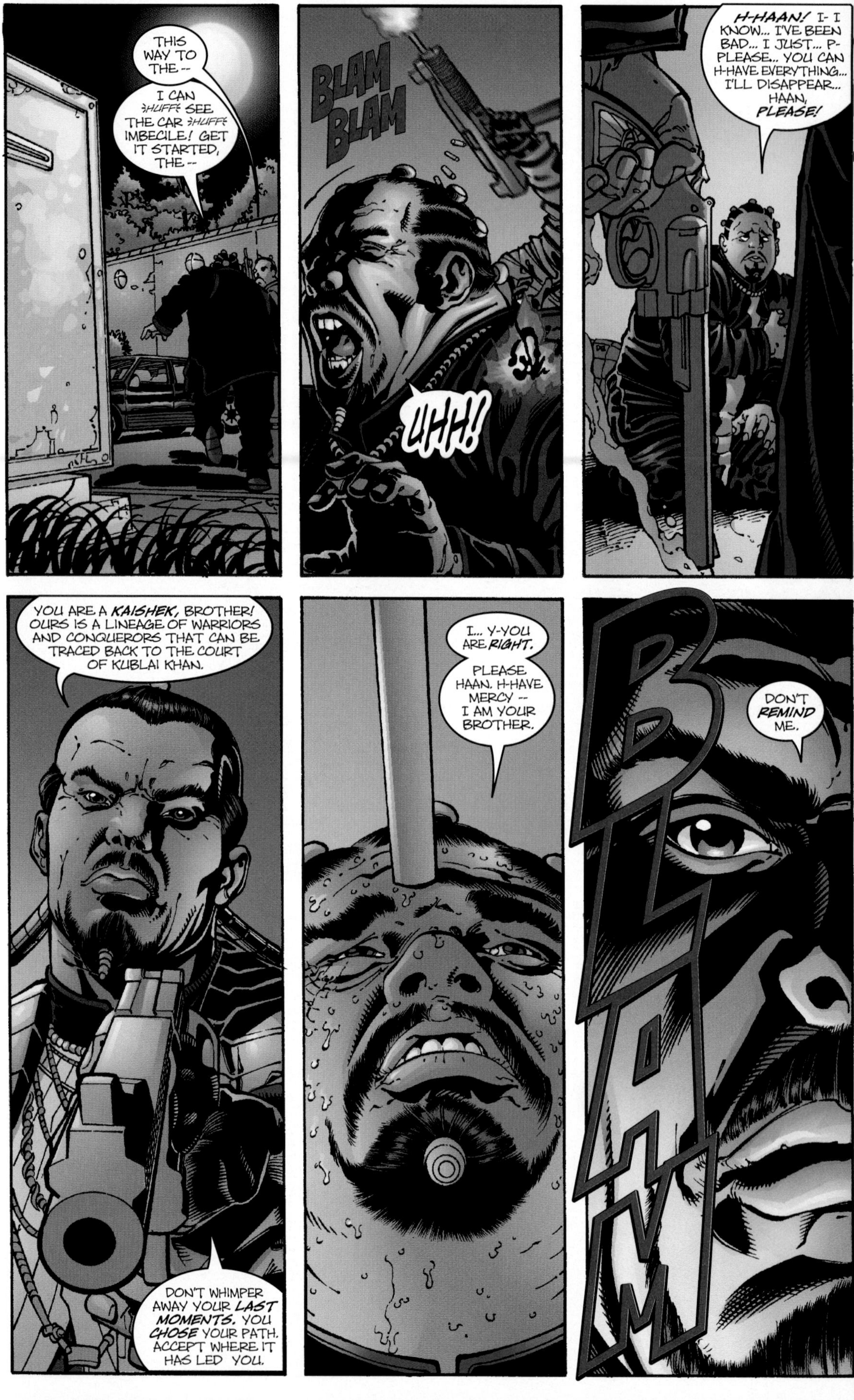
THIS WAY TO THE --
I CAN ⇉HUFF⇇ SEE THE CAR ⇉HUFF⇇ IMBECILE! GET IT STARTED, THE --
BLAM BLAM
UHH!
H-HAAN! I- I KNOW... I'VE BEEN BAD... I JUST... P-PLEASE... YOU CAN H-HAVE EVERYTHING... I'LL DISAPPEAR... HAAN, PLEASE!
YOU ARE A KAISHEK, BROTHER! OURS IS A LINEAGE OF WARRIORS AND CONQUERORS THAT CAN BE TRACED BACK TO THE COURT OF KUBLAI KHAN.
DON'T WHIMPER AWAY YOUR LAST MOMENTS. YOU CHOSE YOUR PATH. ACCEPT WHERE IT HAS LED YOU.
I... Y-YOU ARE RIGHT.
PLEASE HAAN. H-HAVE MERCY -- I AM YOUR BROTHER.
DON'T REMIND ME.
BLAM

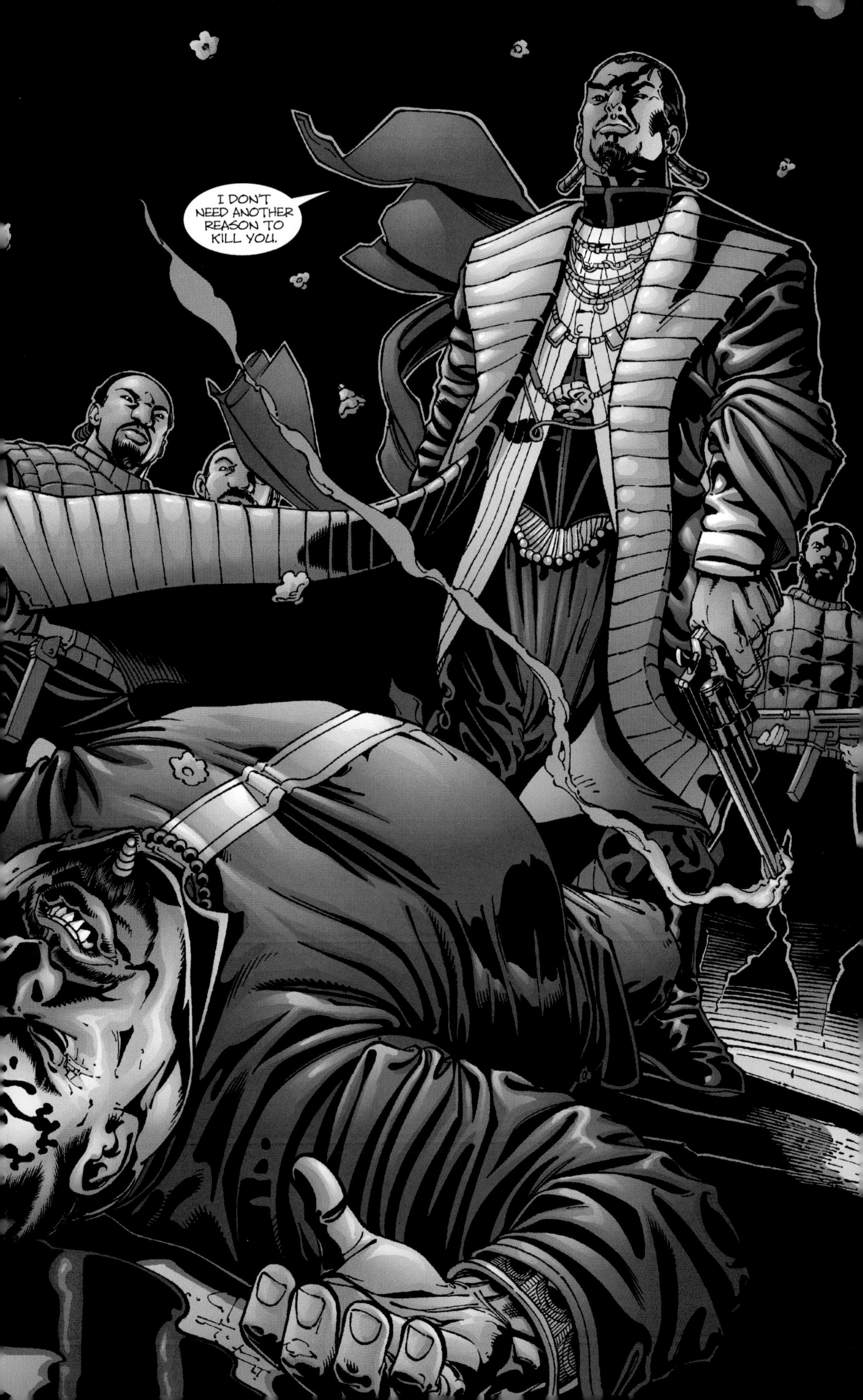
I DON'T NEED ANOTHER REASON TO KILL YOU.

...THIS GARAGE OPENS ONTO A BACK ROAD. GOM'S AND HAAN'S MEN SHOULD BE TOO BUSY FIGHTING EACH OTHER AND WOLVERINE TO NOTICE *YOUR* ESCAPE.

MY AIDE, *TUPA*, WILL DRIVE YOU TO SAFETY.

ALL IS PREPARED, MISTRESS.

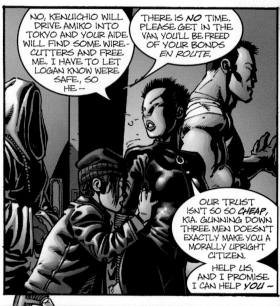

NO, KENUICHIO WILL DRIVE AMIKO INTO TOKYO AND YOUR AIDE WILL FIND SOME WIRE-CUTTERS AND FREE ME. I HAVE TO LET LOGAN KNOW WE'RE SAFE, SO HE --

THERE IS *NO* TIME. PLEASE GET IN THE VAN, YOU'LL BE FREED OF YOUR BONDS *EN ROUTE*.

OUR TRUST ISN'T SO SO *CHEAP*, KIA. GUNNING DOWN THREE MEN DOESN'T EXACTLY MAKE YOU A MORALLY UPRIGHT CITIZEN.

HELP US, AND I PROMISE I CAN HELP *YOU* --

THIS IS THE ONLY WAY YOU CAN HELP ME....

AMIKO...

≥NGHH!≤

PFF PFF

PFF

...NO...

YOU JUST BOUGHT A BROKEN FACE, YOU --

~ RUN ~

WOK

MAKE SURE ALL THREE ARE PROPERLY *BOUND* WHEN THEY AWAKEN.

YES, MISTRESS.

IF ALL GOES WELL, I WILL MEET YOU TOMORROW AT THE *RENDEZVOUS* POINT.

RIGHT NOW, I NEED TO FIND GOM AND SEE WHERE THE PIECES OF MY FAMILY HAVE FALLEN.

MY HEART IS WITH YOU, KIA.

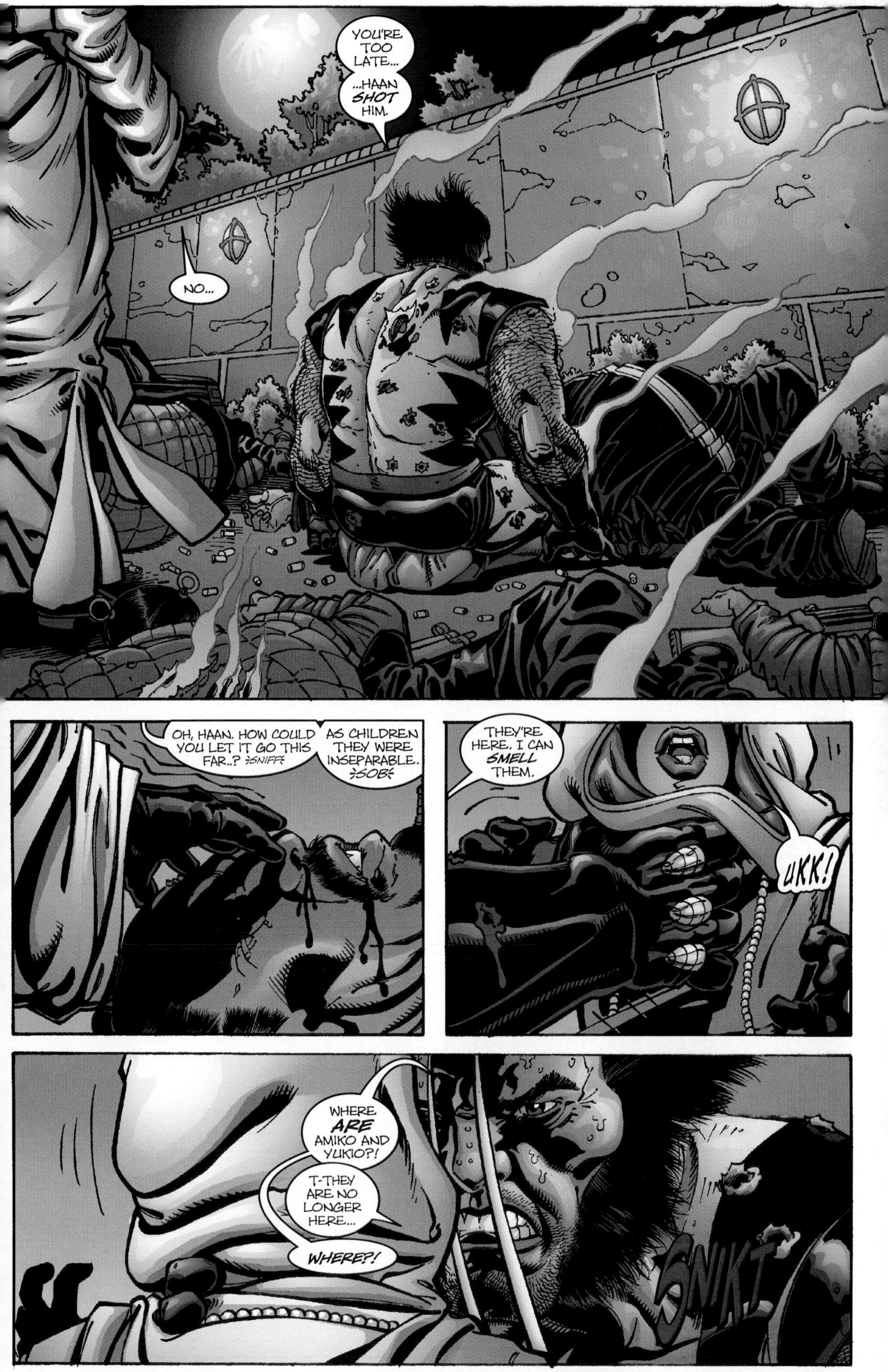
YOU'RE TOO LATE...
...HAAN SHOT HIM.
NO...
OH, HAAN. HOW COULD YOU LET IT GO THIS FAR..? SNIFF
AS CHILDREN THEY WERE INSEPARABLE. SOB
THEY'RE HERE. I CAN SMELL THEM.
UKK!
WHERE ARE AMIKO AND YUKIO?!
T-THEY ARE NO LONGER HERE...
WHERE?!
SNIKT

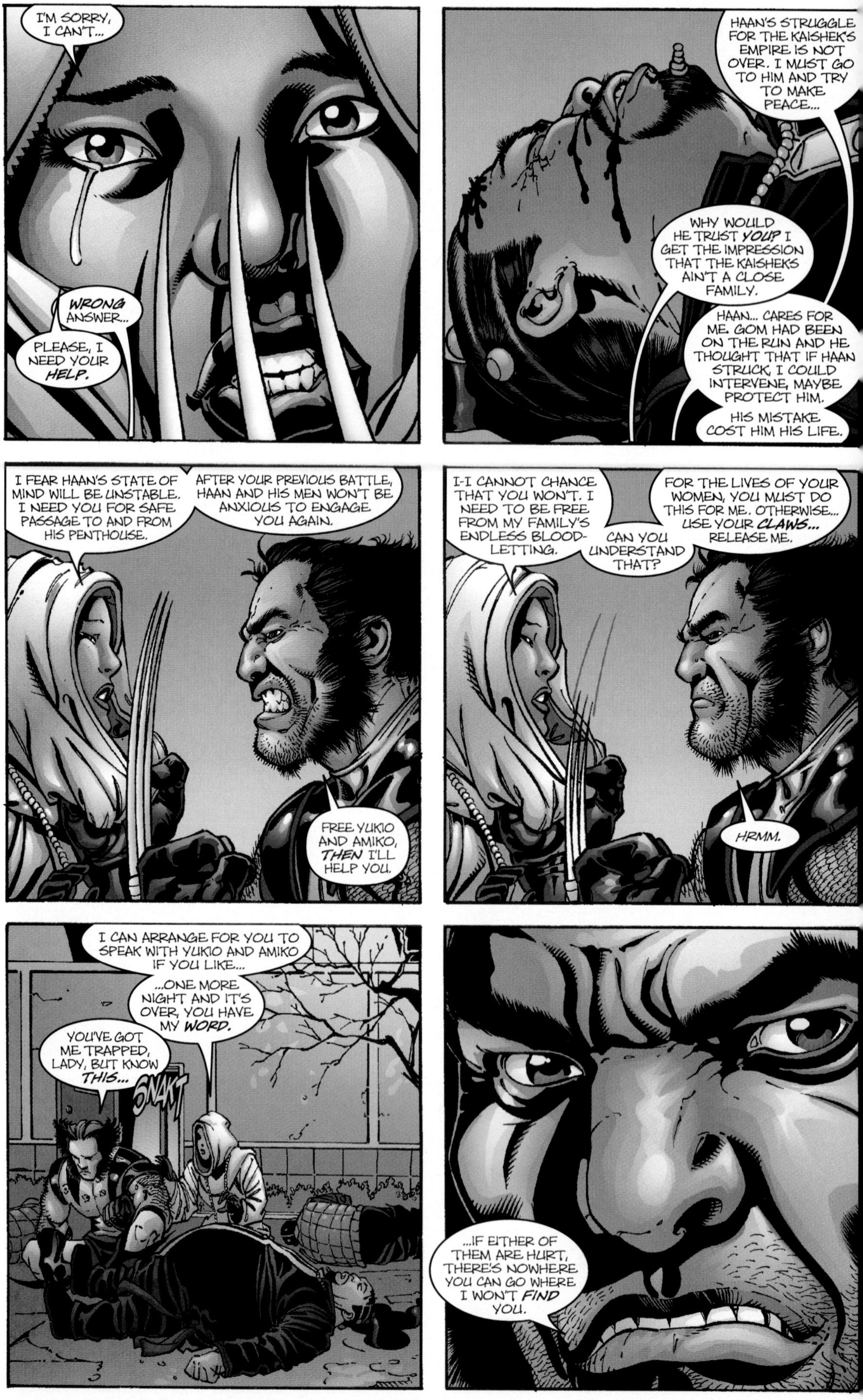
I'M SORRY, I CAN'T...
WRONG ANSWER...
PLEASE, I NEED YOUR HELP.
HAAN'S STRUGGLE FOR THE KAISHEK'S EMPIRE IS NOT OVER. I MUST GO TO HIM AND TRY TO MAKE PEACE...
WHY WOULD HE TRUST YOU? I GET THE IMPRESSION THAT THE KAISHEKS AIN'T A CLOSE FAMILY.
HAAN... CARES FOR ME. GOM HAD BEEN ON THE RUN AND HE THOUGHT THAT IF HAAN STRUCK, I COULD INTERVENE, MAYBE PROTECT HIM.
HIS MISTAKE COST HIM HIS LIFE.
I FEAR HAAN'S STATE OF MIND WILL BE UNSTABLE. I NEED YOU FOR SAFE PASSAGE TO AND FROM HIS PENTHOUSE.
AFTER YOUR PREVIOUS BATTLE, HAAN AND HIS MEN WON'T BE ANXIOUS TO ENGAGE YOU AGAIN.
FREE YUKIO AND AMIKO, THEN I'LL HELP YOU.
I-I CANNOT CHANCE THAT YOU WON'T. I NEED TO BE FREE FROM MY FAMILY'S ENDLESS BLOOD-LETTING.
CAN YOU UNDERSTAND THAT?
FOR THE LIVES OF YOUR WOMEN, YOU MUST DO THIS FOR ME. OTHERWISE... USE YOUR CLAWS... RELEASE ME.
HRMM.
I CAN ARRANGE FOR YOU TO SPEAK WITH YUKIO AND AMIKO IF YOU LIKE...
...ONE MORE NIGHT AND IT'S OVER, YOU HAVE MY WORD.
YOU'VE GOT ME TRAPPED, LADY, BUT KNOW THIS...
SNAKT
...IF EITHER OF THEM ARE HURT, THERE'S NOWHERE YOU CAN GO WHERE I WON'T FIND YOU.

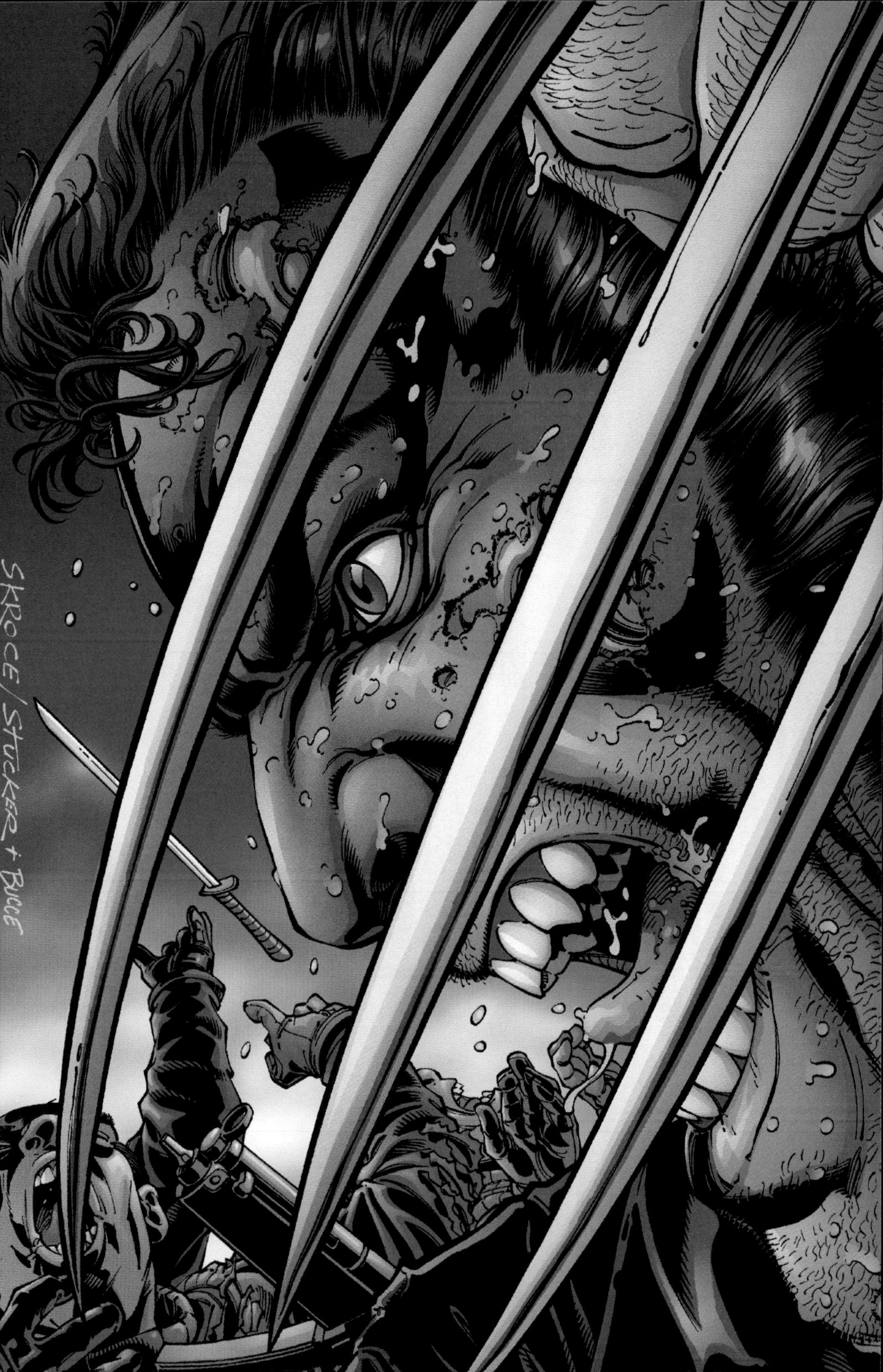
SKROCE/STUCKER + BUCCE

CHAPTER THREE

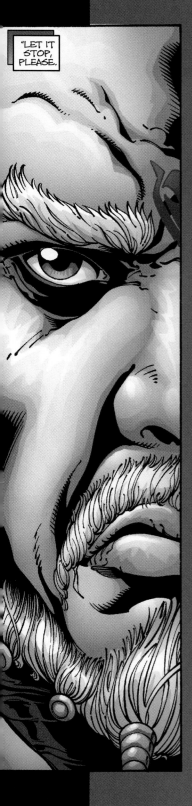

"LET IT STOP, PLEASE.

"I WANT PEACE, YOLYN."

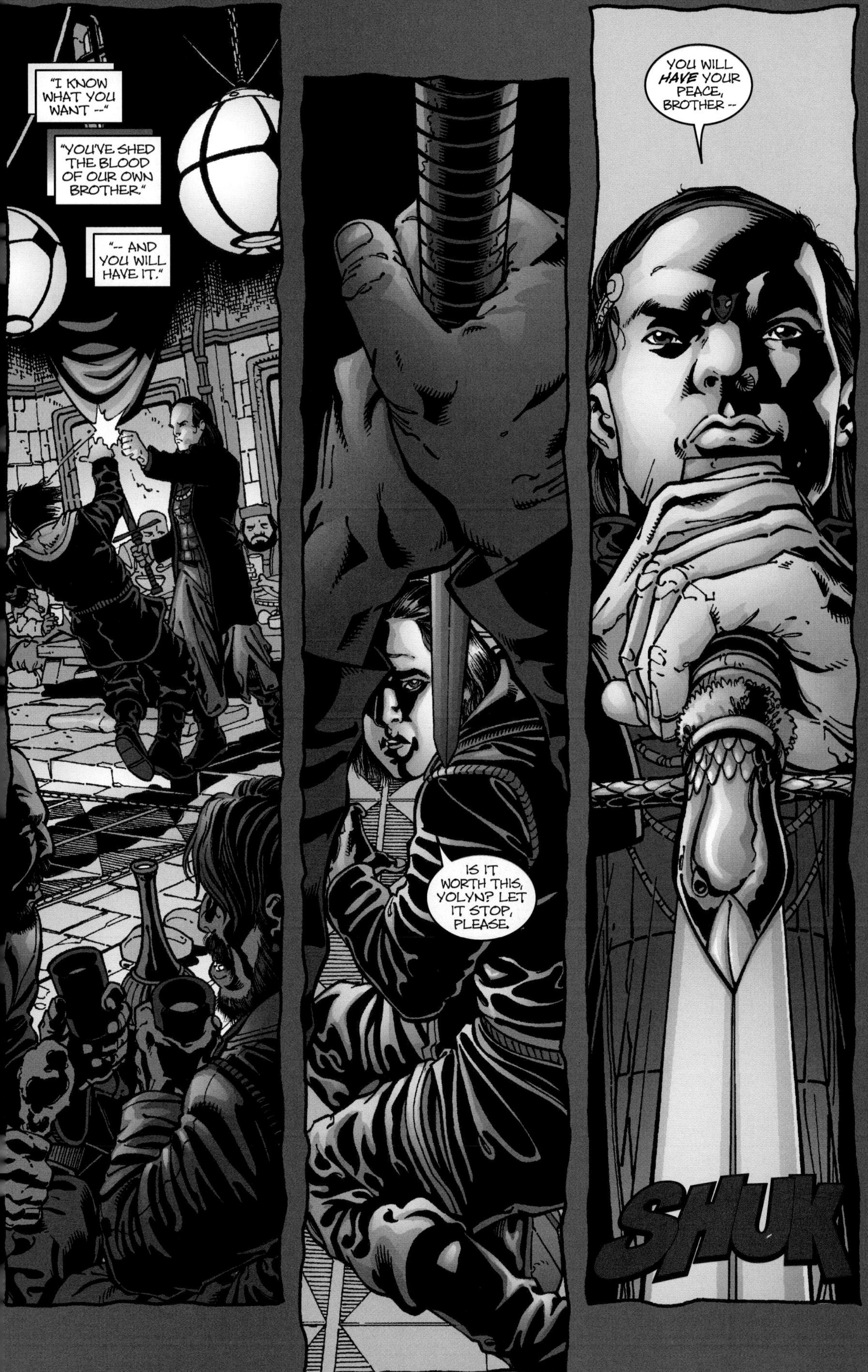
"I KNOW WHAT YOU WANT --"
"YOU'VE SHED THE BLOOD OF OUR OWN BROTHER."
"-- AND YOU WILL HAVE IT."
IS IT WORTH THIS, YOLYN? LET IT STOP, PLEASE.
YOU WILL *HAVE* YOUR PEACE, BROTHER --
SHUK

"-- IN DEATH."

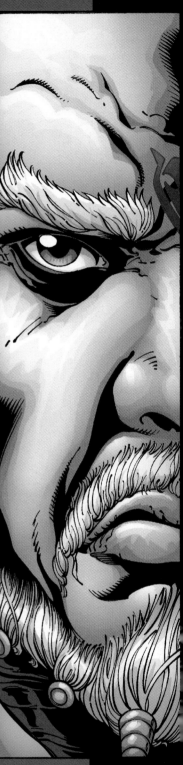

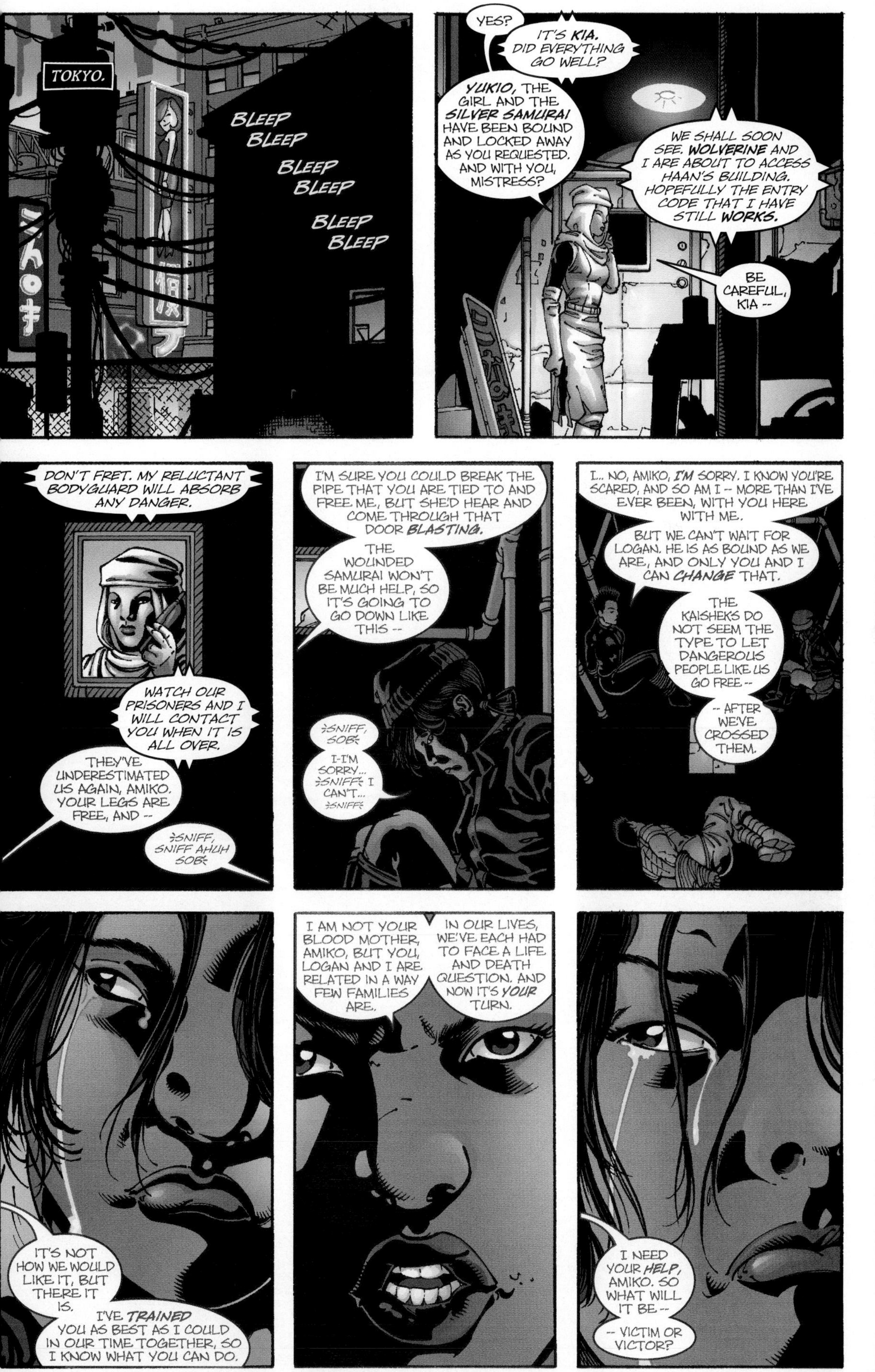
TOKYO.
BLEEP BLEEP BLEEP BLEEP BLEEP BLEEP
YES?
IT'S KIA. DID EVERYTHING GO WELL?
YUKIO, THE GIRL AND THE SILVER SAMURAI HAVE BEEN BOUND AND LOCKED AWAY AS YOU REQUESTED. AND WITH YOU, MISTRESS?
WE SHALL SOON SEE. WOLVERINE AND I ARE ABOUT TO ACCESS HAAN'S BUILDING. HOPEFULLY THE ENTRY CODE THAT I HAVE STILL WORKS.
BE CAREFUL, KIA --
DON'T FRET. MY RELUCTANT BODYGUARD WILL ABSORB ANY DANGER.
WATCH OUR PRISONERS AND I WILL CONTACT YOU WHEN IT IS ALL OVER.
THEY'VE UNDERESTIMATED US AGAIN, AMIKO. YOUR LEGS ARE FREE, AND --
SNIFF, SNIFF AHUH SOB
I'M SURE YOU COULD BREAK THE PIPE THAT YOU ARE TIED TO AND FREE ME, BUT SHE'D HEAR AND COME THROUGH THAT DOOR BLASTING.
THE WOUNDED SAMURAI WON'T BE MUCH HELP, SO IT'S GOING TO GO DOWN LIKE THIS --
SNIFF, SOB
I-I'M SORRY... SNIFF I CAN'T... SNIFF
I... NO, AMIKO, I'M SORRY. I KNOW YOU'RE SCARED, AND SO AM I -- MORE THAN I'VE EVER BEEN, WITH YOU HERE WITH ME.
BUT WE CAN'T WAIT FOR LOGAN. HE IS AS BOUND AS WE ARE, AND ONLY YOU AND I CAN CHANGE THAT.
THE KAISHEKS DO NOT SEEM THE TYPE TO LET DANGEROUS PEOPLE LIKE US GO FREE --
-- AFTER WE'VE CROSSED THEM.
IT'S NOT HOW WE WOULD LIKE IT, BUT THERE IT IS.
I'VE TRAINED YOU AS BEST AS I COULD IN OUR TIME TOGETHER, SO I KNOW WHAT YOU CAN DO.
I AM NOT YOUR BLOOD MOTHER, AMIKO, BUT YOU, LOGAN AND I ARE RELATED IN A WAY FEW FAMILIES ARE.
IN OUR LIVES, WE'VE EACH HAD TO FACE A LIFE AND DEATH QUESTION. AND NOW IT'S YOUR TURN.
I NEED YOUR HELP, AMIKO. SO WHAT WILL IT BE --
-- VICTIM OR VICTOR?

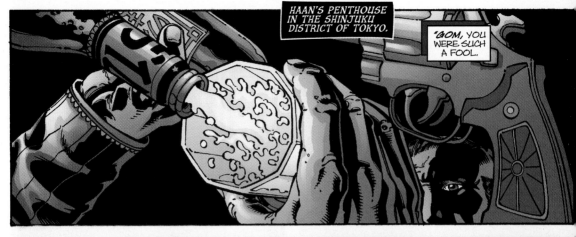

HAAN'S PENTHOUSE IN THE SHINJUKU DISTRICT OF TOKYO.

"GOM, YOU WERE SUCH A FOOL.

"YOUR GAINING CONTROL OF THE *KAISHEK EMPIRE* WAS A FANTASY...

"...A FANTASY WITH A FATAL PRICE.

...MERCY ...I AM YOUR BROTHER

"YOUR ARROGANCE AND IGNORANCE KILLED YOU, GOM...

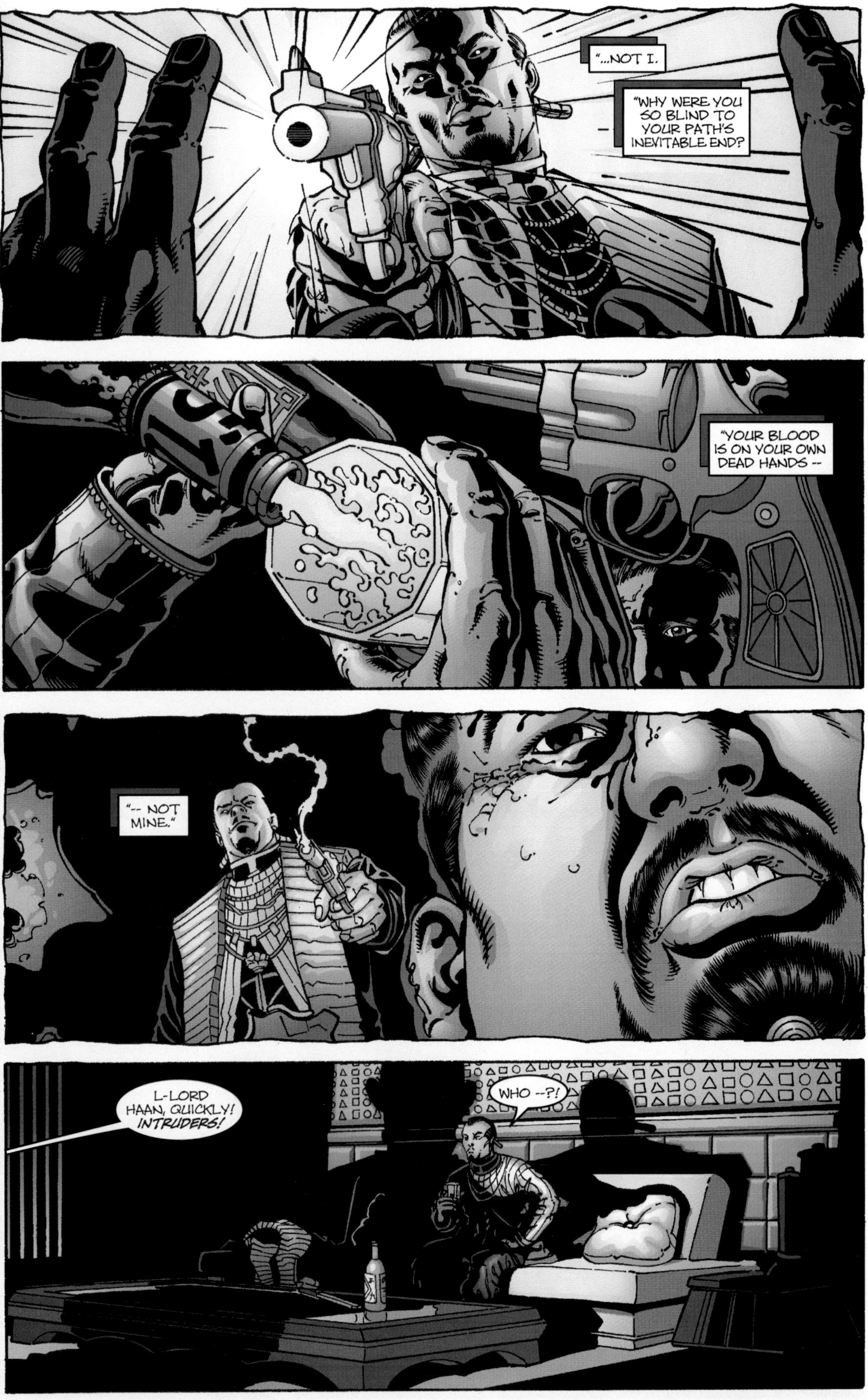
"...NOT I.
"WHY WERE YOU SO BLIND TO YOUR PATH'S INEVITABLE END?
"YOUR BLOOD IS ON YOUR OWN DEAD HANDS --
"-- NOT MINE."
L-LORD HAAN, QUICKLY! INTRUDERS!
WHO --?!

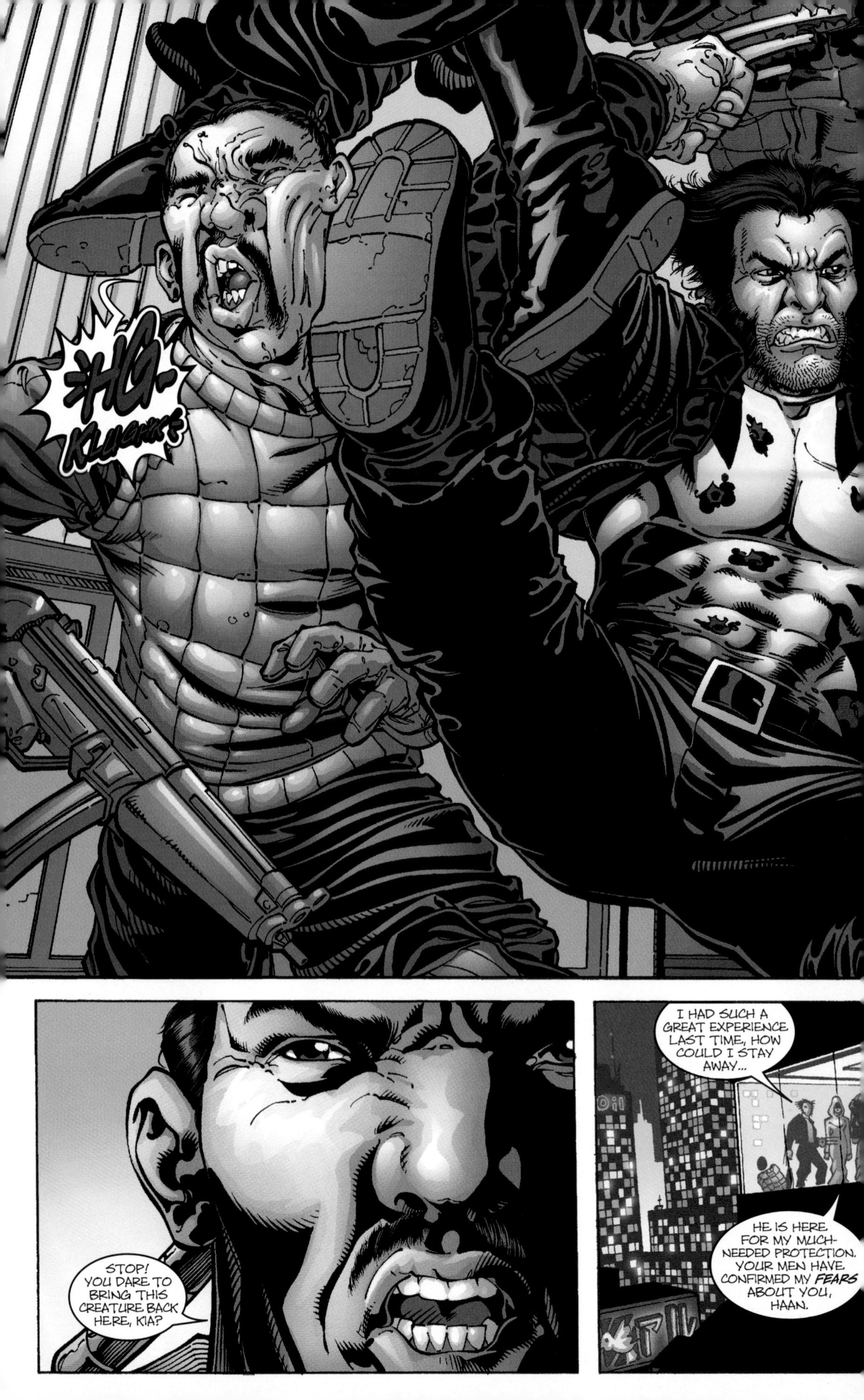
HG-KLUCHK!
STOP! YOU DARE TO BRING THIS CREATURE BACK HERE, KIA?
I HAD SUCH A GREAT EXPERIENCE LAST TIME, HOW COULD I STAY AWAY...
HE IS HERE FOR MY MUCH-NEEDED PROTECTION. YOUR MEN HAVE CONFIRMED MY FEARS ABOUT YOU, HAAN.

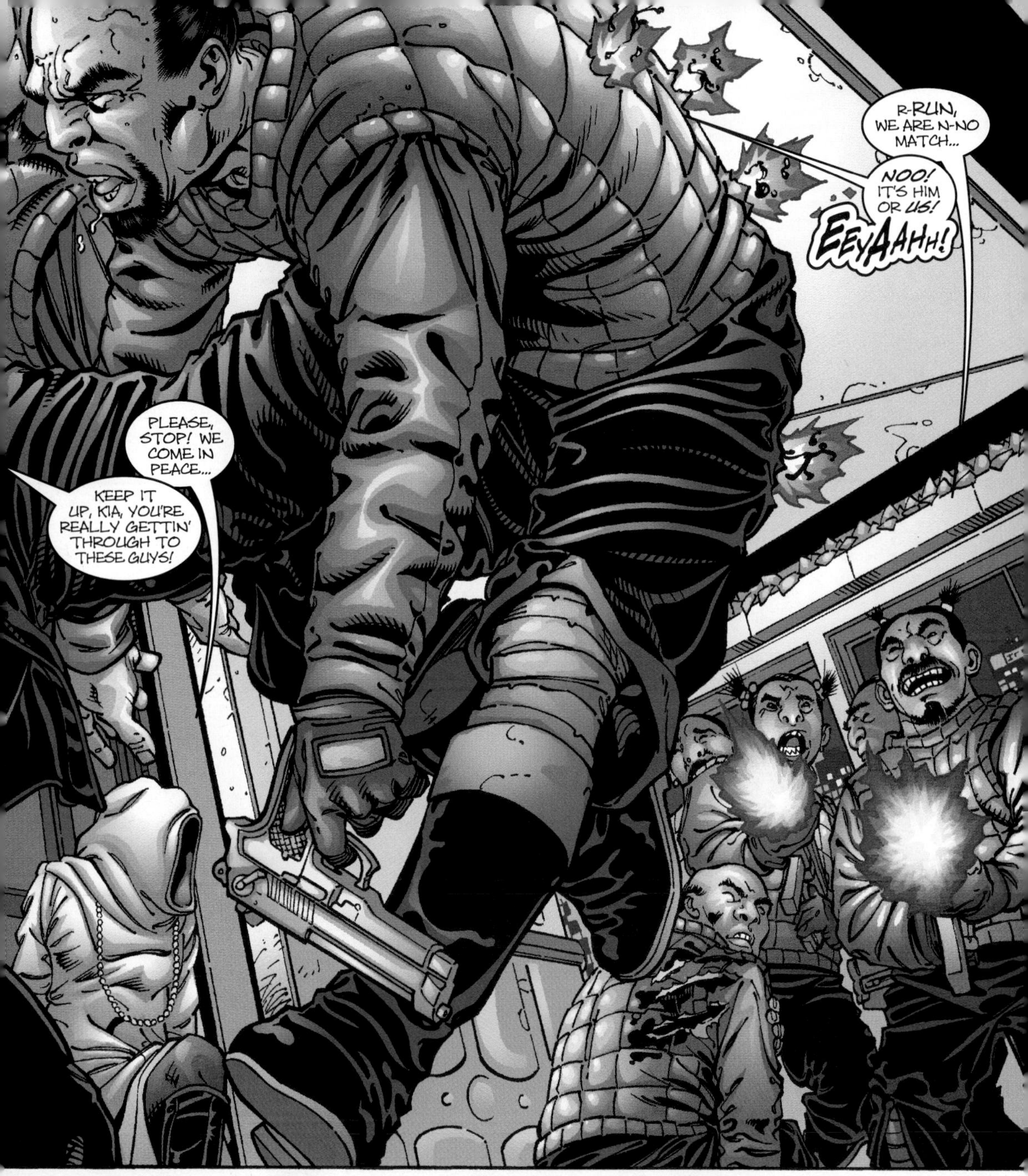
R-RUN, WE ARE N-NO MATCH...
NOO! IT'S HIM OR US!
EEYAAHH!
PLEASE, STOP! WE COME IN PEACE...
KEEP IT UP, KIA, YOU'RE REALLY GETTIN' THROUGH TO THESE GUYS!

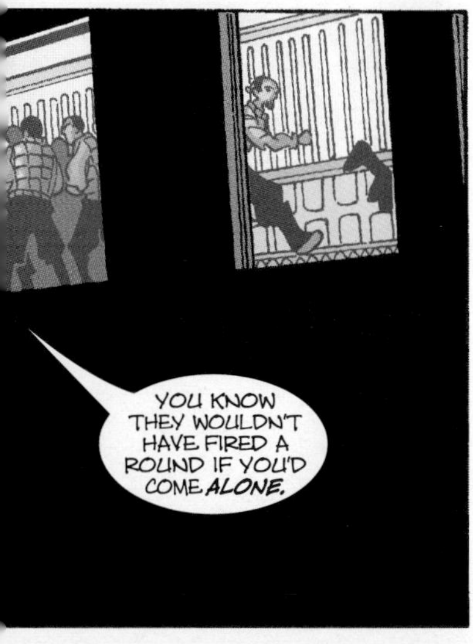
YOU KNOW THEY WOULDN'T HAVE FIRED A ROUND IF YOU'D COME ALONE.

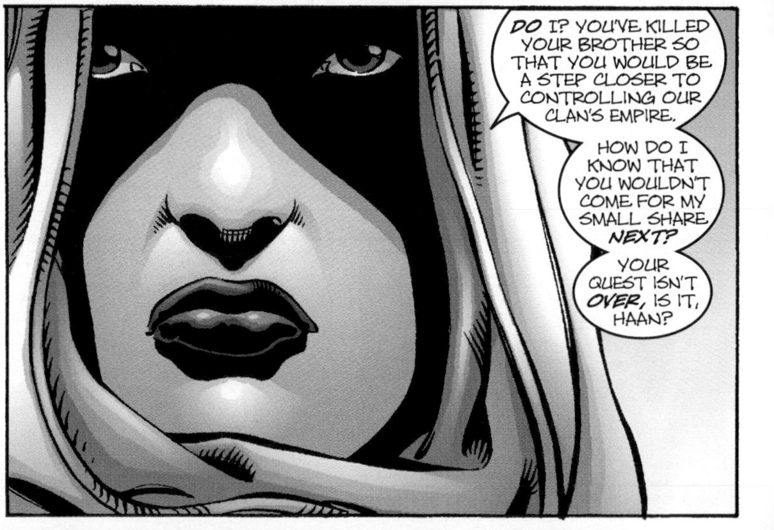
DO I? YOU'VE KILLED YOUR BROTHER SO THAT YOU WOULD BE A STEP CLOSER TO CONTROLLING OUR CLAN'S EMPIRE.
HOW DO I KNOW THAT YOU WOULDN'T COME FOR MY SMALL SHARE NEXT?
YOUR QUEST ISN'T OVER, IS IT, HAAN?

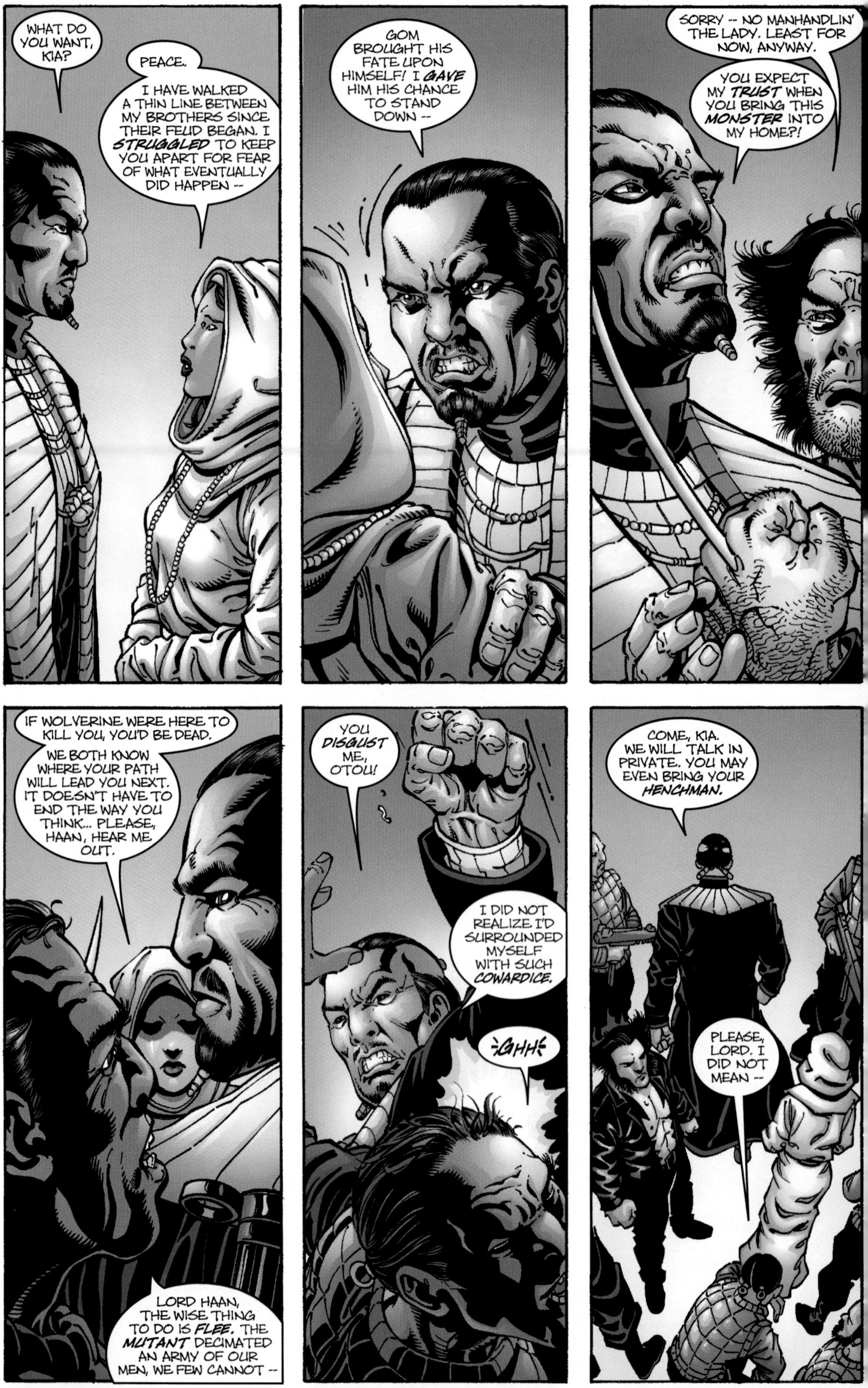
WHAT DO YOU WANT, KIA?
PEACE.
I HAVE WALKED A THIN LINE BETWEEN MY BROTHERS SINCE THEIR FEUD BEGAN. I STRUGGLED TO KEEP YOU APART FOR FEAR OF WHAT EVENTUALLY DID HAPPEN --
GOM BROUGHT HIS FATE UPON HIMSELF! I GAVE HIM HIS CHANCE TO STAND DOWN --
SORRY -- NO MANHANDLIN' THE LADY. LEAST FOR NOW, ANYWAY.
YOU EXPECT MY TRUST WHEN YOU BRING THIS MONSTER INTO MY HOME?!
IF WOLVERINE WERE HERE TO KILL YOU, YOU'D BE DEAD.
WE BOTH KNOW WHERE YOUR PATH WILL LEAD YOU NEXT. IT DOESN'T HAVE TO END THE WAY YOU THINK... PLEASE, HAAN, HEAR ME OUT.
LORD HAAN, THE WISE THING TO DO IS FLEE. THE MUTANT DECIMATED AN ARMY OF OUR MEN, WE FEW CANNOT --
YOU DISGUST ME, OTOU!
I DID NOT REALIZE I'D SURROUNDED MYSELF WITH SUCH COWARDICE.
GHH
COME, KIA. WE WILL TALK IN PRIVATE. YOU MAY EVEN BRING YOUR HENCHMAN.
PLEASE, LORD. I DID NOT MEAN --

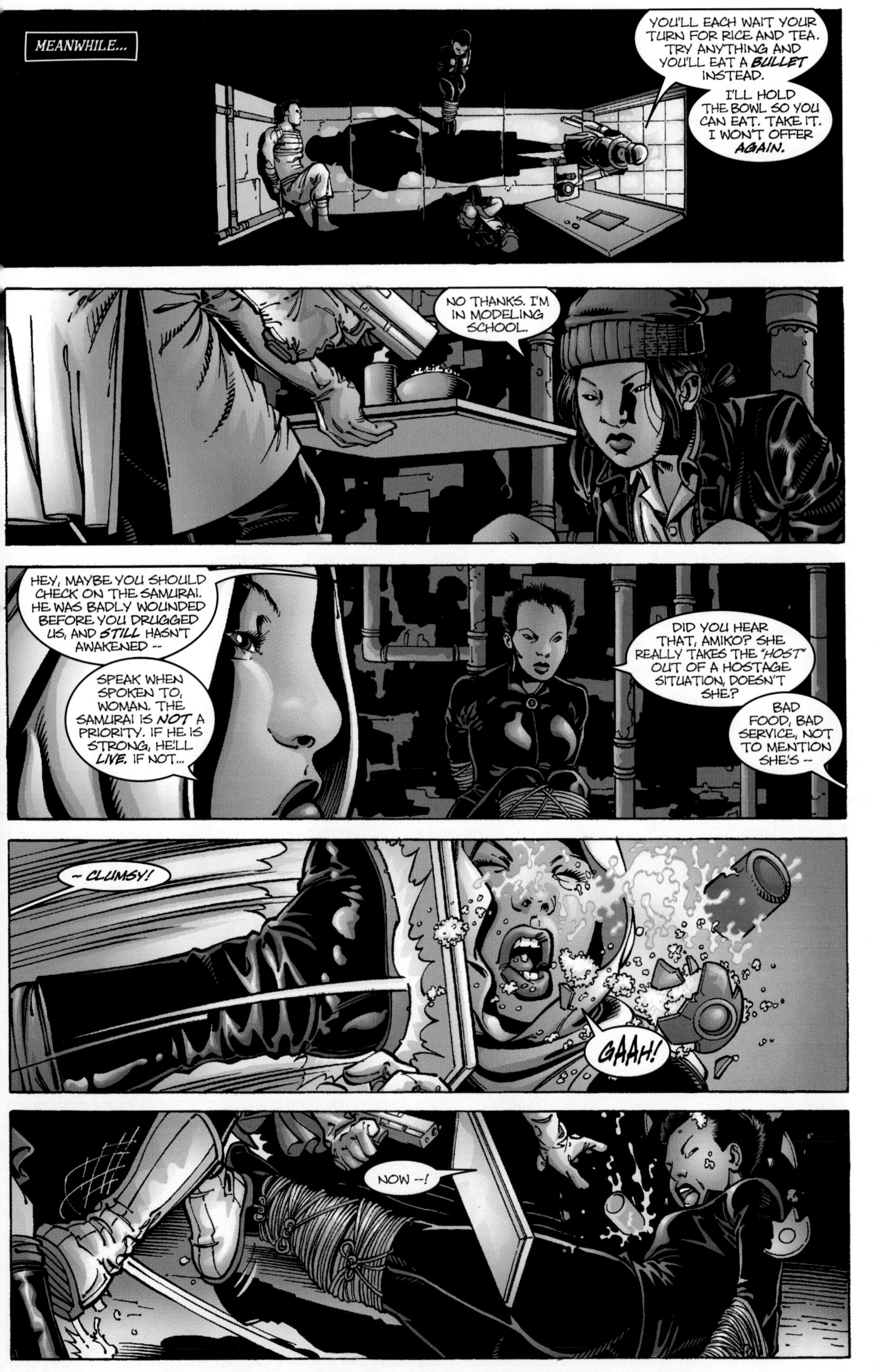
MEANWHILE...
YOU'LL EACH WAIT YOUR TURN FOR RICE AND TEA. TRY ANYTHING AND YOU'LL EAT A *BULLET* INSTEAD.
I'LL HOLD THE BOWL SO YOU CAN EAT. TAKE IT. I WON'T OFFER *AGAIN.*
NO THANKS. I'M IN MODELING SCHOOL.
HEY, MAYBE YOU SHOULD CHECK ON THE SAMURAI. HE WAS BADLY WOUNDED BEFORE YOU DRUGGED US, AND *STILL* HASN'T AWAKENED --
SPEAK WHEN SPOKEN TO, WOMAN. THE SAMURAI IS *NOT* A PRIORITY. IF HE IS STRONG, HE'LL *LIVE.* IF NOT...
DID YOU HEAR THAT, AMIKO? SHE REALLY TAKES THE *"HOST"* OUT OF A HOSTAGE SITUATION, DOESN'T SHE?
BAD FOOD, BAD SERVICE, NOT TO MENTION SHE'S --
-- *CLUMSY!*
GAAH!
NOW --!

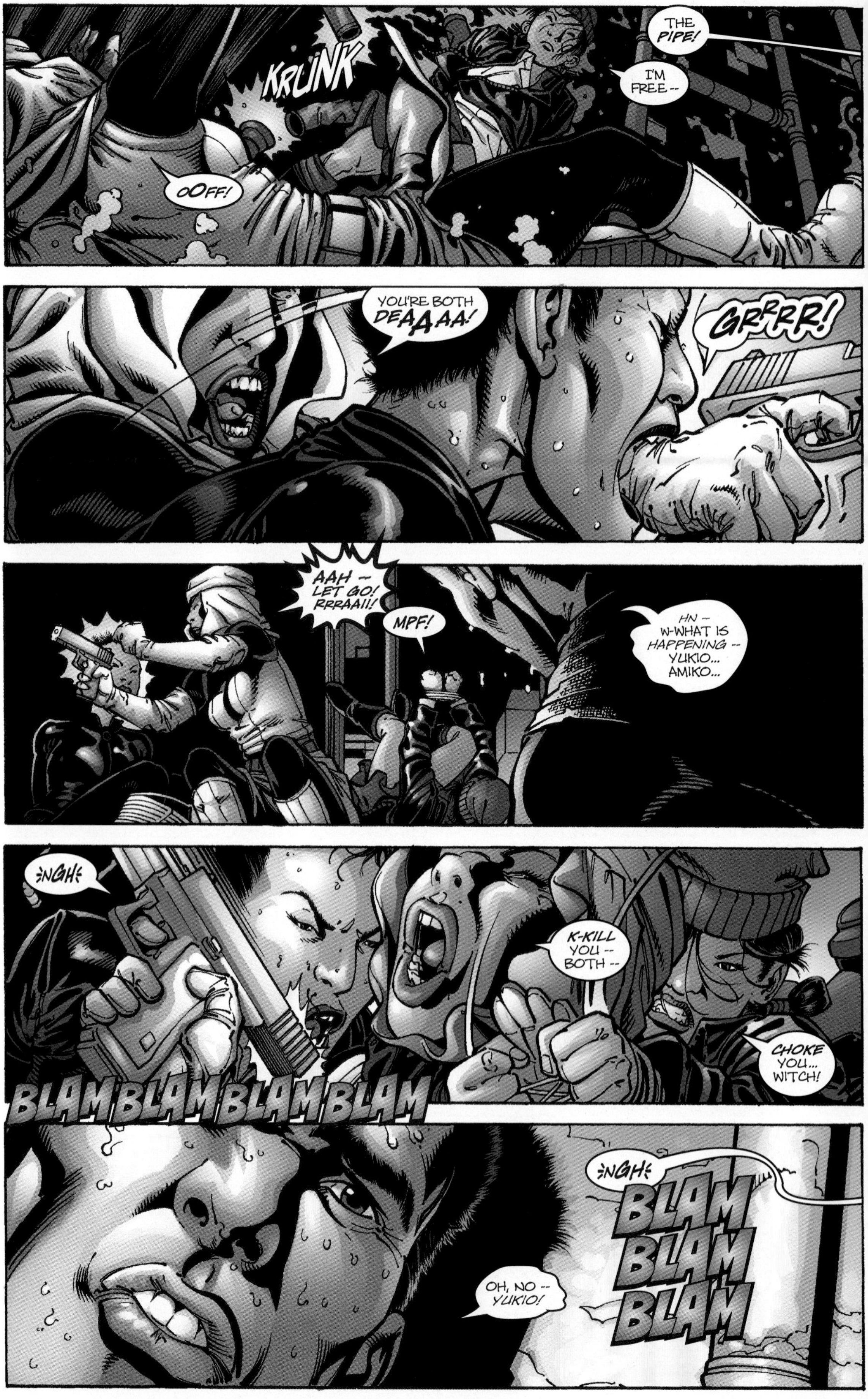
KRUNK
THE PIPE!
I'M FREE --
OOFF!
YOU'RE BOTH DEAAAA!
GRRRR!
AAH -- LET GO! RRRAAII!
MPF!
HN -- W-WHAT IS HAPPENING -- YUKIO... AMIKO...
NGH
K-KILL YOU -- BOTH --
CHOKE YOU... WITCH!
BLAM BLAM BLAM BLAM
NGH
BLAM BLAM BLAM
OH, NO -- YUKIO!

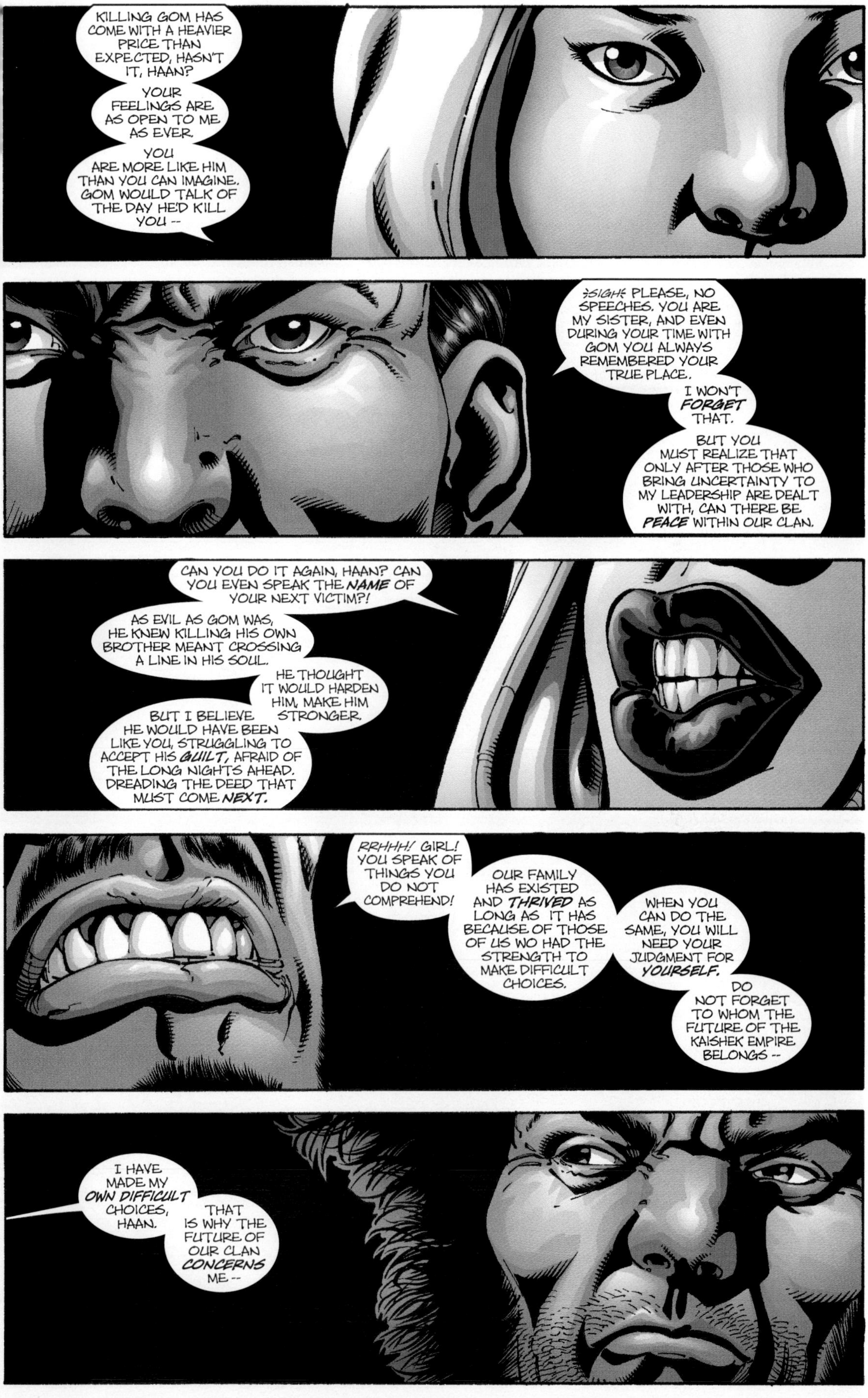
KILLING GOM HAS COME WITH A HEAVIER PRICE THAN EXPECTED, HASN'T IT, HAAN?
YOUR FEELINGS ARE AS OPEN TO ME AS EVER.
YOU ARE MORE LIKE HIM THAN YOU CAN IMAGINE. GOM WOULD TALK OF THE DAY HE'D KILL YOU --
SIGH PLEASE, NO SPEECHES. YOU ARE MY SISTER, AND EVEN DURING YOUR TIME WITH GOM YOU ALWAYS REMEMBERED YOUR TRUE PLACE.
I WON'T FORGET THAT.
BUT YOU MUST REALIZE THAT ONLY AFTER THOSE WHO BRING UNCERTAINTY TO MY LEADERSHIP ARE DEALT WITH, CAN THERE BE PEACE WITHIN OUR CLAN.
CAN YOU DO IT AGAIN, HAAN? CAN YOU EVEN SPEAK THE NAME OF YOUR NEXT VICTIM?!
AS EVIL AS GOM WAS, HE KNEW KILLING HIS OWN BROTHER MEANT CROSSING A LINE IN HIS SOUL.
HE THOUGHT IT WOULD HARDEN HIM, MAKE HIM STRONGER.
BUT I BELIEVE HE WOULD HAVE BEEN LIKE YOU, STRUGGLING TO ACCEPT HIS GUILT, AFRAID OF THE LONG NIGHTS AHEAD. DREADING THE DEED THAT MUST COME NEXT.
RRHHH! GIRL! YOU SPEAK OF THINGS YOU DO NOT COMPREHEND!
OUR FAMILY HAS EXISTED AND THRIVED AS LONG AS IT HAS BECAUSE OF THOSE OF US WO HAD THE STRENGTH TO MAKE DIFFICULT CHOICES.
WHEN YOU CAN DO THE SAME, YOU WILL NEED YOUR JUDGMENT FOR YOURSELF.
DO NOT FORGET TO WHOM THE FUTURE OF THE KAISHEK EMPIRE BELONGS --
I HAVE MADE MY OWN DIFFICULT CHOICES, HAAN.
THAT IS WHY THE FUTURE OF OUR CLAN CONCERNS ME --

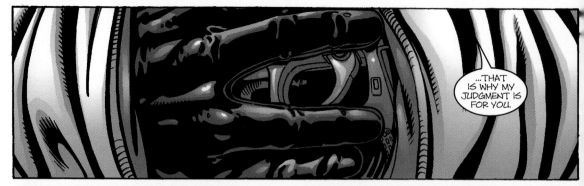

...THAT IS WHY MY JUDGMENT IS FOR YOU.

BLEEP BLEEP

BLEEP BLEEP

BLEEP BLEEP

THAT YOUR CEL, DARLIN'? BETTER ANSWER IT. COULD BE SOMETHING ABOUT THE GIRLS.

BLEEP BLEEP

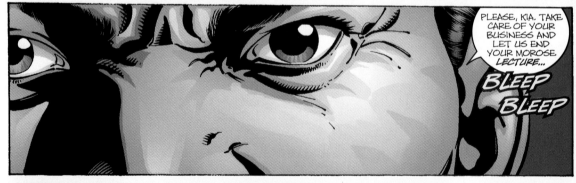

PLEASE, KIA. TAKE CARE OF YOUR BUSINESS AND LET US END YOUR MOROSE LECTURE...

BLEEP BLEEP

BLEEP

TUPA, NOW IS NOT THE TI --

LOGAN, WE'RE FREE! GET HER!

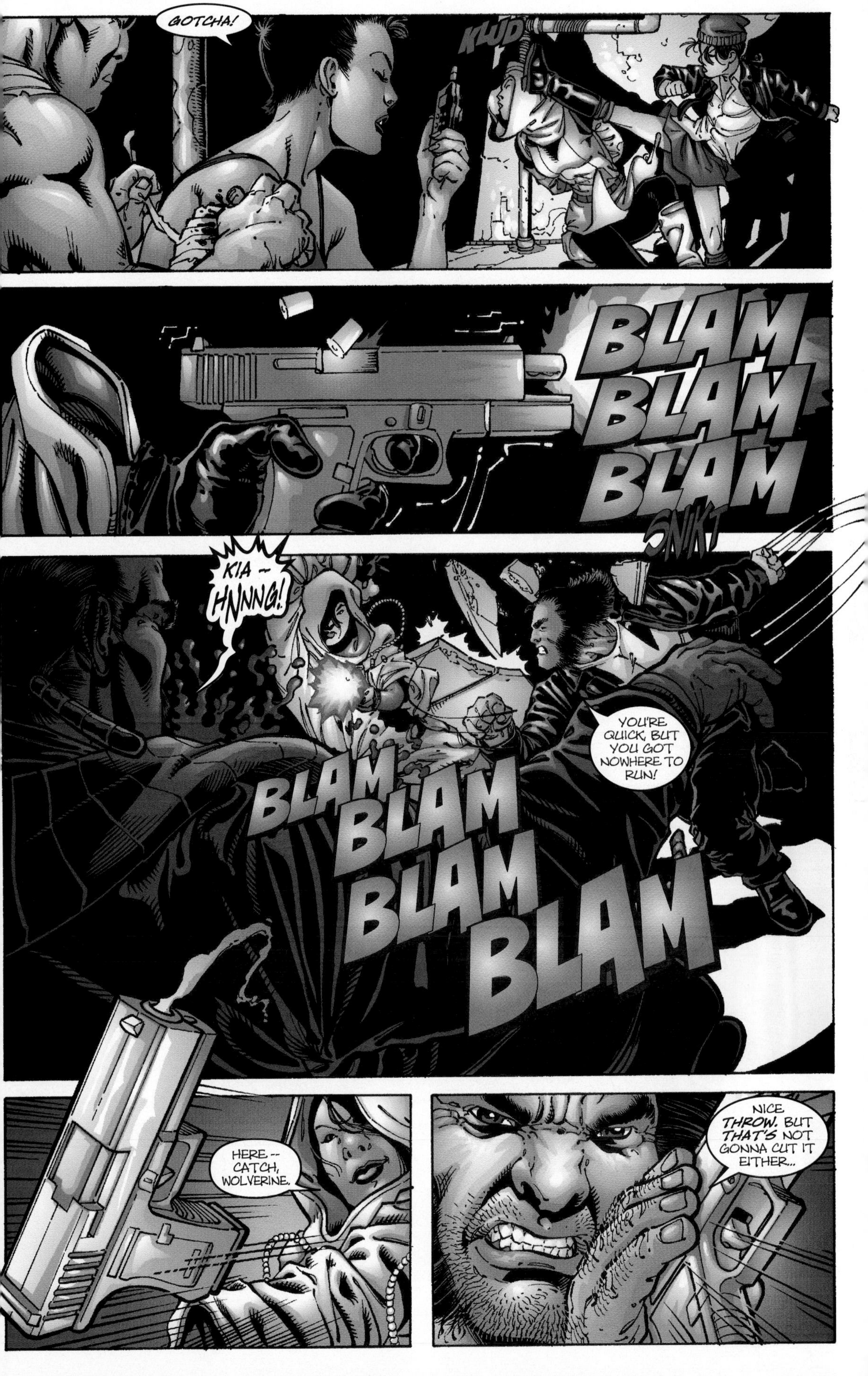

GOTCHA!
KLUD
BLAM
BLAM
BLAM
SNIKT
KIA -- HNNNG!
YOU'RE QUICK, BUT YOU GOT NOWHERE TO RUN!
BLAM
BLAM
BLAM
BLAM
HERE -- CATCH, WOLVERINE.
NICE THROW. BUT THAT'S NOT GONNA CUT IT EITHER...

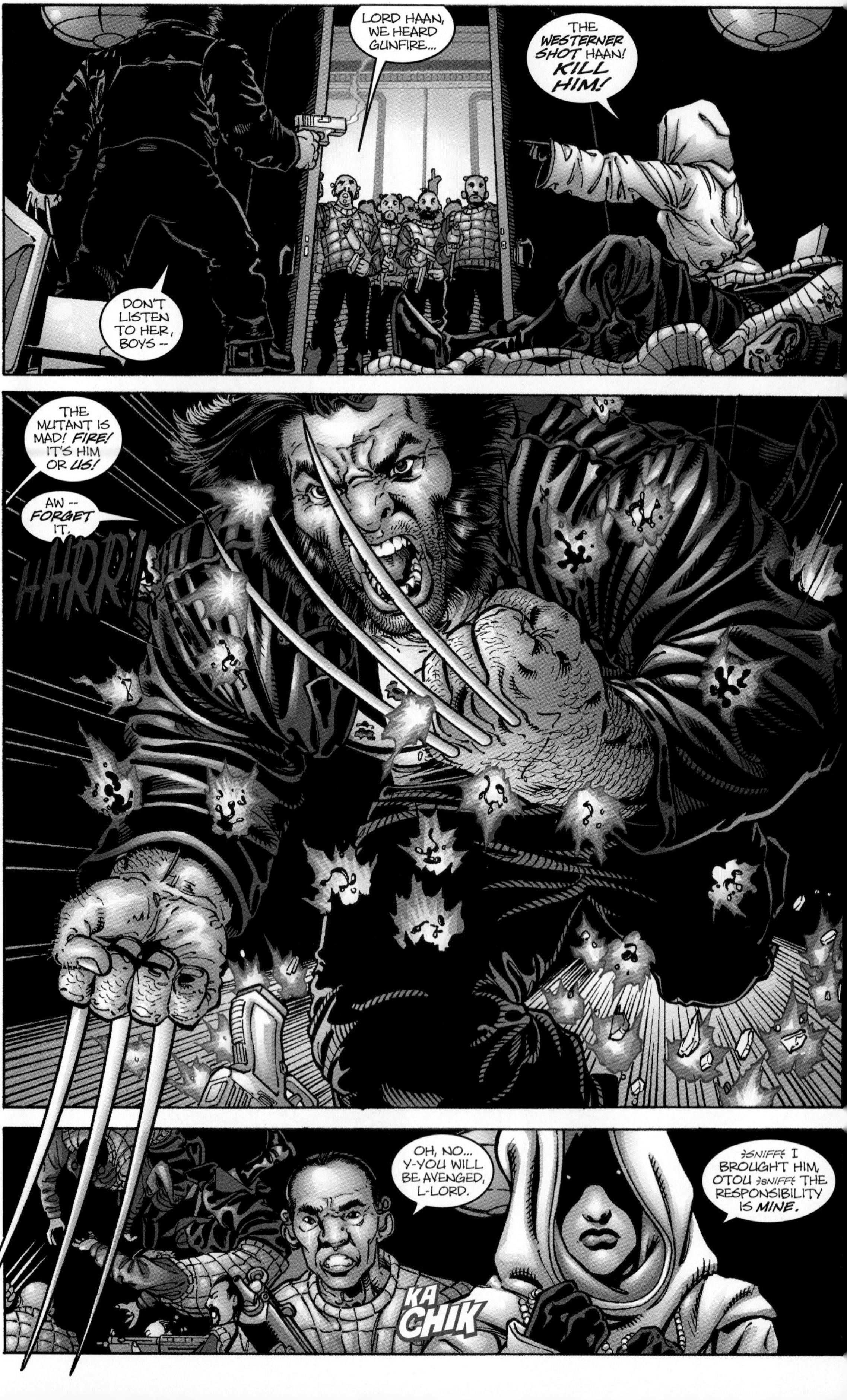
LORD HAAN, WE HEARD GUNFIRE...
THE WESTERNER SHOT HAAN! KILL HIM!
DON'T LISTEN TO HER, BOYS --
THE MUTANT IS MAD! FIRE! IT'S HIM OR US!
AW -- FORGET IT.
HRRR!
OH, NO... Y-YOU WILL BE AVENGED, L-LORD.
SNIFF I BROUGHT HIM, OTOU SNIFF THE RESPONSIBILITY IS MINE.
KA CHIK

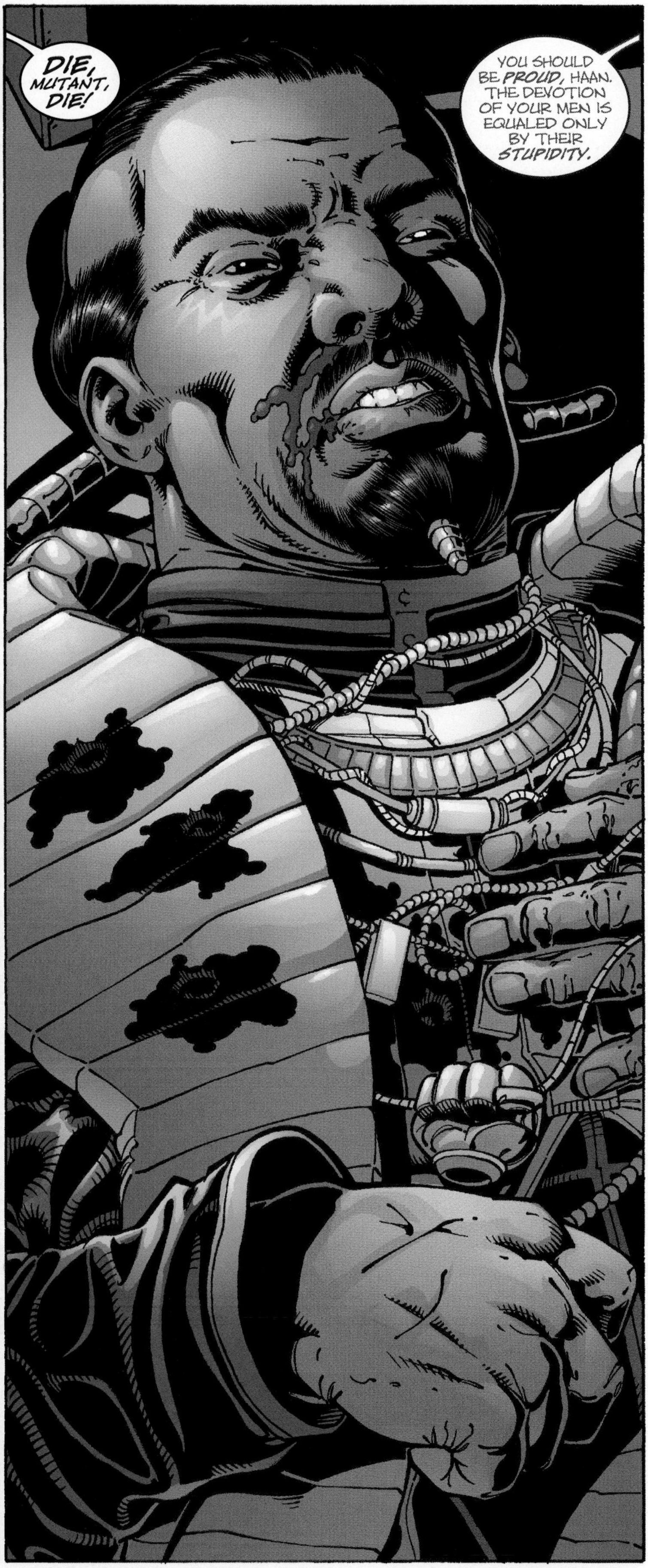
DIE, MUTANT, DIE!
YOU SHOULD BE PROUD, HAAN. THE DEVOTION OF YOUR MEN IS EQUALED ONLY BY THEIR STUPIDITY.

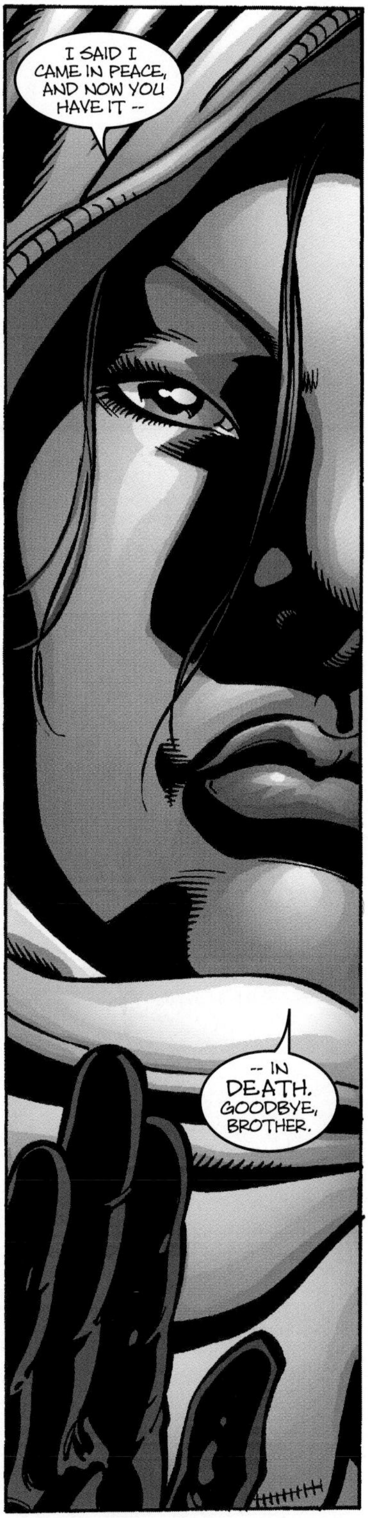
I SAID I CAME IN PEACE, AND NOW YOU HAVE IT --
-- IN DEATH. GOODBYE, BROTHER.

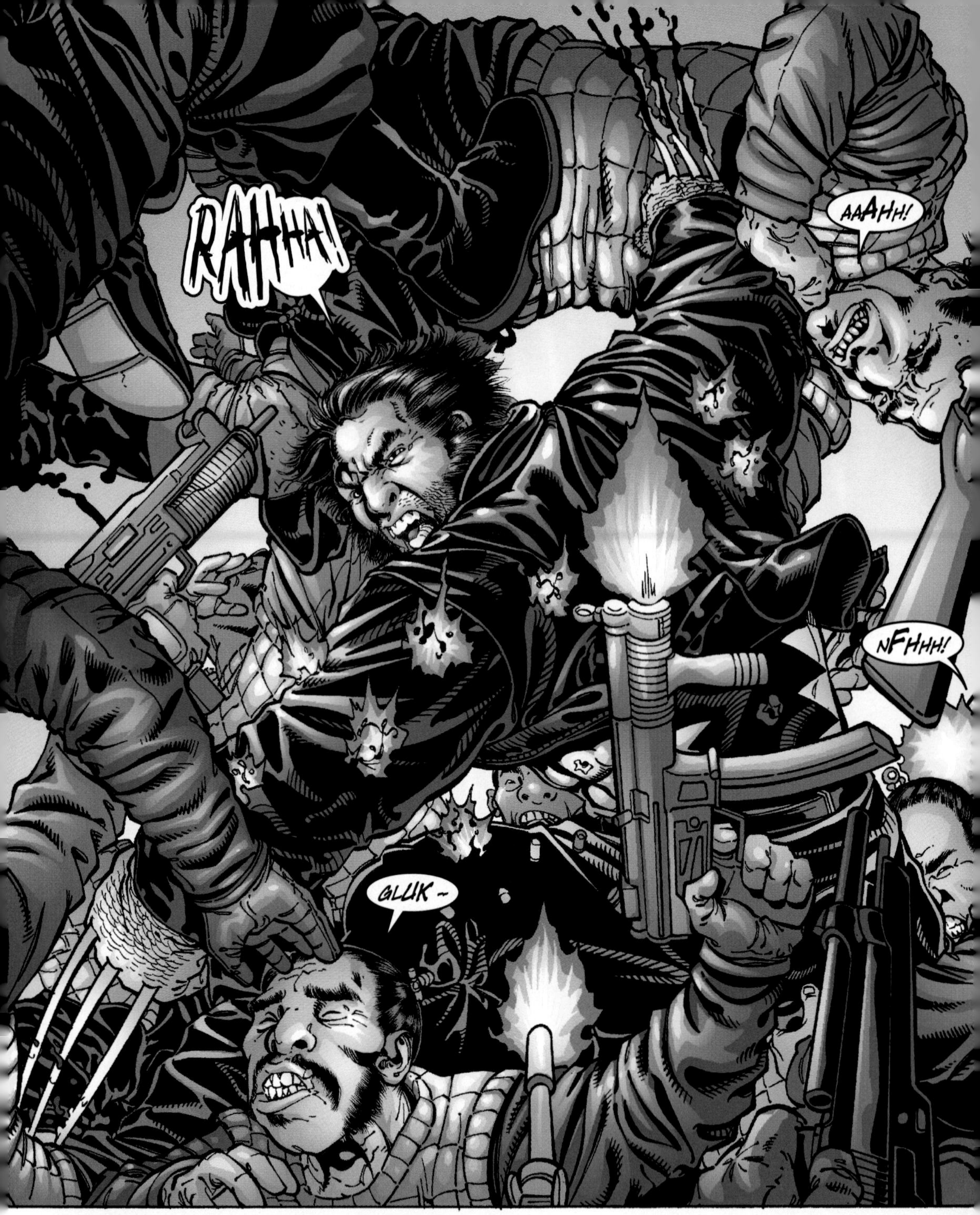
RAHHA!
AAAHH!
NFHHH!
GLUK --

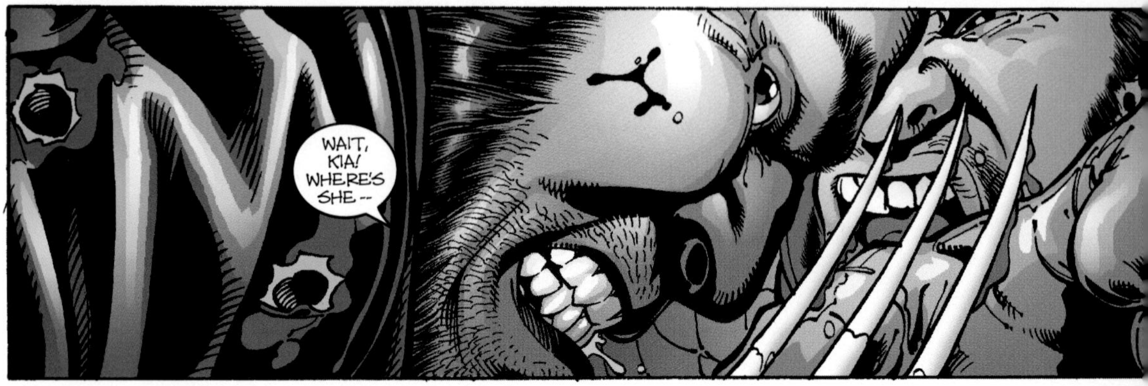
WAIT, KIA! WHERE'S SHE --

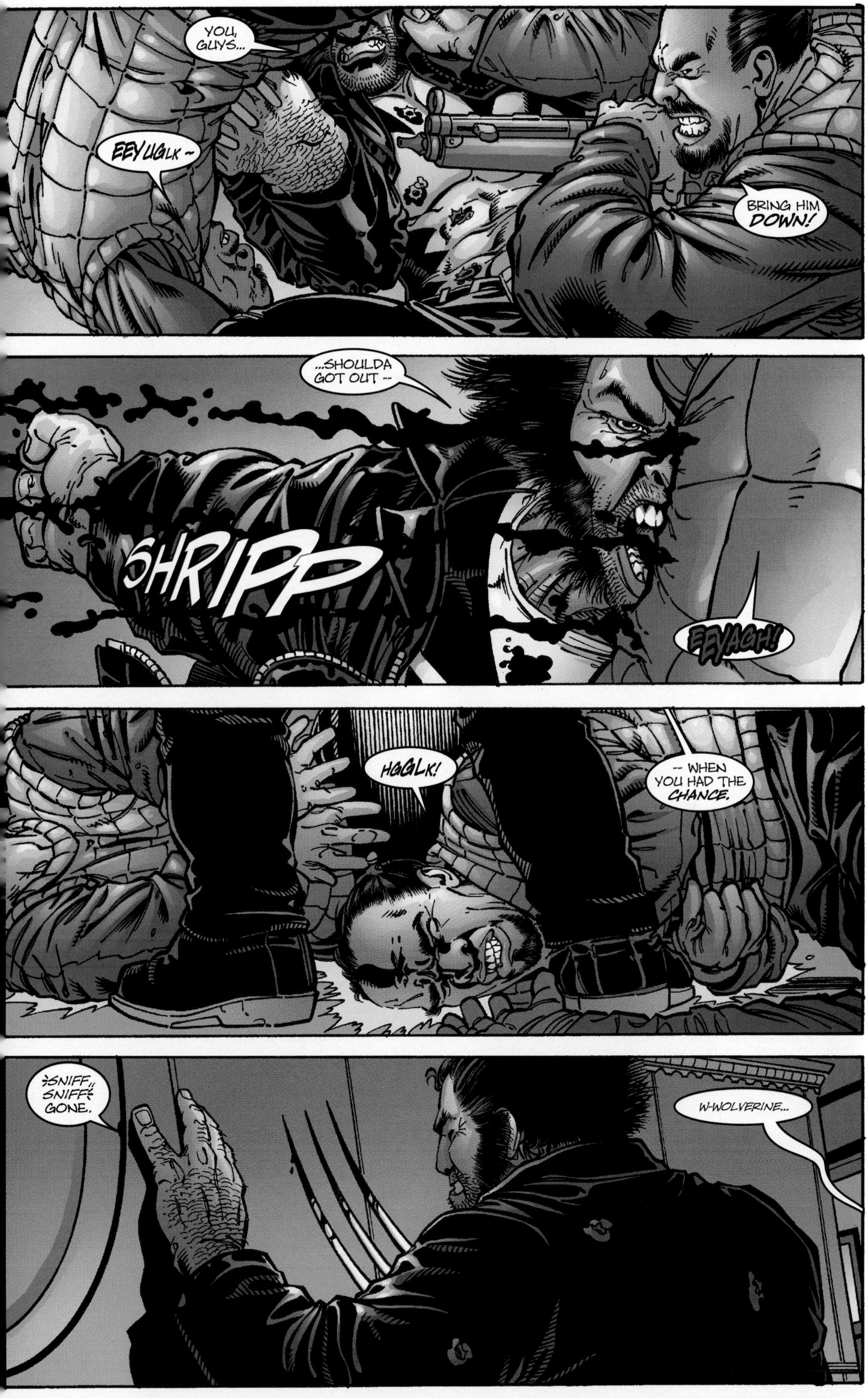
YOU, GUYS...
EEYUGLK --
BRING HIM DOWN!
...SHOULDA GOT OUT --
SHRIPP
EEYAGH!
HGGLK!
-- WHEN YOU HAD THE CHANCE.
SNIFF *SNIFF* GONE.
W-WOLVERINE...

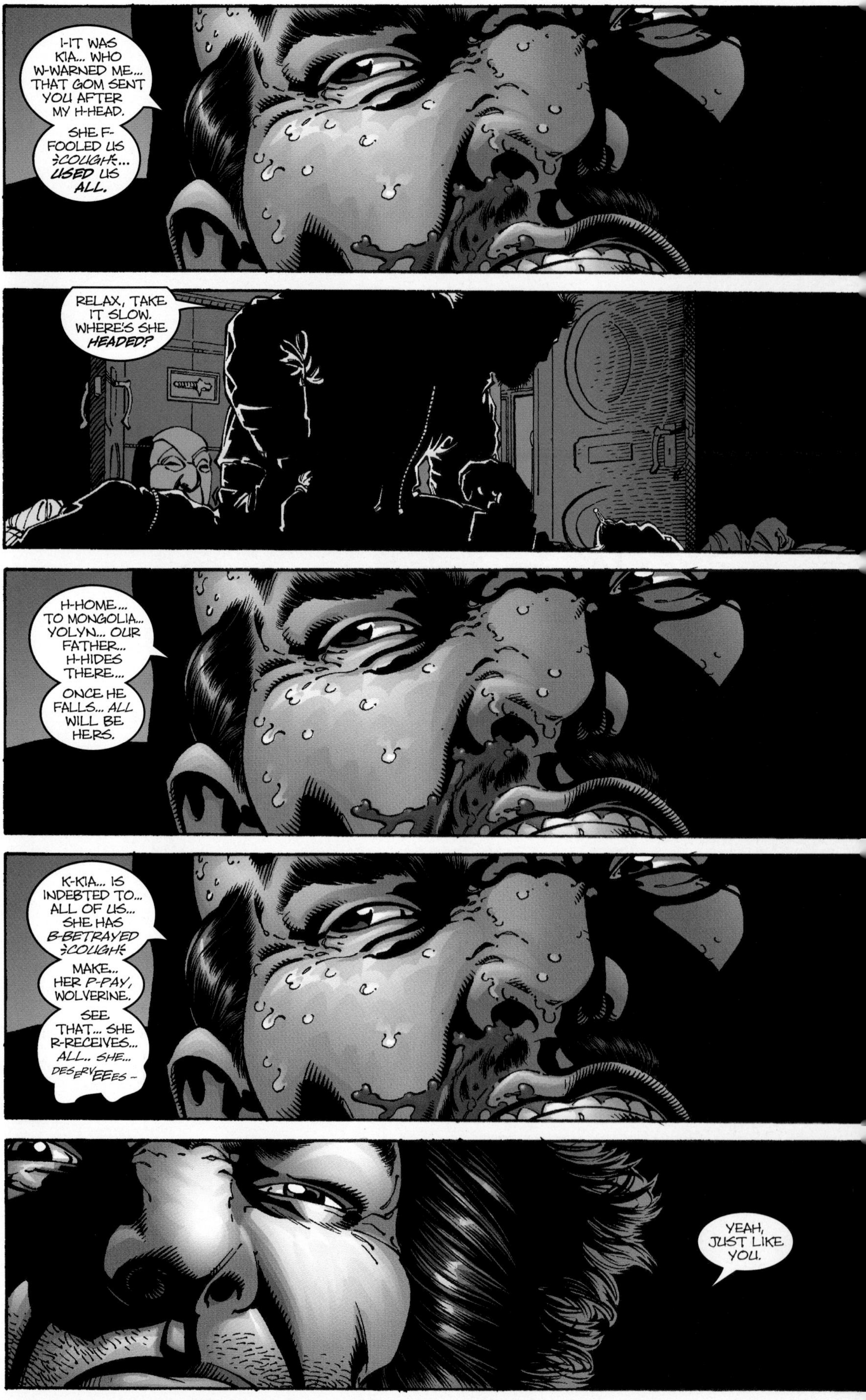
I-IT WAS KIA... WHO W-WARNED ME... THAT GOM SENT YOU AFTER MY H-HEAD.
SHE F-FOOLED US ≷COUGH≶... USED US ALL.
RELAX, TAKE IT SLOW. WHERE'S SHE HEADED?
H-HOME... TO MONGOLIA... YOLYN... OUR FATHER... H-HIDES THERE...
ONCE HE FALLS... ALL WILL BE HERS.
K-KIA... IS INDEBTED TO... ALL OF US... SHE HAS B-BETRAYED ≷COUGH≶
MAKE... HER P-PAY, WOLVERINE.
SEE THAT... SHE R-RECEIVES... ALL.. SHE... DESERVEEEs --
YEAH, JUST LIKE YOU.

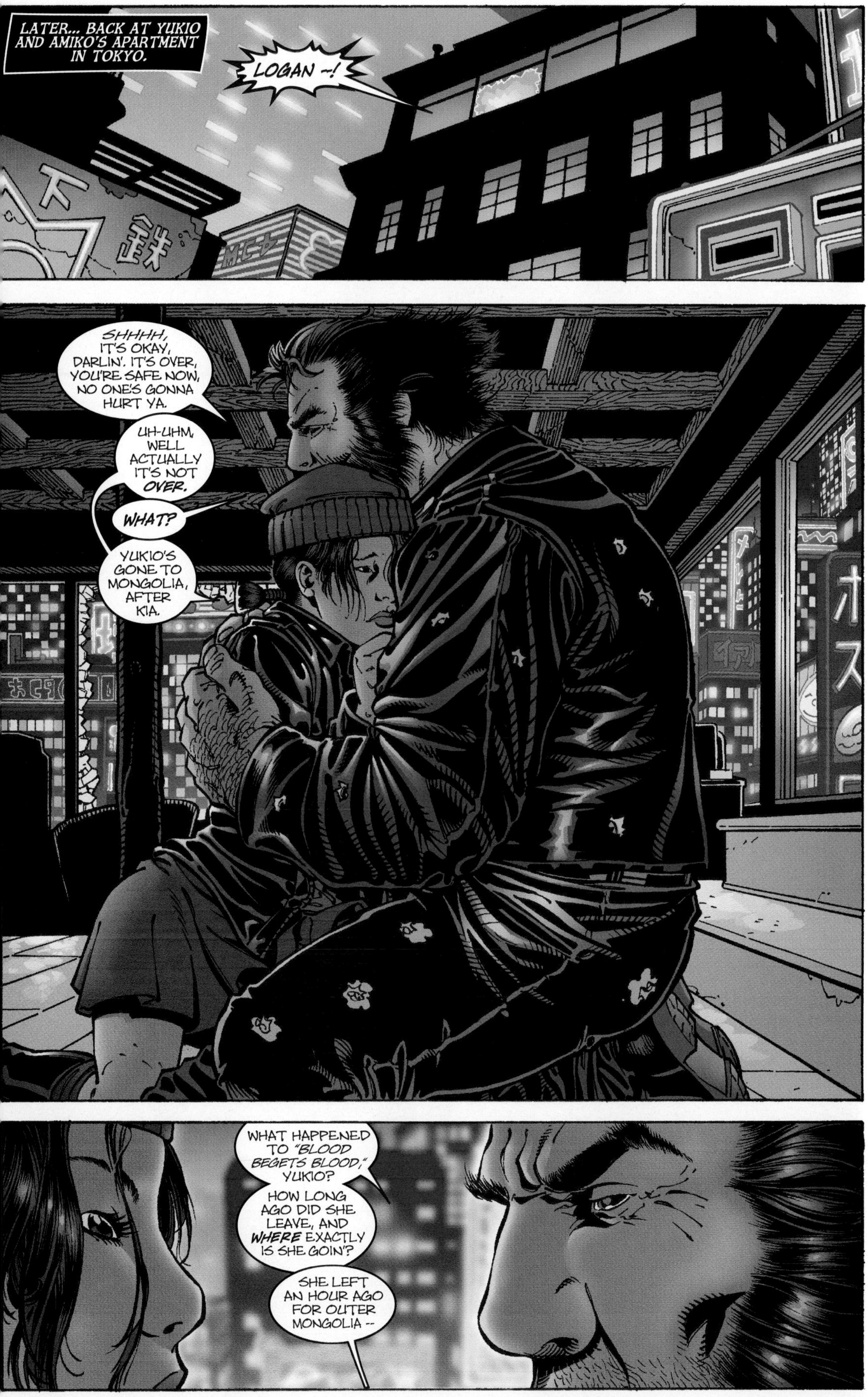
LATER... BACK AT YUKIO AND AMIKO'S APARTMENT IN TOKYO.
LOGAN --!
SHHHH, IT'S OKAY, DARLIN'. IT'S OVER, YOU'RE SAFE NOW, NO ONE'S GONNA HURT YA.
UH-UHM, WELL ACTUALLY IT'S NOT OVER.
WHAT?
YUKIO'S GONE TO MONGOLIA, AFTER KIA.
WHAT HAPPENED TO "BLOOD BEGETS BLOOD," YUKIO?
HOW LONG AGO DID SHE LEAVE, AND WHERE EXACTLY IS SHE GOIN'?
SHE LEFT AN HOUR AGO FOR OUTER MONGOLIA --

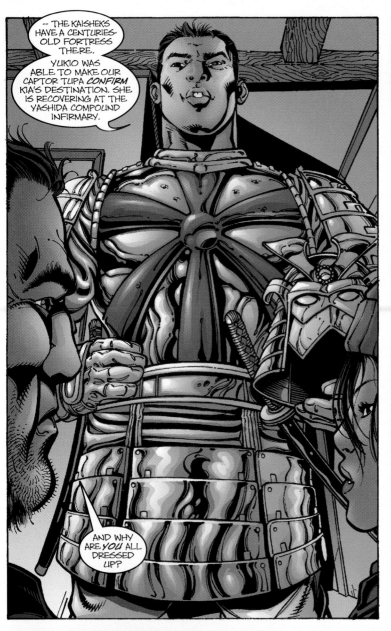

-- THE KAISHEKS HAVE A CENTURIES-OLD FORTRESS THERE.

YUKIO WAS ABLE TO MAKE OUR CAPTOR TUPA *CONFIRM* KIA'S DESTINATION. SHE IS RECOVERING AT THE YASHIDA COMPOUND INFIRMARY.

AND WHY ARE *YOU* ALL DRESSED UP?

I'M COMING *WITH* YOU. YOU'LL NEED MY HELP AND WHAT'S LEFT OF MY RESOURCES TO GET YOU THERE IN TIME.

YOU'RE IN NO SHAPE TO FIGHT, KENUICHIO AND I'M PRETTY TIRED OF SAVIN' YOUR TIN-PLATED BUTT.

LOGAN, I HAVE LOST ALMOST *EVERYTHING* TO THE KAISHEKS.

DO NOT EXPECT ME TO STAND IDLY BY WHILE YOU --

BE GRATEFUL YOU'RE ALIVE AND HAVE A SECOND CHANCE. AFTER ALL YOU'VE DONE IN YOUR LIFE, I'M NOT SURE YOU *DESERVE* IT.

DON'T GIVE ME THAT *"IT'S TOO DANGEROUS FOR YOU, AMIKO"* BULL! I'M COMING, WHETHER YOU --

RELAX! -- YOU *BOTH* CAN COME.

SEEMS LIKE THE ONLY WAY TO KEEP YOU SAFE IS TO NOT LET YOU OUTTA MY SIGHT.

SHRRIP

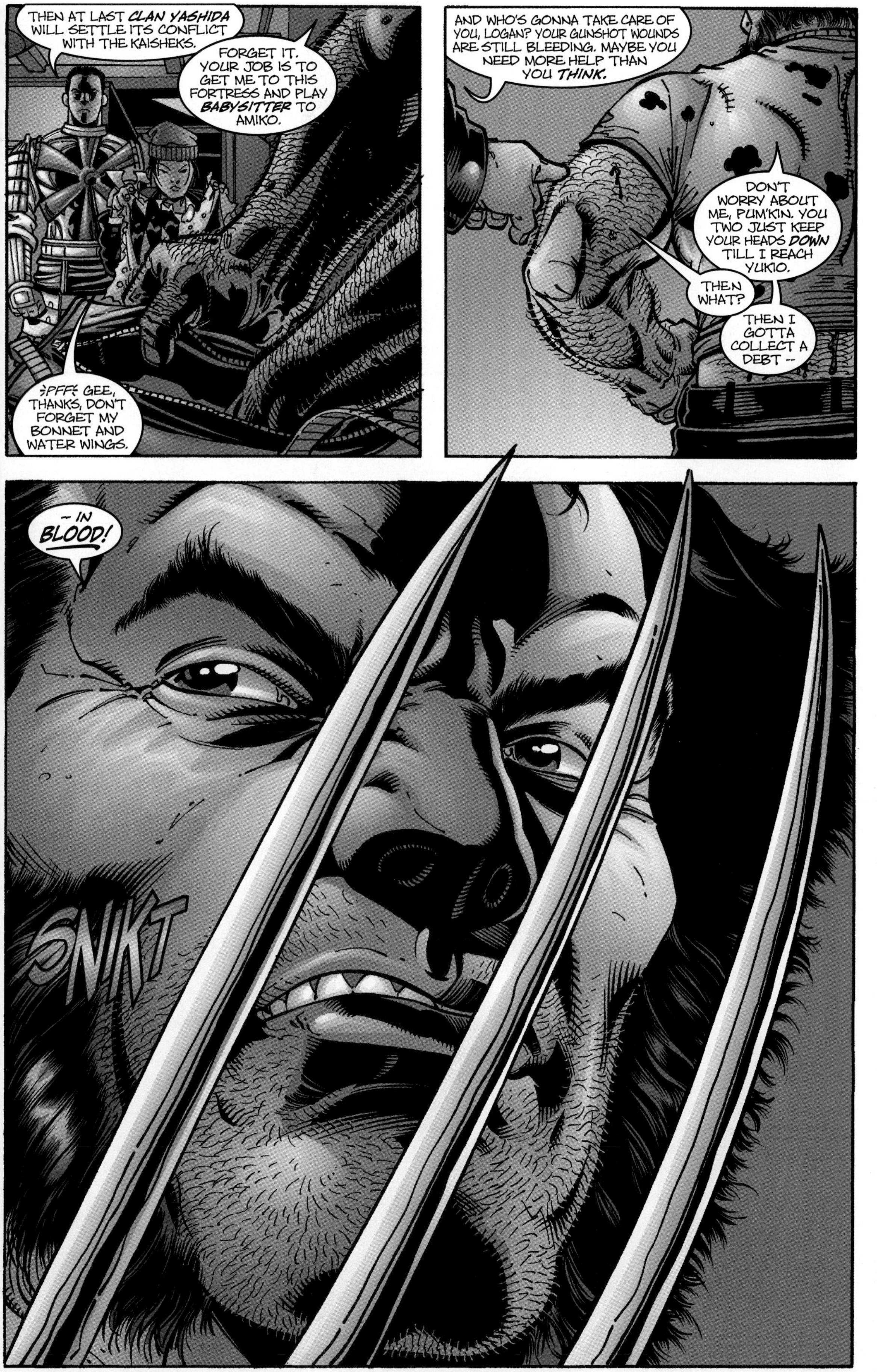
THEN AT LAST CLAN YASHIDA WILL SETTLE ITS CONFLICT WITH THE KAISHEKS.
FORGET IT. YOUR JOB IS TO GET ME TO THIS FORTRESS AND PLAY BABYSITTER TO AMIKO.
PFF GEE, THANKS, DON'T FORGET MY BONNET AND WATER WINGS.
AND WHO'S GONNA TAKE CARE OF YOU, LOGAN? YOUR GUNSHOT WOUNDS ARE STILL BLEEDING. MAYBE YOU NEED MORE HELP THAN YOU THINK.
DON'T WORRY ABOUT ME, PUM'KIN. YOU TWO JUST KEEP YOUR HEADS DOWN TILL I REACH YUKIO.
THEN WHAT?
THEN I GOTTA COLLECT A DEBT --
-- IN BLOOD!
SNIKT

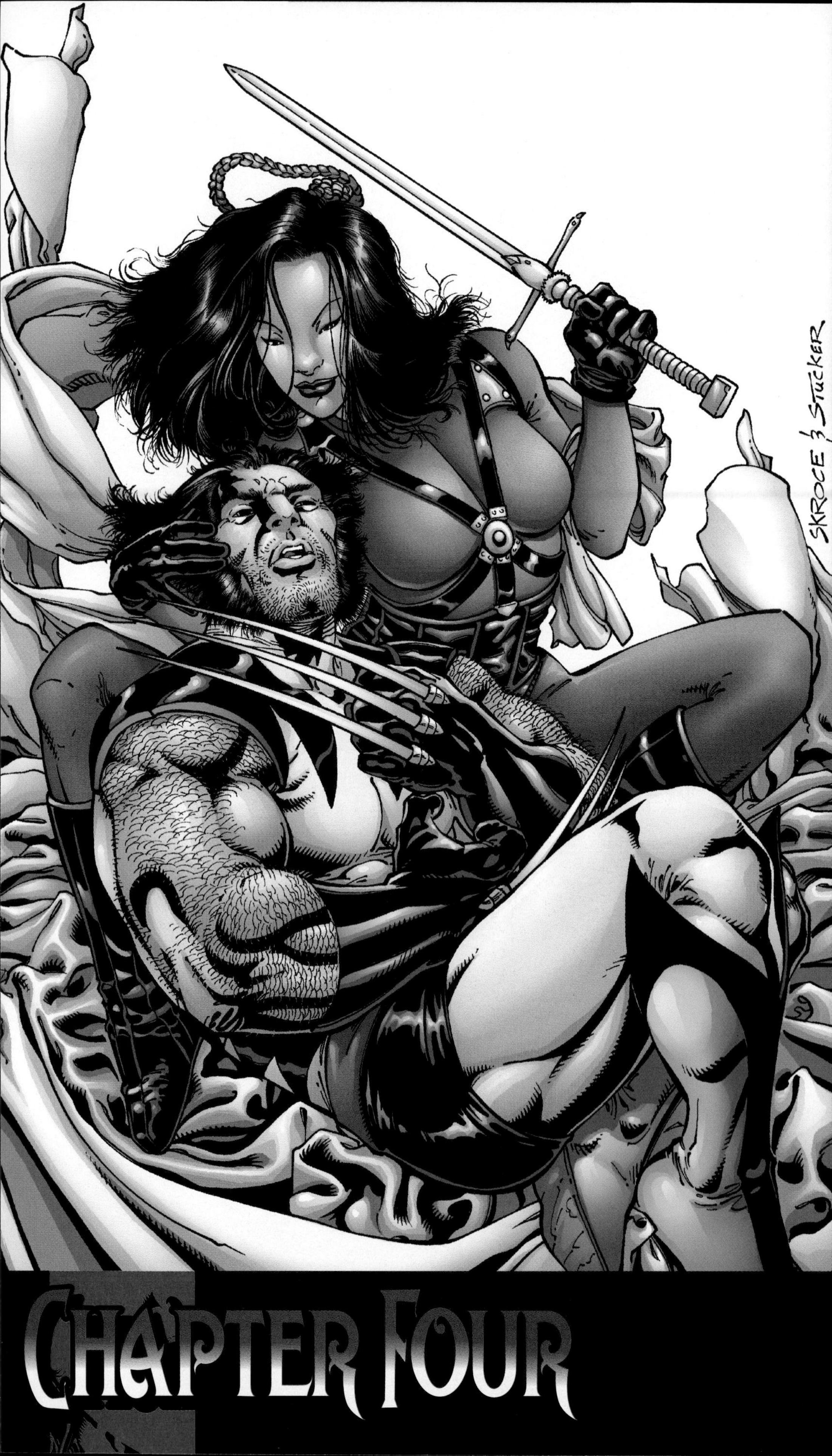
SKROCE & STUCKER

CHAPTER FOUR

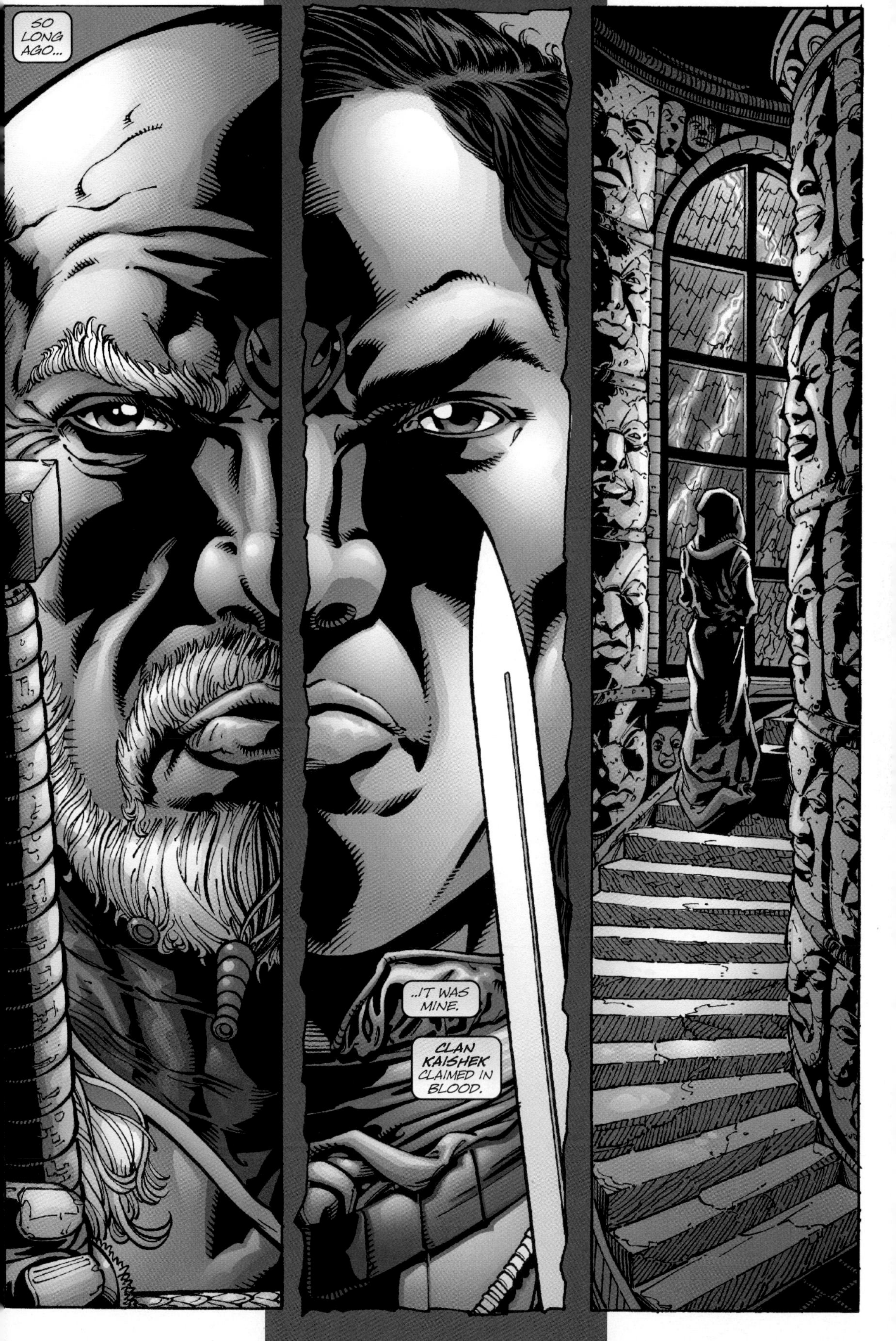

SO LONG AGO...
..IT WAS MINE.
CLAN KAISHEK CLAIMED IN BLOOD.

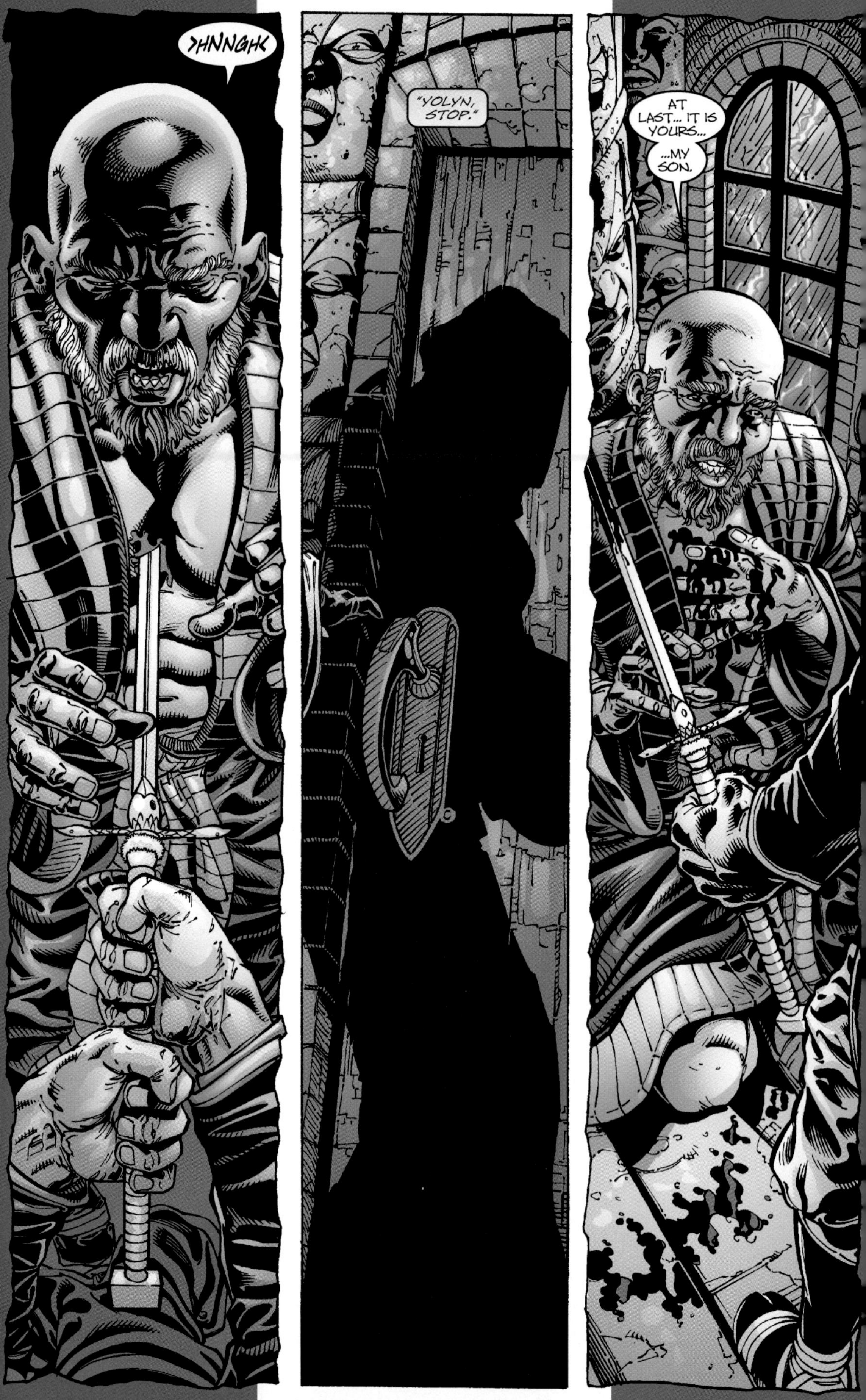
>HNNGH<
"YOLYN, STOP."
AT LAST... IT IS YOURS...
...MY SON.

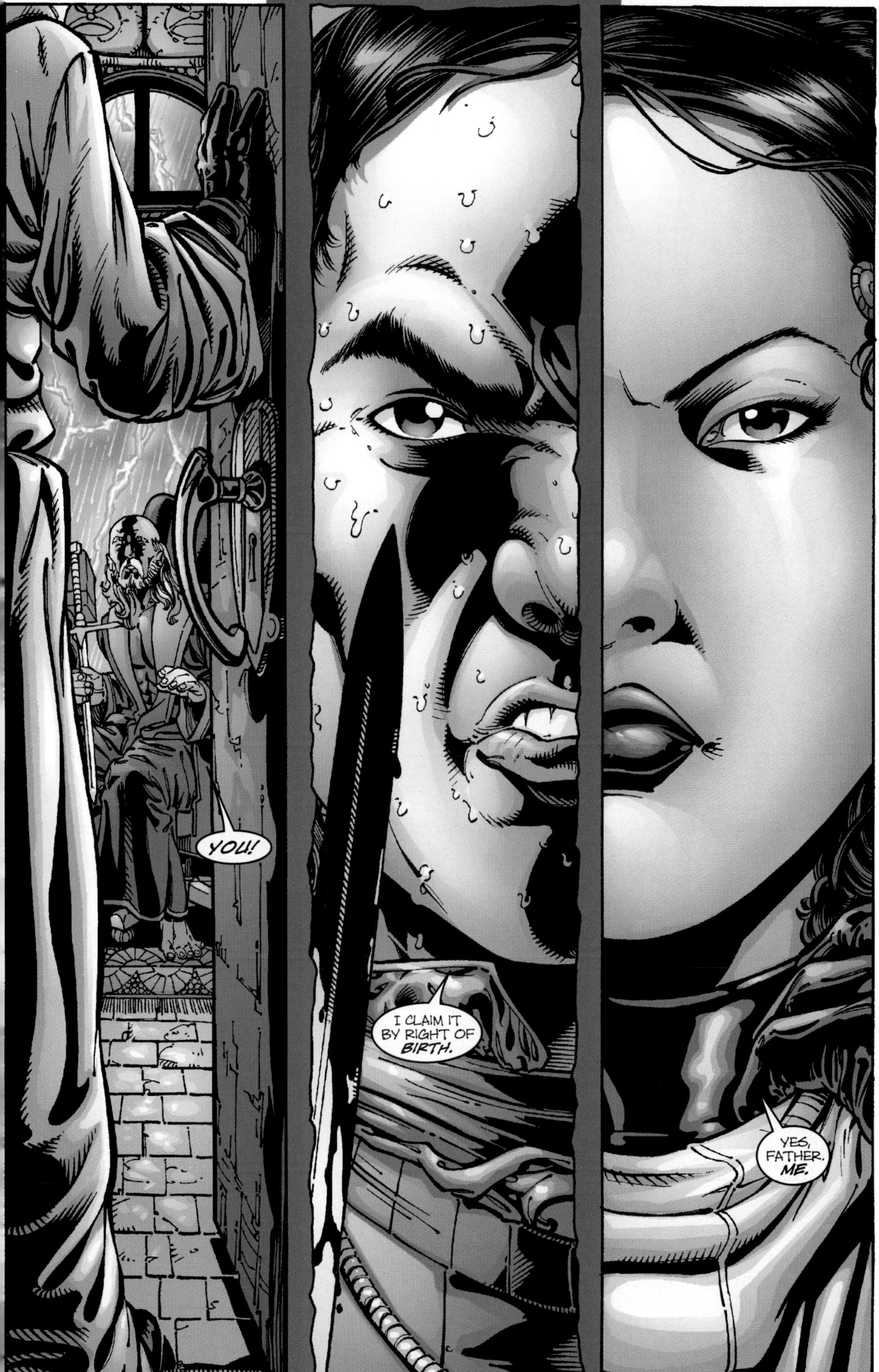
YOU!
I CLAIM IT BY RIGHT OF BIRTH.
YES, FATHER. ME.

"I CLAIM IT IN *BLOOD.*"

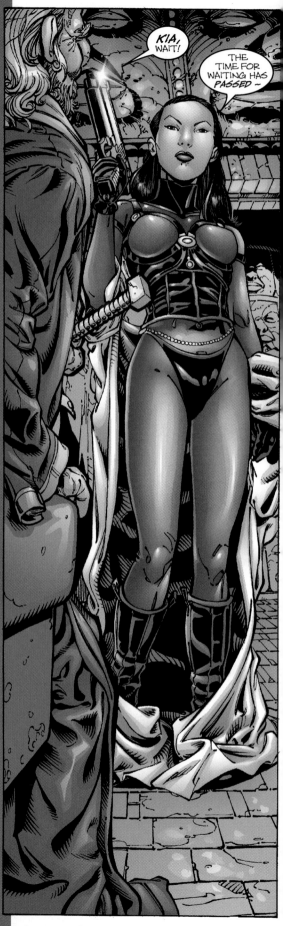

KIA, WAIT!

THE TIME FOR WAITING HAS *PASSED* ~

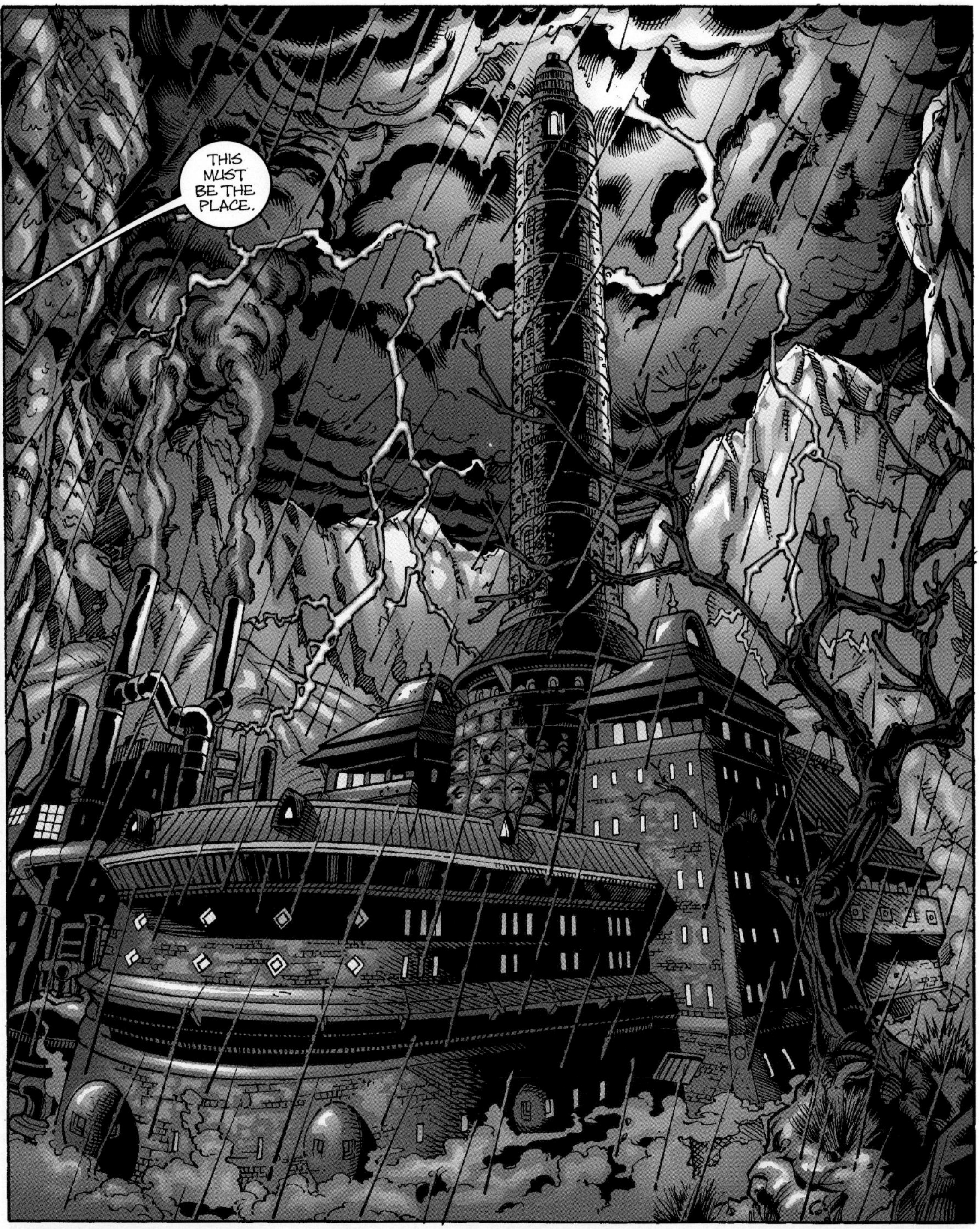
THIS MUST BE THE PLACE.

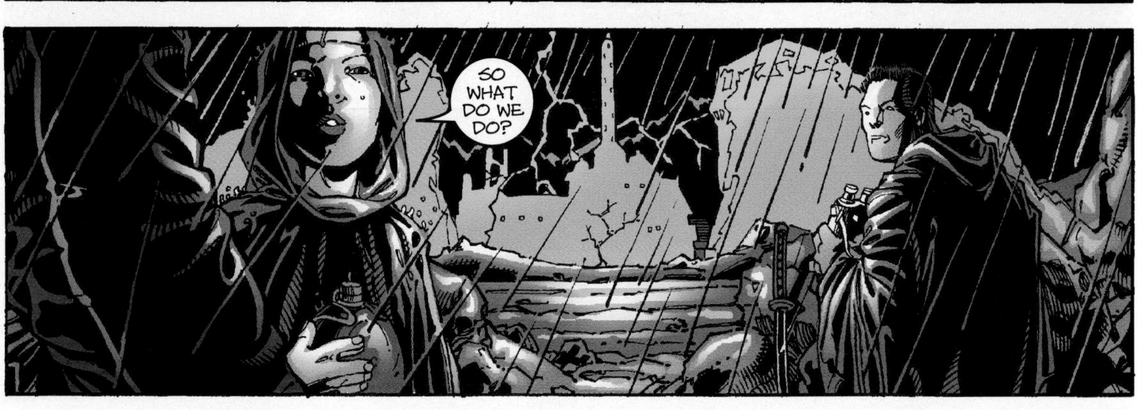
SO WHAT DO WE DO?

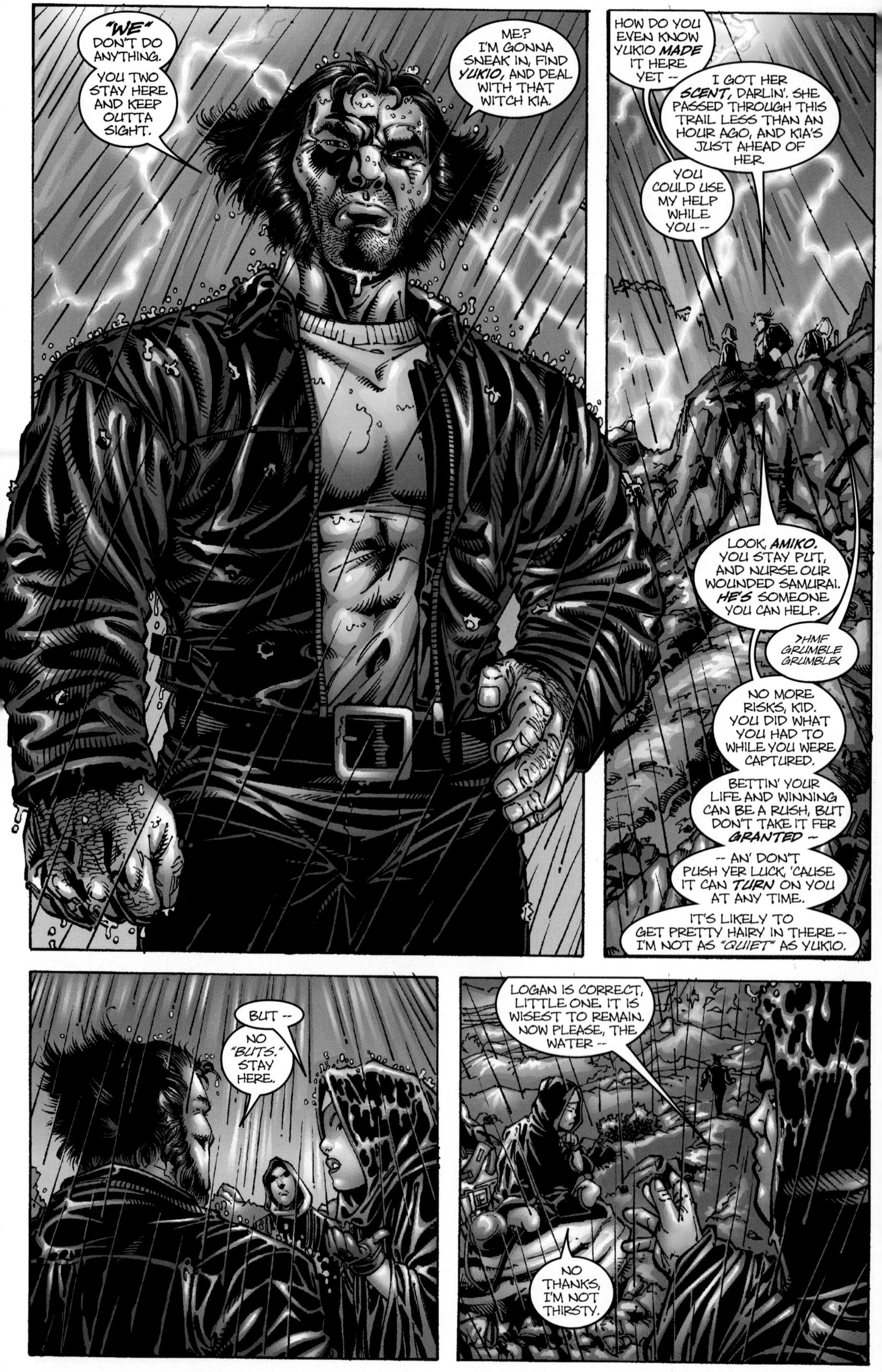
"WE" DON'T DO ANYTHING.
YOU TWO STAY HERE AND KEEP OUTTA SIGHT.
ME? I'M GONNA SNEAK IN, FIND YUKIO, AND DEAL WITH THAT WITCH KIA.
HOW DO YOU EVEN KNOW YUKIO MADE IT HERE YET --
I GOT HER SCENT, DARLIN'. SHE PASSED THROUGH THIS TRAIL LESS THAN AN HOUR AGO, AND KIA'S JUST AHEAD OF HER.
YOU COULD USE MY HELP WHILE YOU --
LOOK, AMIKO. YOU STAY PUT, AND NURSE OUR WOUNDED SAMURAI. HE'S SOMEONE YOU CAN HELP.
>HMF GRUMBLE GRUMBLE<
NO MORE RISKS, KID. YOU DID WHAT YOU HAD TO WHILE YOU WERE CAPTURED.
BETTIN' YOUR LIFE AND WINNING CAN BE A RUSH, BUT DON'T TAKE IT FER GRANTED --
-- AN' DON'T PUSH YER LUCK, 'CAUSE IT CAN TURN ON YOU AT ANY TIME.
IT'S LIKELY TO GET PRETTY HAIRY IN THERE -- I'M NOT AS "QUIET" AS YUKIO.
BUT --
NO "BUTS." STAY HERE.
LOGAN IS CORRECT, LITTLE ONE. IT IS WISEST TO REMAIN. NOW PLEASE, THE WATER --
NO THANKS, I'M NOT THIRSTY.

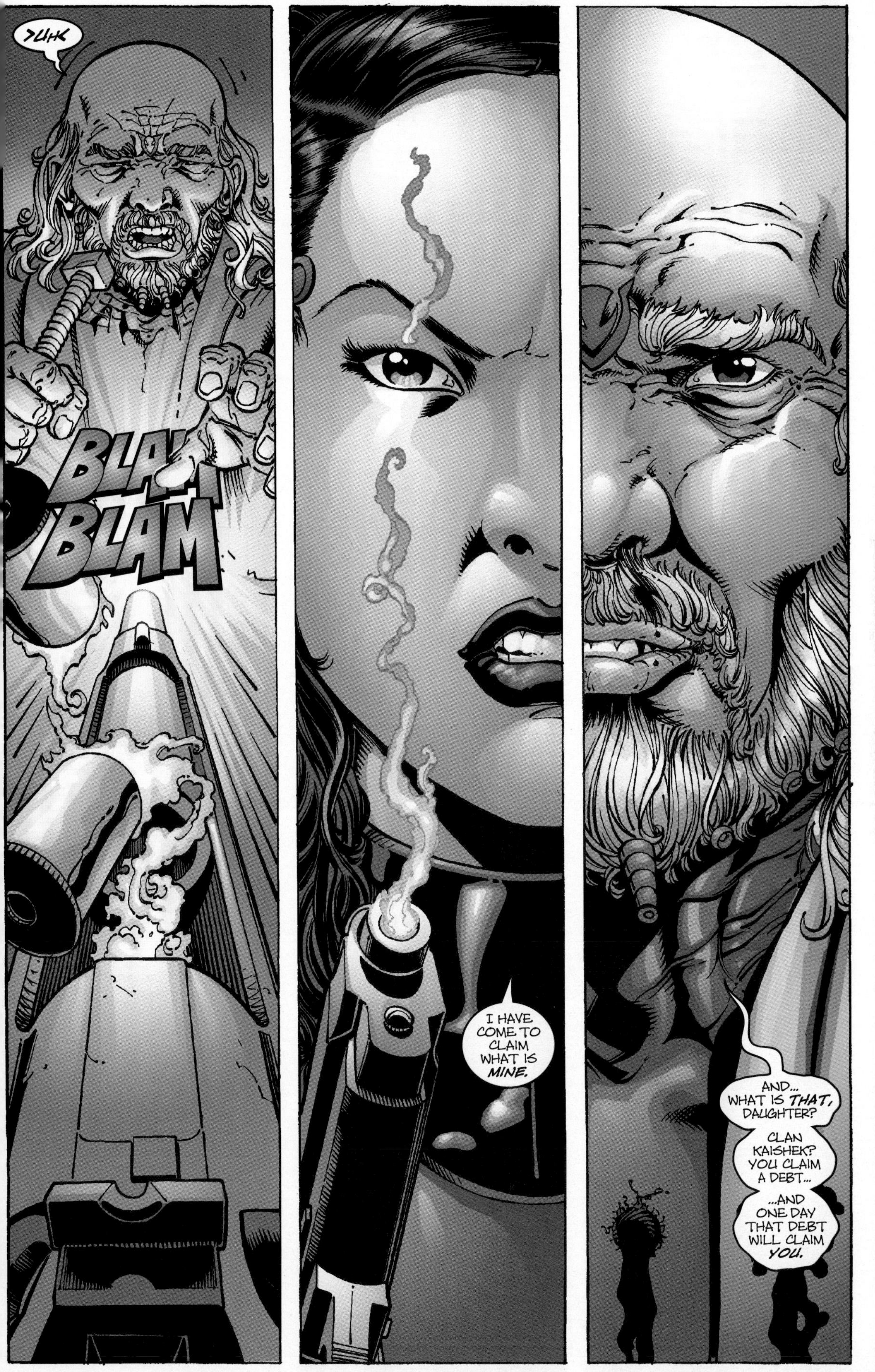
UHK
BLAM
I HAVE COME TO CLAIM WHAT IS *MINE.*
AND... WHAT IS *THAT,* DAUGHTER?
CLAN KAISHEK? YOU CLAIM A DEBT...
...AND ONE DAY THAT DEBT WILL CLAIM *YOU.*

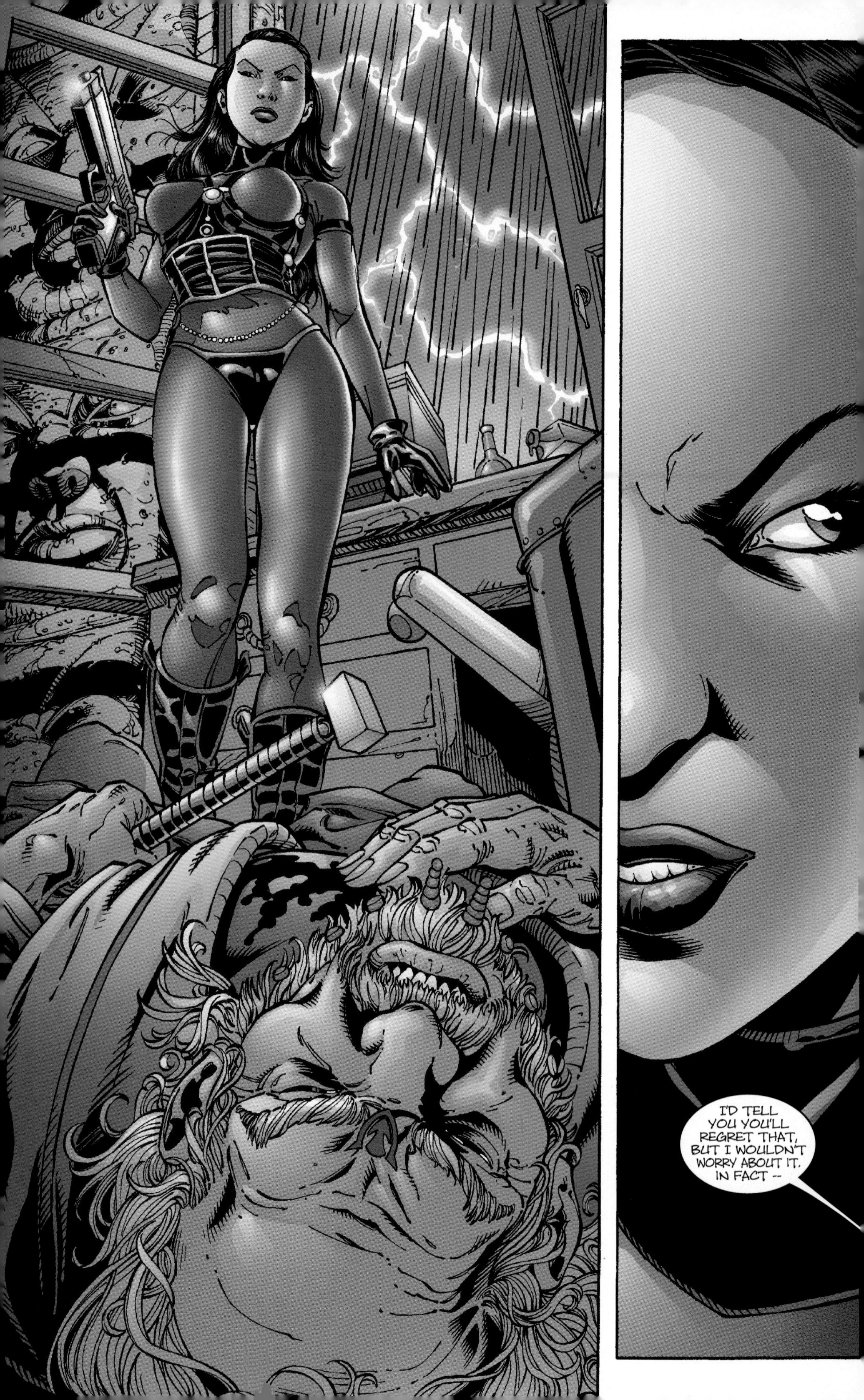
I'D TELL YOU YOU'LL REGRET THAT, BUT I WOULDN'T WORRY ABOUT IT. IN FACT --

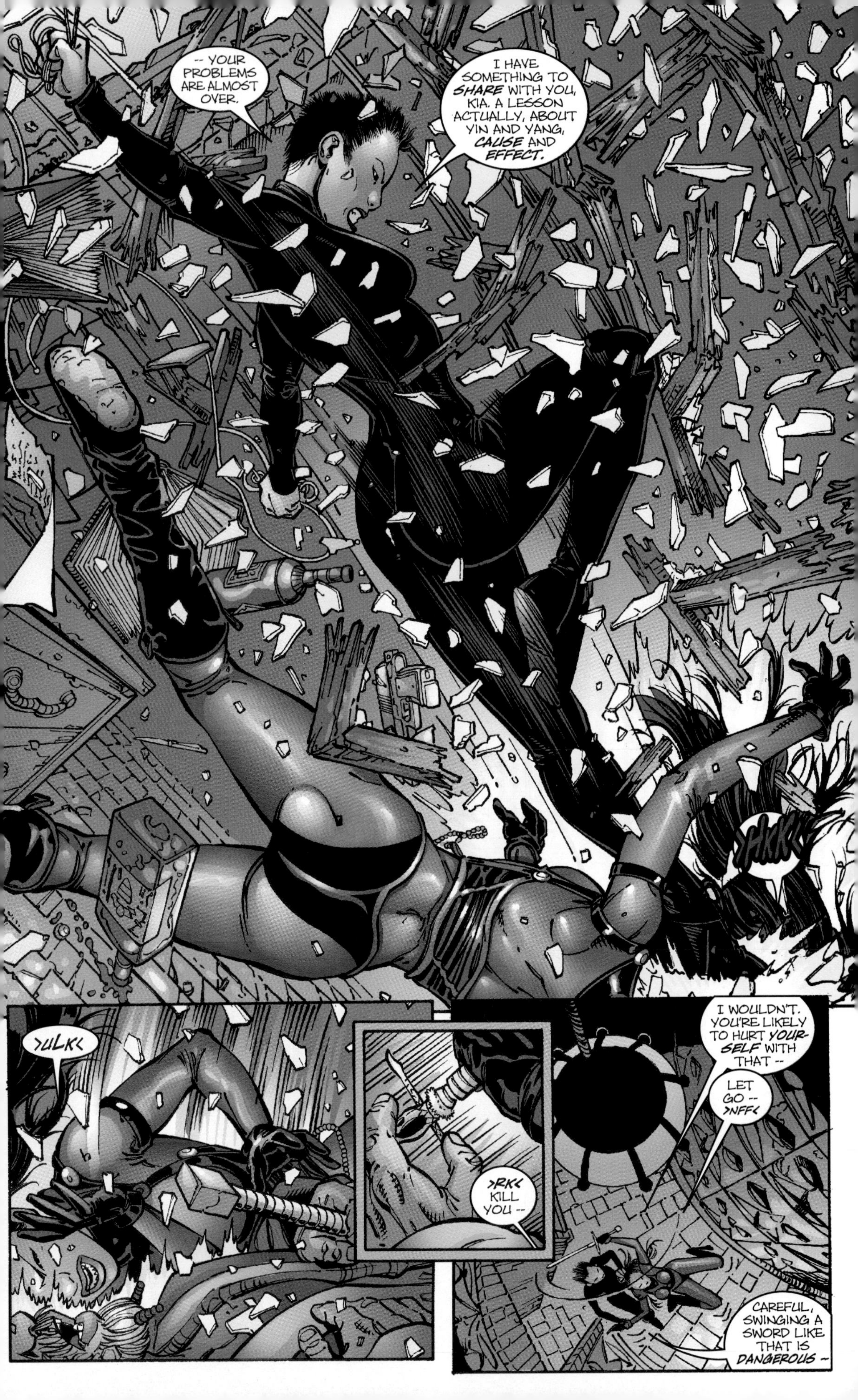

-- YOUR PROBLEMS ARE ALMOST OVER.
I HAVE SOMETHING TO SHARE WITH YOU, KIA. A LESSON ACTUALLY, ABOUT YIN AND YANG, CAUSE AND EFFECT.
>HKK<
>ULK<
>RK< KILL YOU --
I WOULDN'T. YOU'RE LIKELY TO HURT YOURSELF WITH THAT --
LET GO -- >NFF<
CAREFUL, SWINGING A SWORD LIKE THAT IS DANGEROUS --

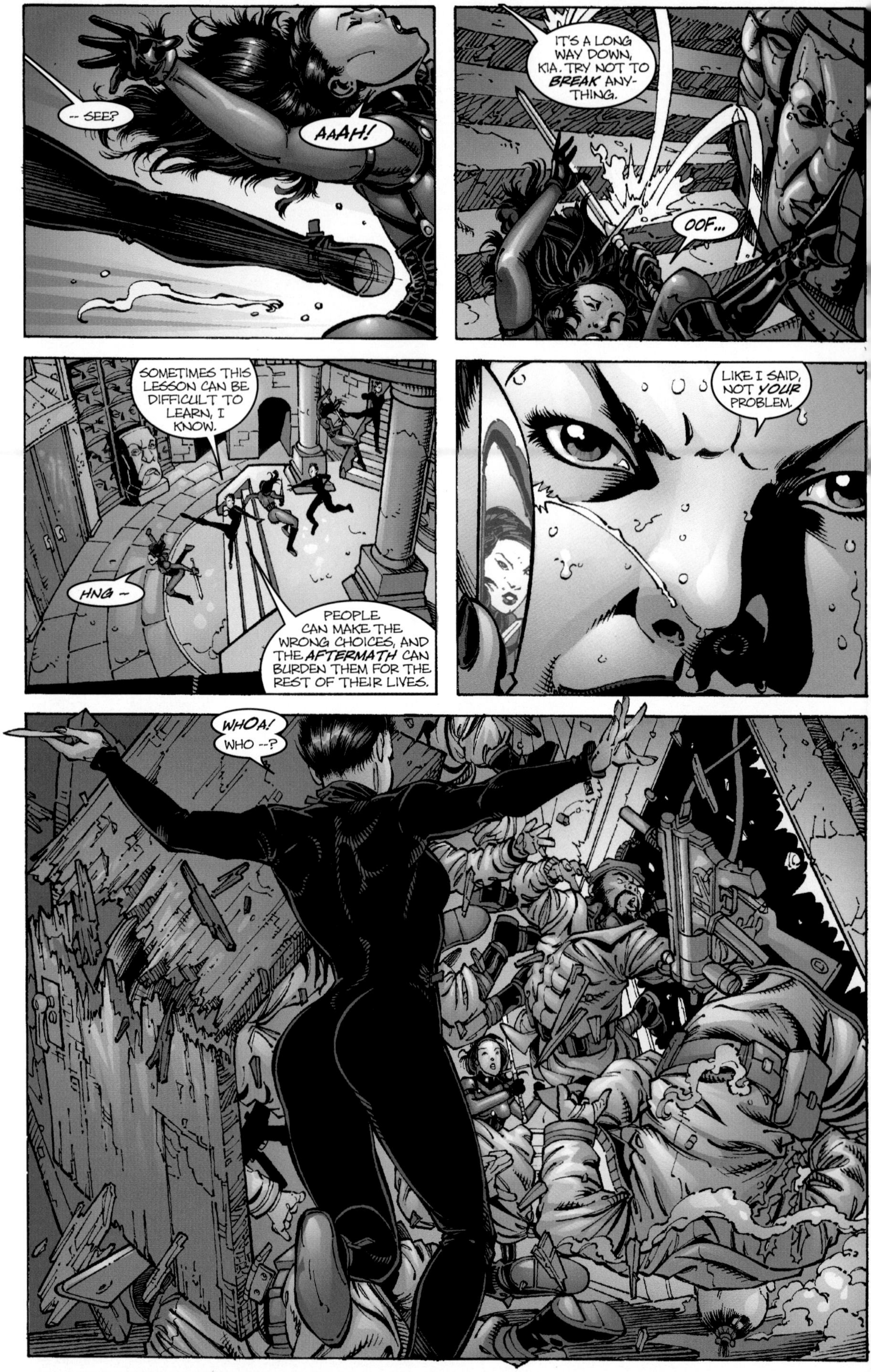
-- SEE?
AAAH!
IT'S A LONG WAY DOWN, KIA. TRY NOT TO BREAK ANY-THING.
OOF...
SOMETIMES THIS LESSON CAN BE DIFFICULT TO LEARN, I KNOW.
HNG --
PEOPLE CAN MAKE THE WRONG CHOICES, AND THE AFTERMATH CAN BURDEN THEM FOR THE REST OF THEIR LIVES.
LIKE I SAID, NOT YOUR PROBLEM.
WHOA! WHO --?

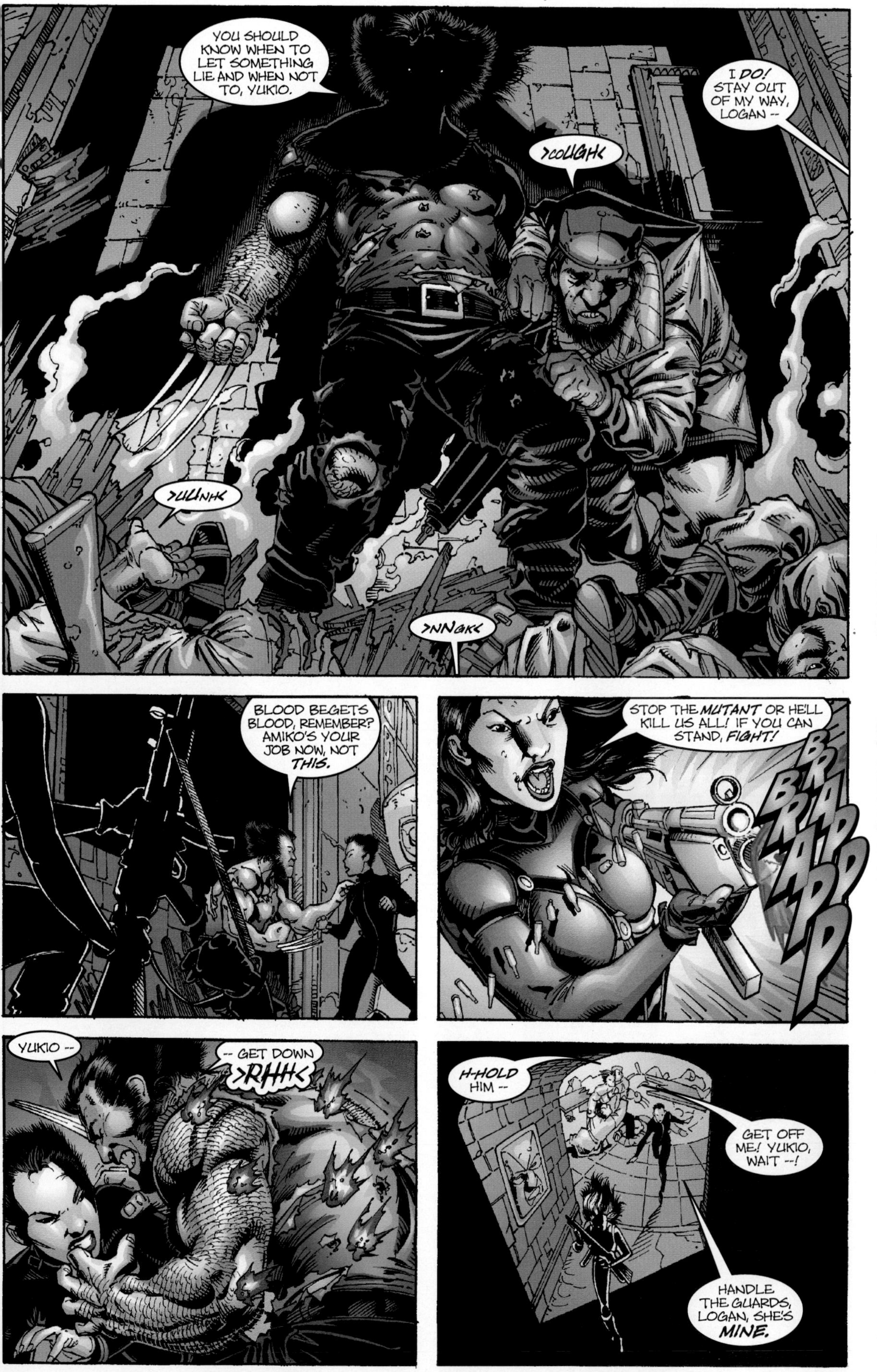
YOU SHOULD KNOW WHEN TO LET SOMETHING LIE AND WHEN NOT TO, YUKIO.
I DO! STAY OUT OF MY WAY, LOGAN --
>COUGH<
>UUNH<
>NNGK<
BLOOD BEGETS BLOOD, REMEMBER? AMIKO'S YOUR JOB NOW, NOT THIS.
STOP THE MUTANT OR HE'LL KILL US ALL! IF YOU CAN STAND, FIGHT!
BRRAPPP
BRRAPPP
YUKIO --
-- GET DOWN
>RHH<
H-HOLD HIM --
GET OFF ME! YUKIO, WAIT --!
HANDLE THE GUARDS, LOGAN, SHE'S MINE.

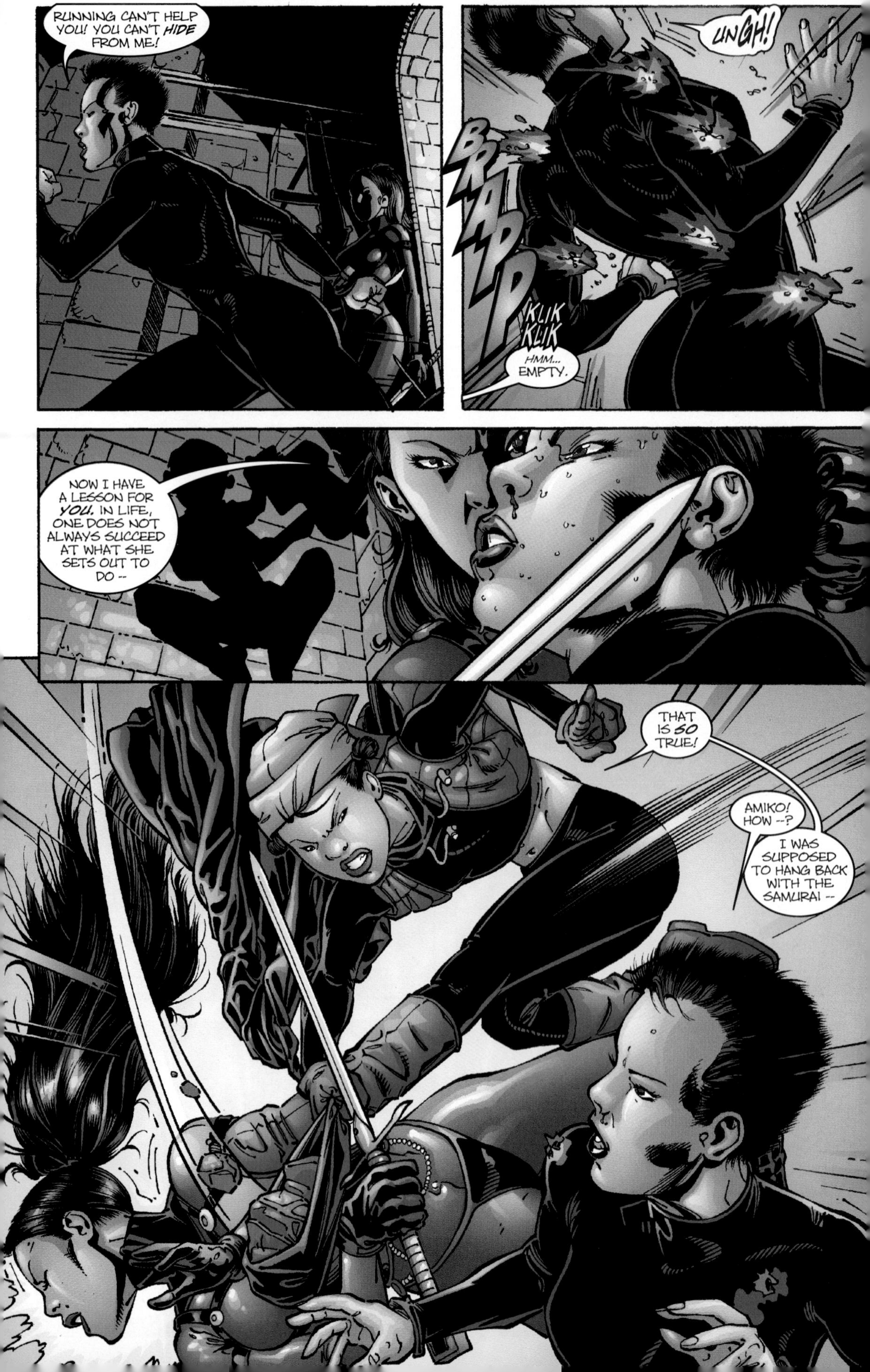

RUNNING CAN'T HELP YOU! YOU CAN'T *HIDE* FROM ME!
UNGH!
BRRAP
KLIK KLIK
HMM... EMPTY.
NOW I HAVE A LESSON FOR *YOU.* IN LIFE, ONE DOES NOT ALWAYS SUCCEED AT WHAT SHE SETS OUT TO DO --
THAT IS *SO* TRUE!
AMIKO! HOW --?
I WAS SUPPOSED TO HANG BACK WITH THE SAMURAI --

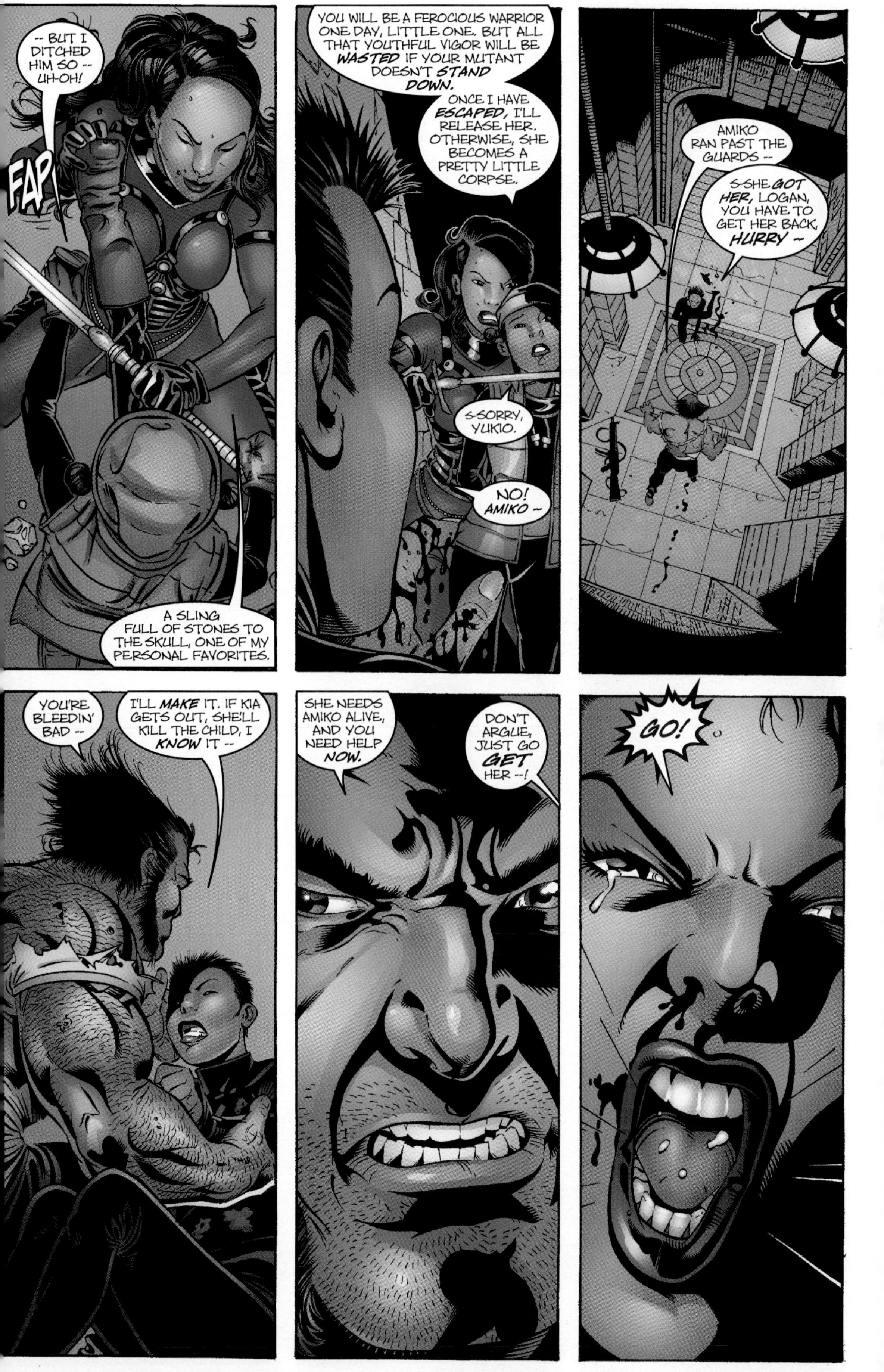

-- BUT I DITCHED HIM SO -- UH-OH!
FAP
A SLING FULL OF STONES TO THE SKULL, ONE OF MY PERSONAL FAVORITES.
YOU WILL BE A FEROCIOUS WARRIOR ONE DAY, LITTLE ONE. BUT ALL THAT YOUTHFUL VIGOR WILL BE WASTED IF YOUR MUTANT DOESN'T STAND DOWN.
ONCE I HAVE ESCAPED, I'LL RELEASE HER. OTHERWISE, SHE BECOMES A PRETTY LITTLE CORPSE.
S-SORRY, YUKIO.
NO! AMIKO --
AMIKO RAN PAST THE GUARDS --
S-SHE GOT HER, LOGAN, YOU HAVE TO GET HER BACK, HURRY --
YOU'RE BLEEDIN' BAD --
I'LL MAKE IT. IF KIA GETS OUT, SHE'LL KILL THE CHILD, I KNOW IT --
SHE NEEDS AMIKO ALIVE, AND YOU NEED HELP NOW.
DON'T ARGUE, JUST GO GET HER --!
GO!

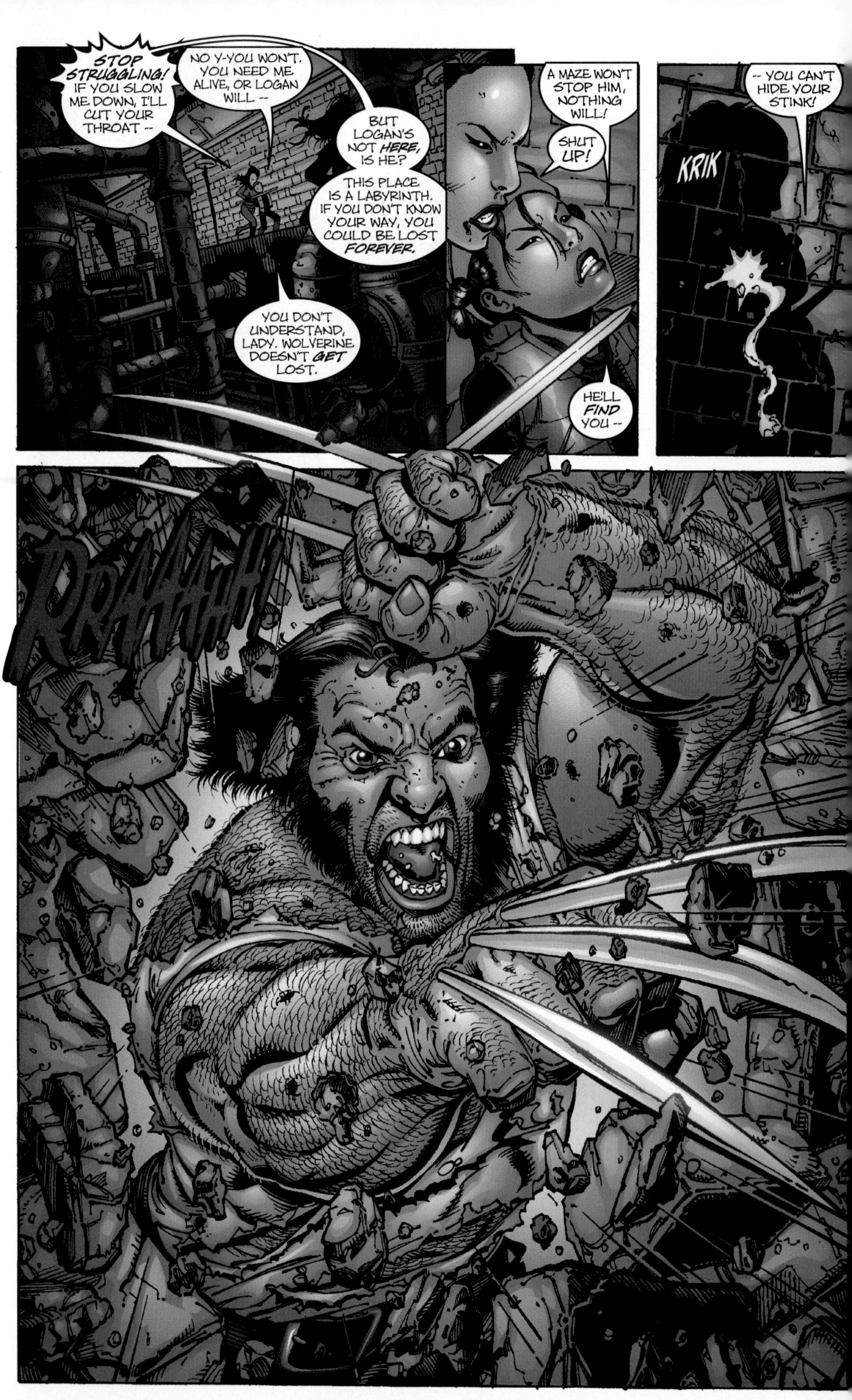
STOP STRUGGLING! IF YOU SLOW ME DOWN, I'LL CUT YOUR THROAT --
NO Y-YOU WON'T. YOU NEED ME ALIVE, OR LOGAN WILL --
BUT LOGAN'S NOT HERE, IS HE?
THIS PLACE IS A LABYRINTH. IF YOU DON'T KNOW YOUR WAY, YOU COULD BE LOST FOREVER.
YOU DON'T UNDERSTAND, LADY. WOLVERINE DOESN'T GET LOST.
A MAZE WON'T STOP HIM, NOTHING WILL!
SHUT UP!
HE'LL FIND YOU --
-- YOU CAN'T HIDE YOUR STINK!
KRIK
RRAAAHH!

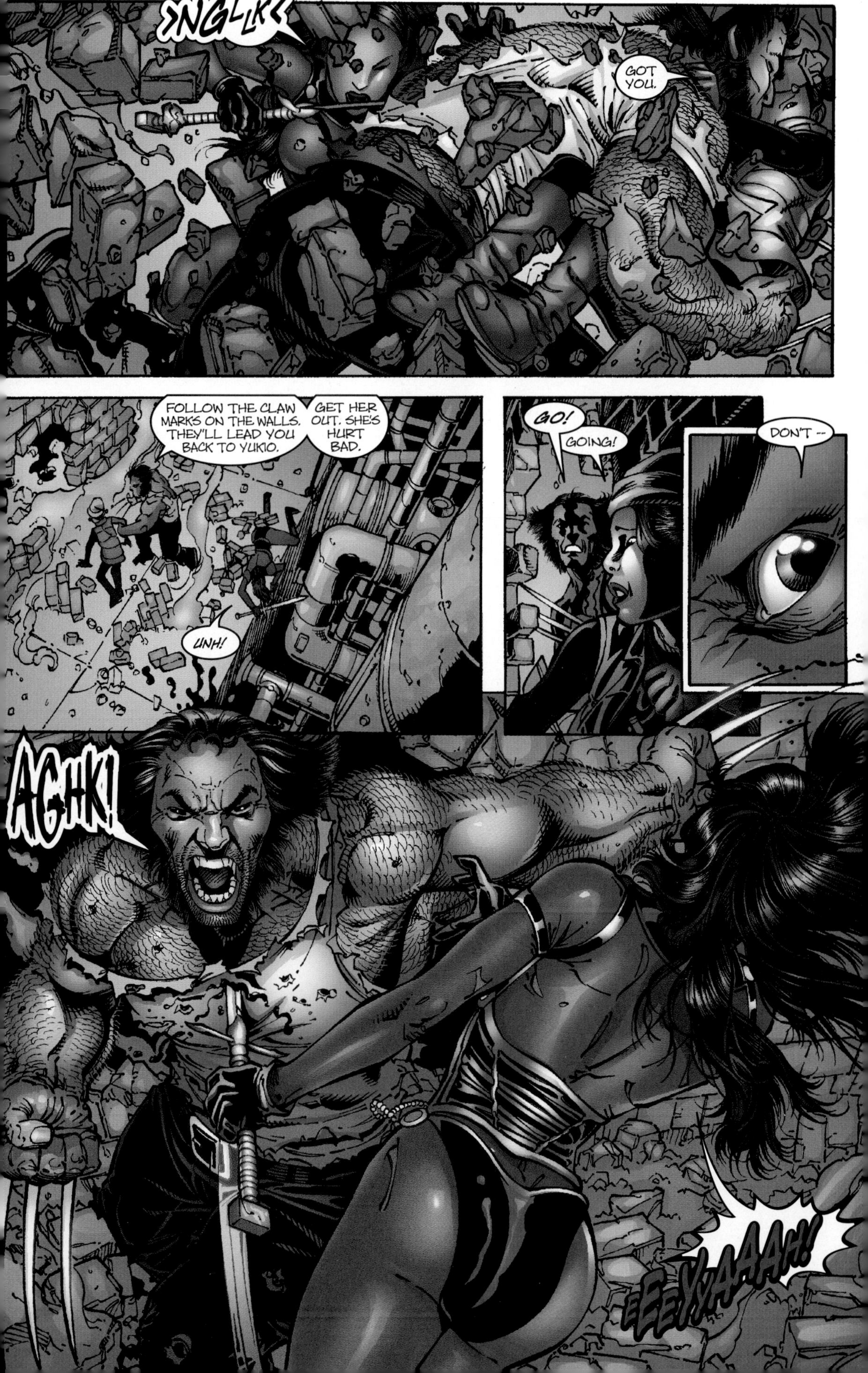

NGLLK
GOT YOU.
FOLLOW THE CLAW MARKS ON THE WALLS. THEY'LL LEAD YOU BACK TO YUKIO.
GET HER OUT. SHE'S HURT BAD.
UNH!
GO!
GOING!
DON'T --
AGHK!
EEEYAAAAH!

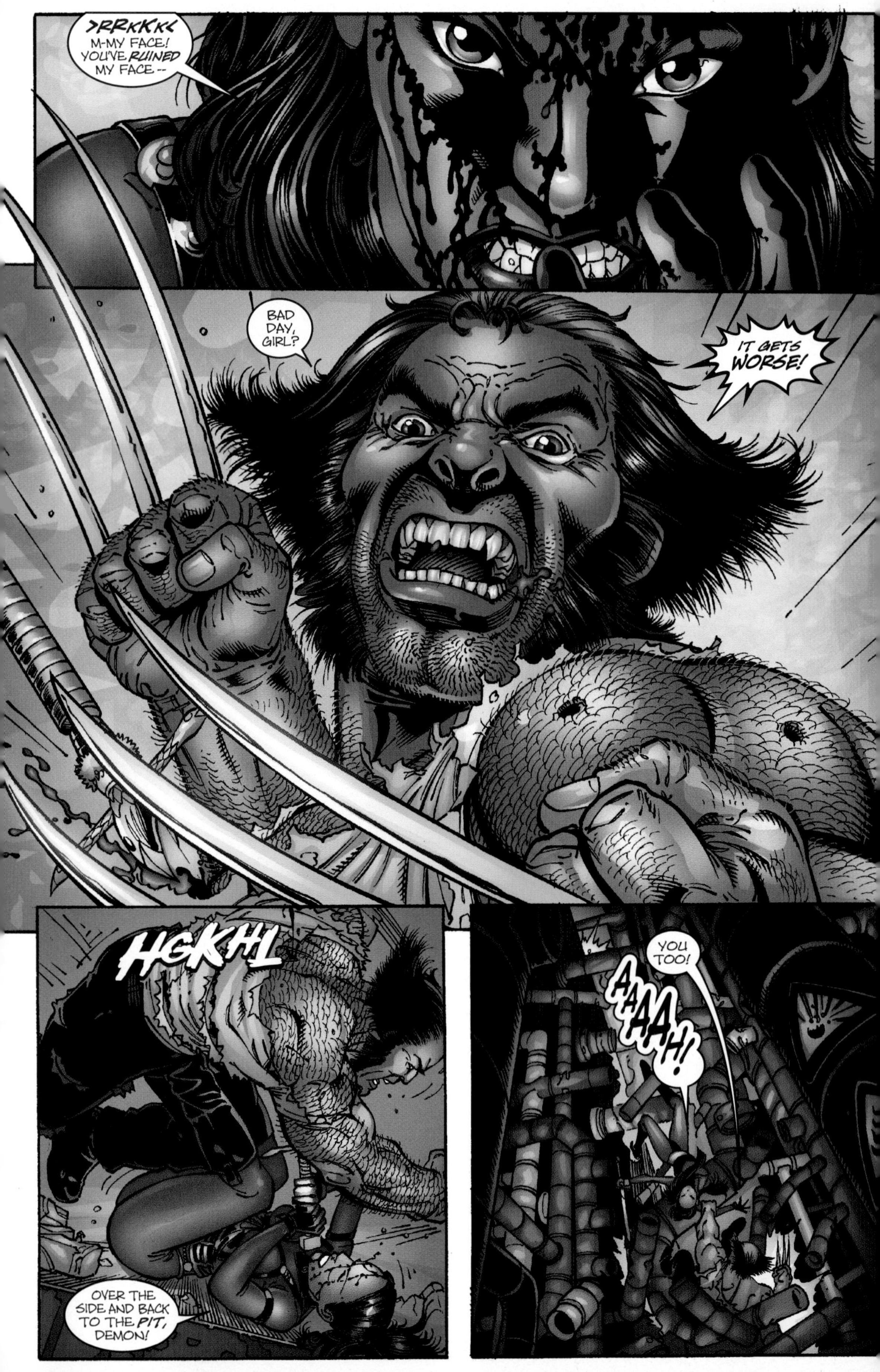
>RRKKK< M-MY FACE! YOU'VE RUINED MY FACE --
BAD DAY, GIRL?
IT GETS WORSE!
HGKHL
OVER THE SIDE AND BACK TO THE PIT, DEMON!
YOU TOO!
AAAAH!

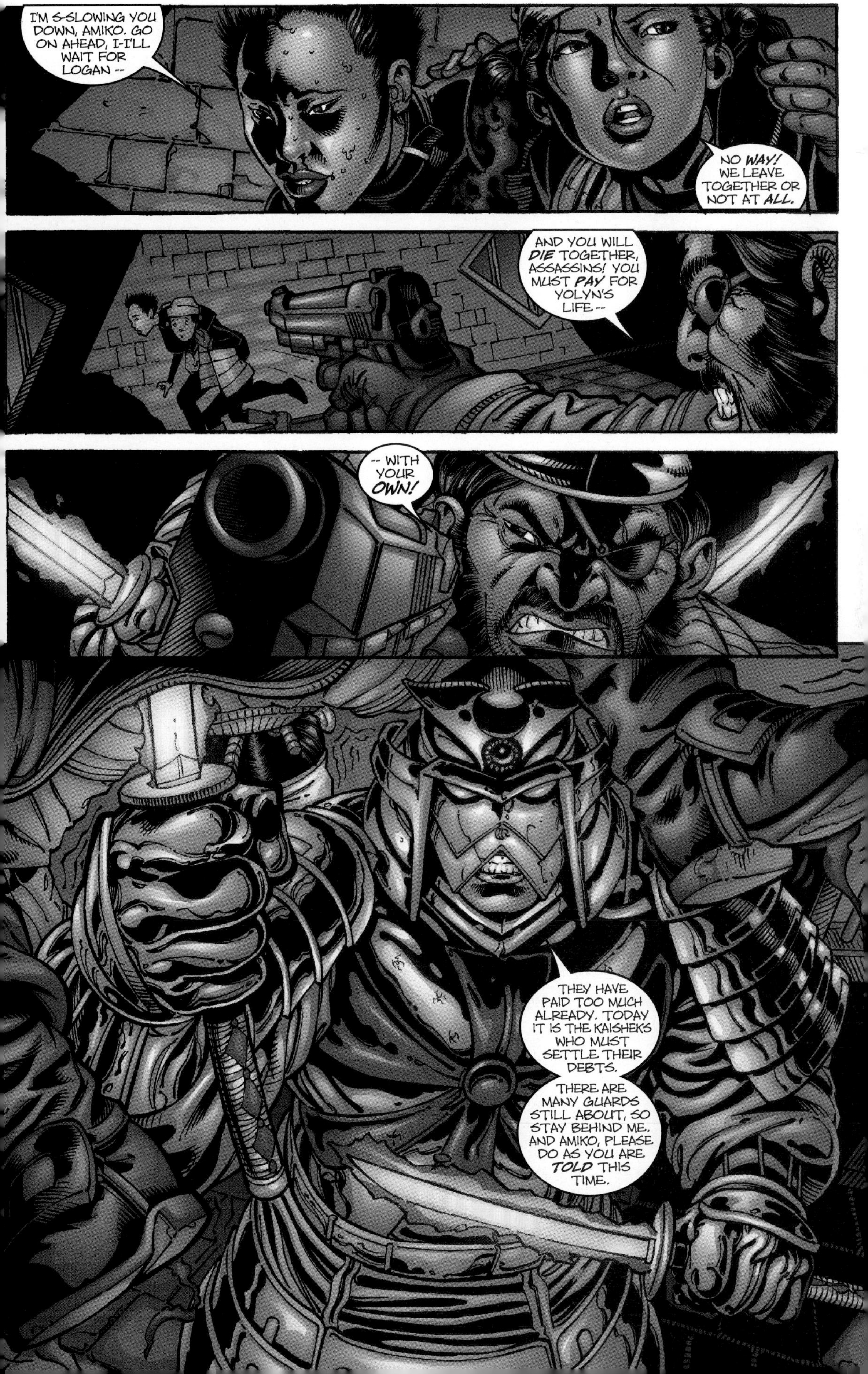
I'M S-SLOWING YOU DOWN, AMIKO. GO ON AHEAD, I-I'LL WAIT FOR LOGAN --
NO *WAY!* WE LEAVE TOGETHER OR NOT AT *ALL.*
AND YOU WILL *DIE* TOGETHER, ASSASSINS! YOU MUST *PAY* FOR YOLYN'S LIFE --
-- WITH YOUR *OWN!*
THEY HAVE PAID TOO MUCH ALREADY. TODAY IT IS THE KAISHEKS WHO MUST SETTLE THEIR DEBTS.
THERE ARE MANY GUARDS STILL ABOUT, SO STAY BEHIND ME. AND AMIKO, PLEASE DO AS YOU ARE *TOLD* THIS TIME.

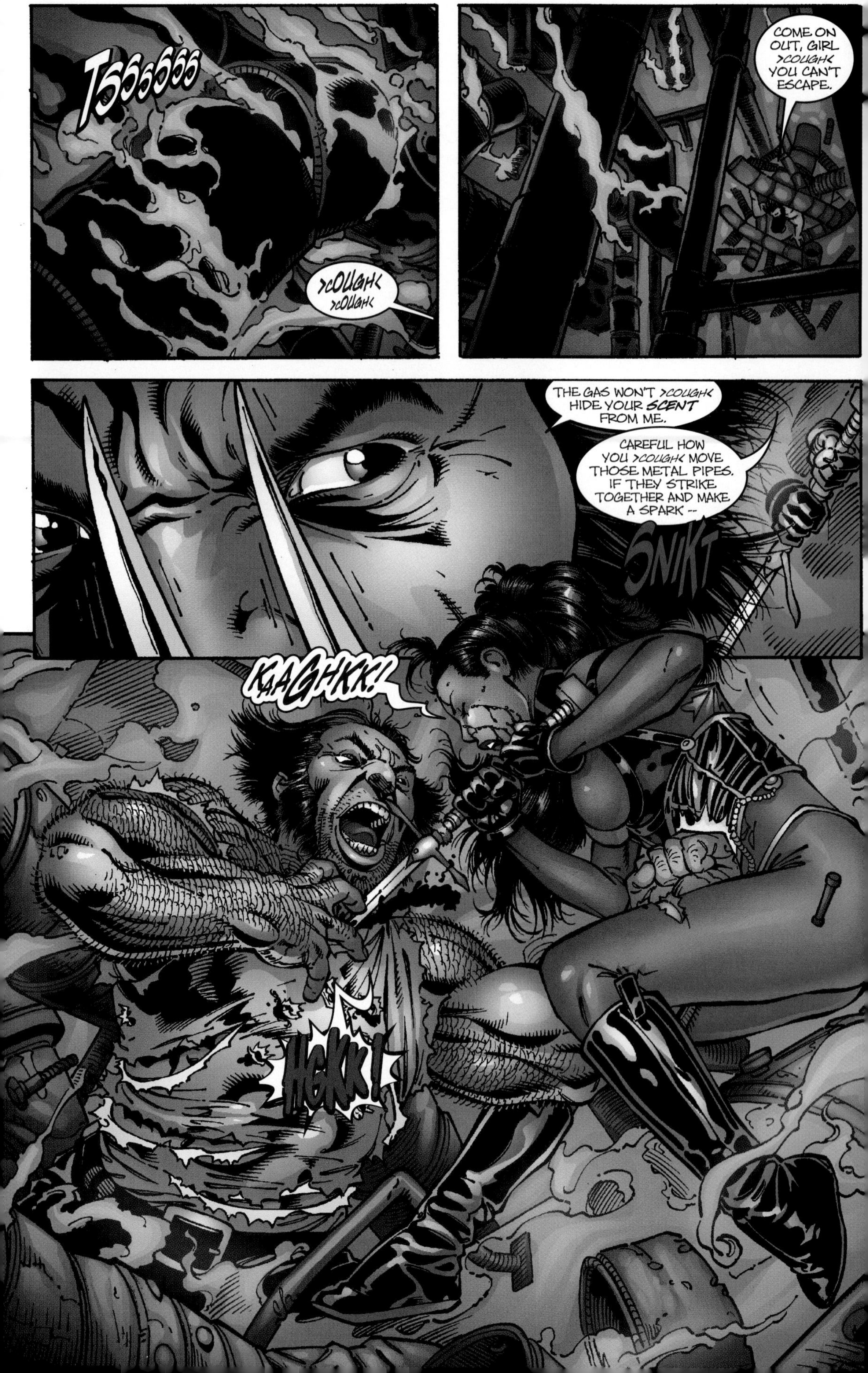
TSSSSSS
>COUGH< >COUGH<
COME ON OUT, GIRL >COUGH< YOU CAN'T ESCAPE.
THE GAS WON'T >COUGH< HIDE YOUR SCENT FROM ME.
CAREFUL HOW YOU >COUGH< MOVE THOSE METAL PIPES. IF THEY STRIKE TOGETHER AND MAKE A SPARK --
SNIKT
KAAGHKK!
HGKK!

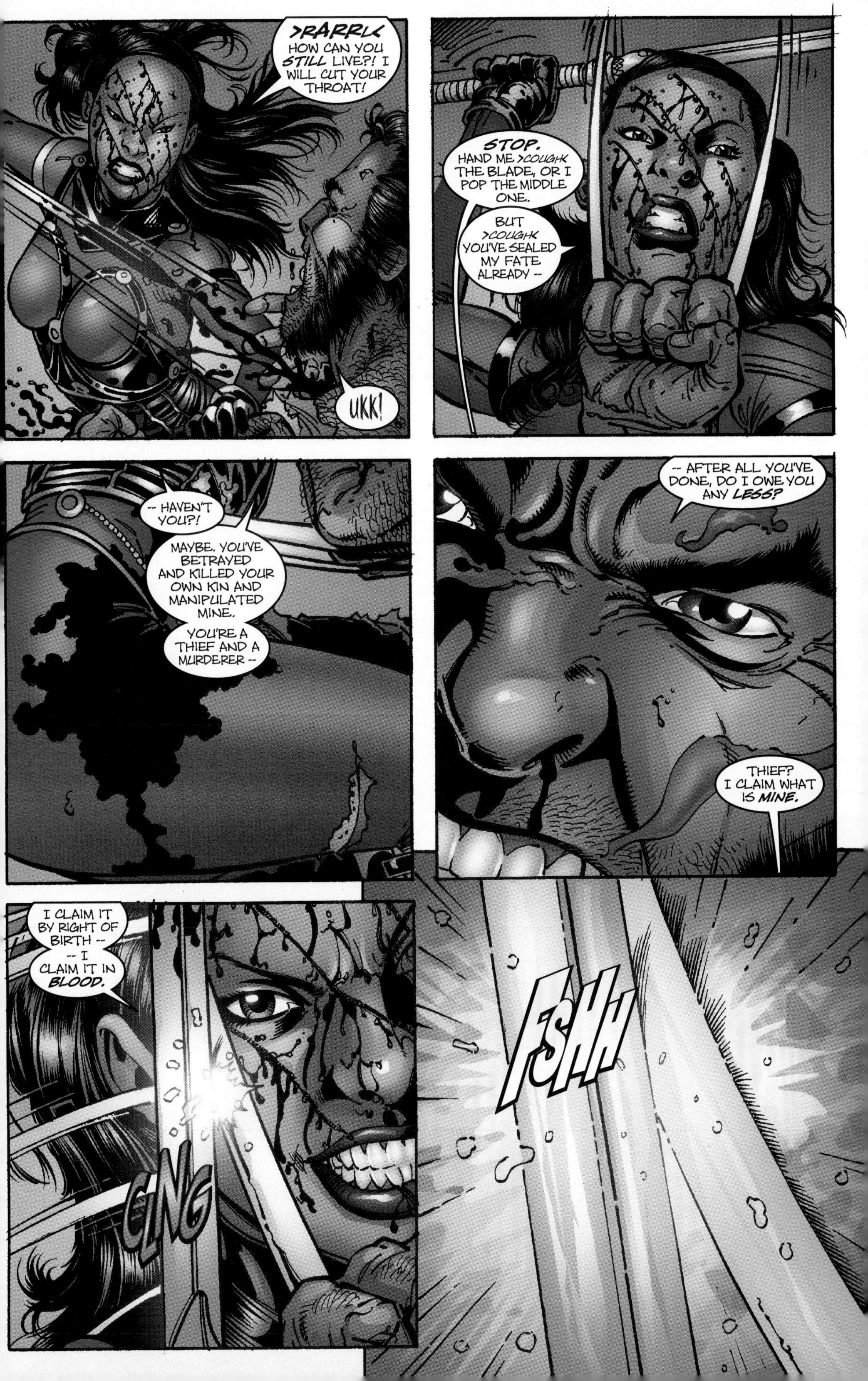
>RARRL< HOW CAN YOU STILL LIVE?! I WILL CUT YOUR THROAT!
UKK!
STOP. HAND ME >COUGH< THE BLADE, OR I POP THE MIDDLE ONE.
BUT >COUGH< YOU'VE SEALED MY FATE ALREADY --
-- HAVEN'T YOU?!
MAYBE. YOU'VE BETRAYED AND KILLED YOUR OWN KIN AND MANIPULATED MINE.
YOU'RE A THIEF AND A MURDERER --
-- AFTER ALL YOU'VE DONE, DO I OWE YOU ANY LESS?
THIEF? I CLAIM WHAT IS MINE.
I CLAIM IT BY RIGHT OF BIRTH --
-- I CLAIM IT IN BLOOD.
CLNG
FSHH

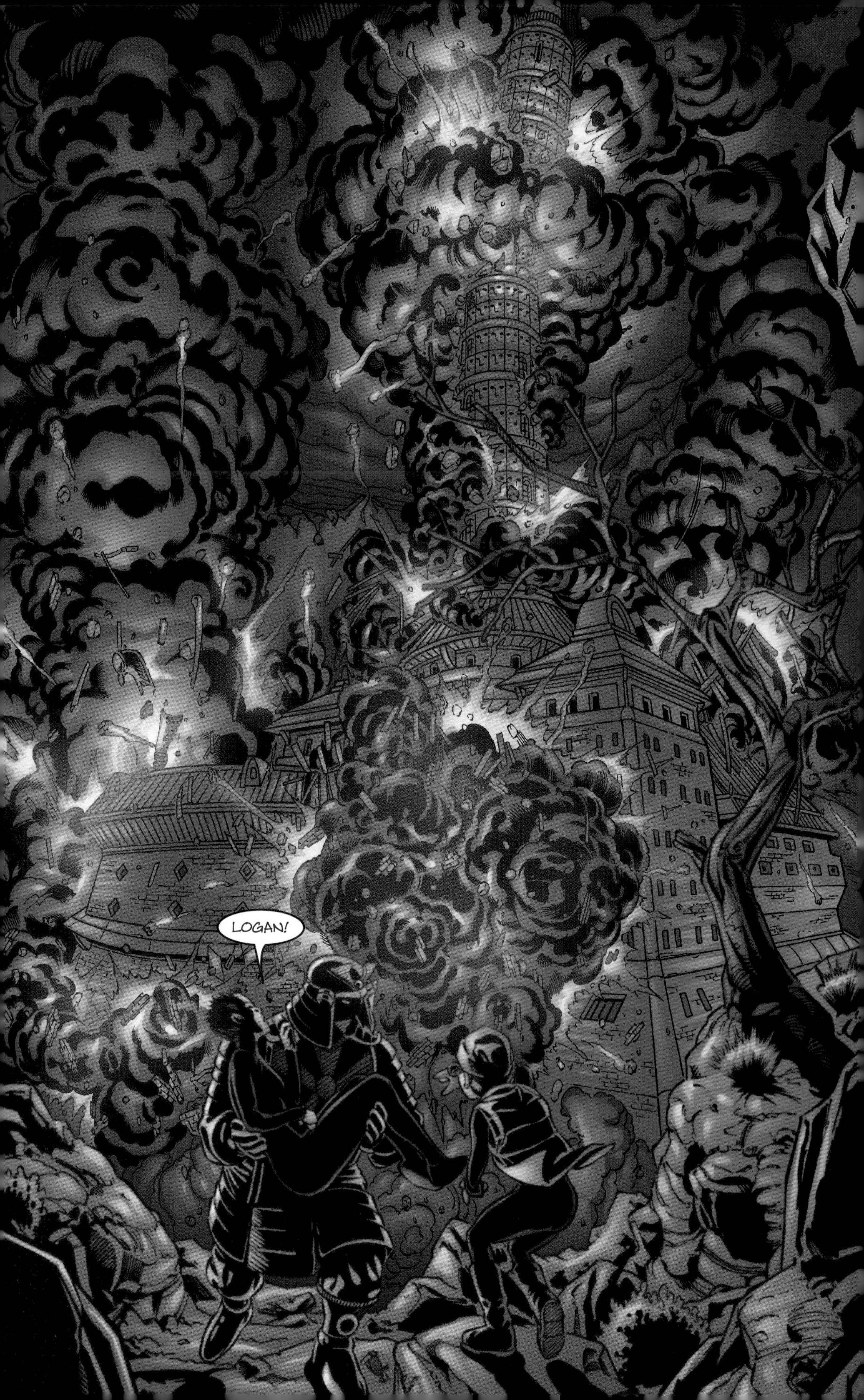
LOGAN!

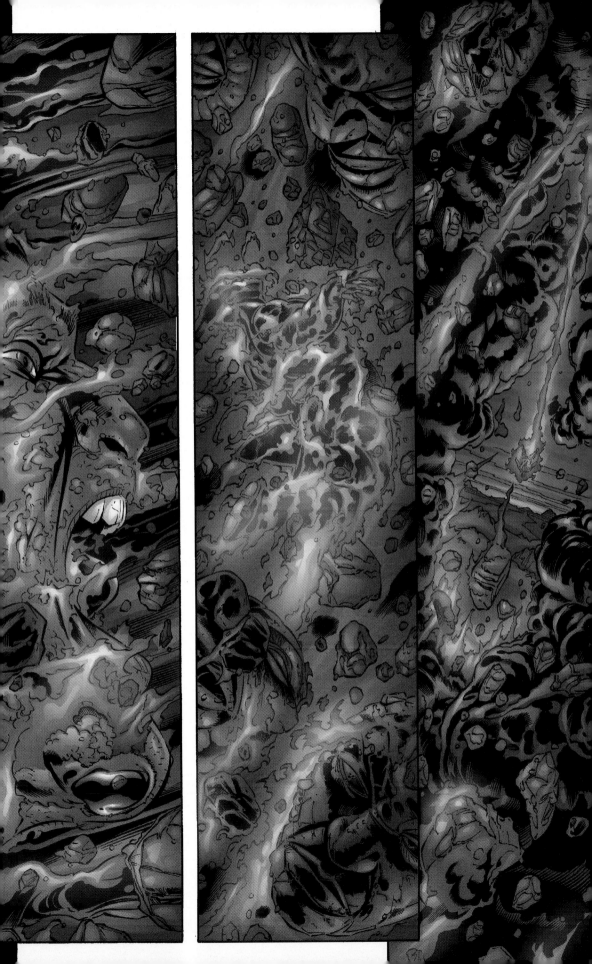

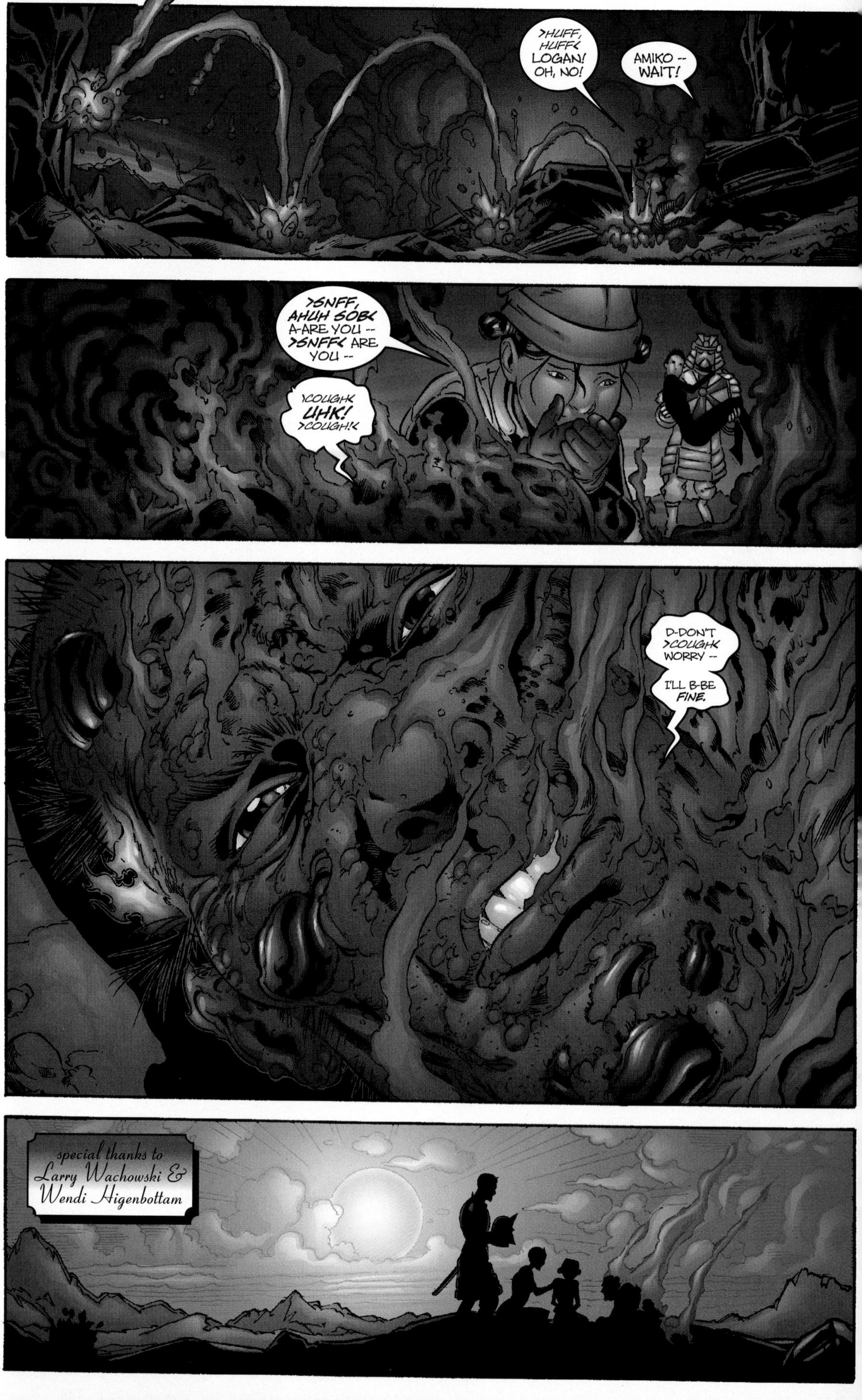
>HUFF, HUFF< LOGAN! OH, NO!
AMIKO -- WAIT!
>SNFF, AHUH SOB< A-ARE YOU -- >SNFF< ARE YOU --
>COUGH< UHK! >COUGH!<
D-DON'T >COUGH< WORRY --
I'LL B-BE FINE.
special thanks to Larry Wachowski & Wendi Higenbottam

WOLVERINE®

SKETCHBOOK

by STEVE SKROCE

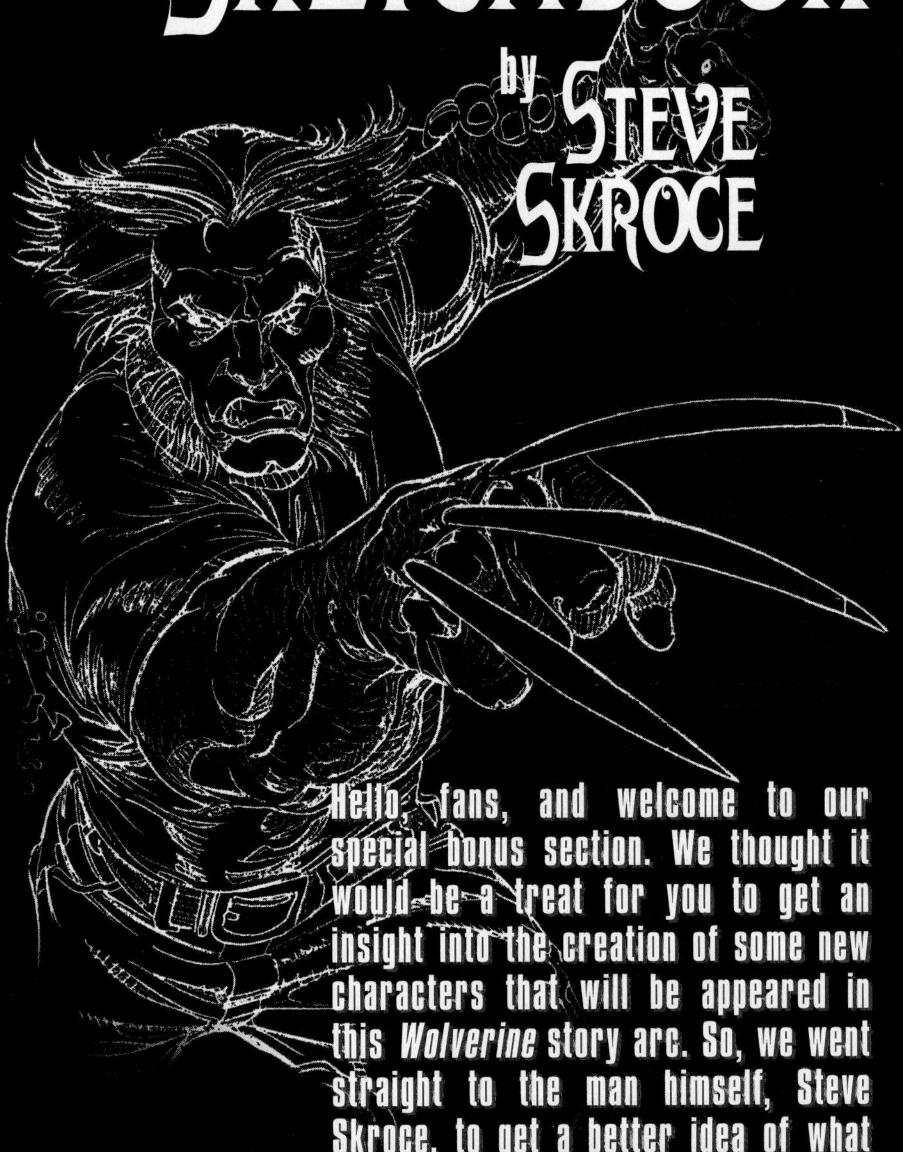

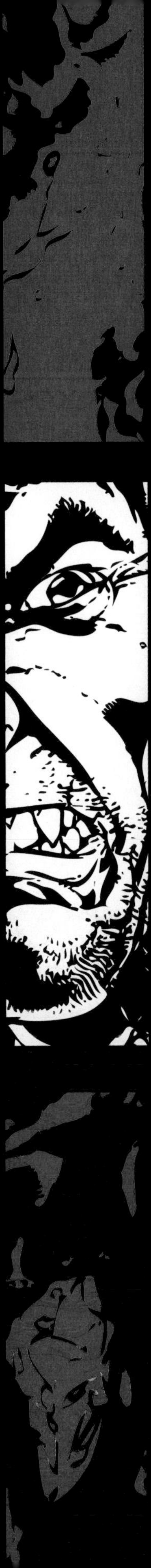

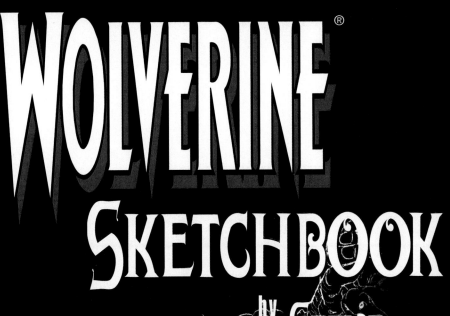

Hello, fans, and welcome to our special bonus section. We thought it would be a treat for you to get an insight into the creation of some new characters that will be appeared in this *Wolverine* story arc. So, we went straight to the man himself, Steve Skroce, to get a better idea of what he was thinking when doing these designs. Enjoy!

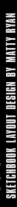

SKETCHBOOK LAYOUT DESIGN BY MATTY RYAN

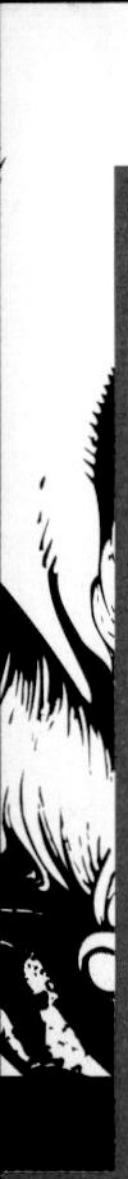

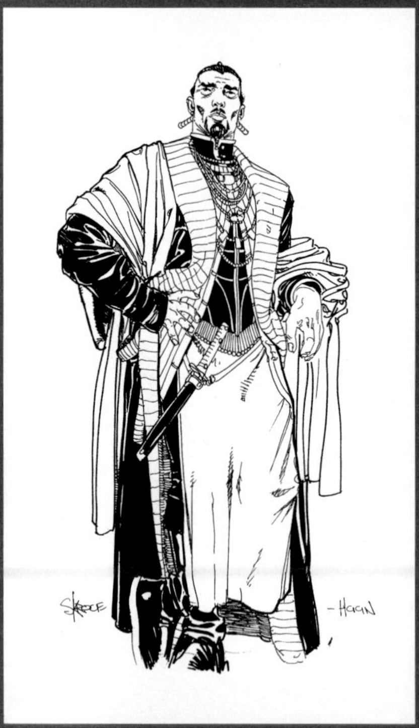

HAAN

"I wanted Han to look very rich and regal, so I gave him a sort of trench coat robe, and underneath that this chain. The haircut and chain were taken from the work of photographer Leni Riefenstahl who took pictures of this one African tribe. I thought it was a great look and it fit the character perfectly."

"The vest, something I lifted from a fashion magazine, is influenced by the Edwardian dandy from 19th century England."

"With all the three characters, I definitely wanted to add a question mark by using all three styles. You really don't know where they came from."

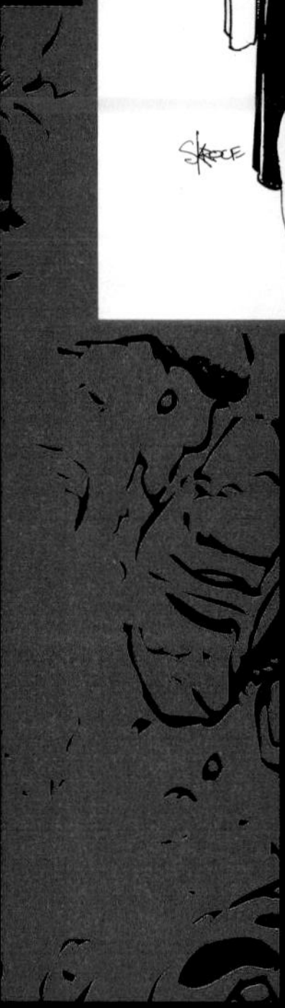

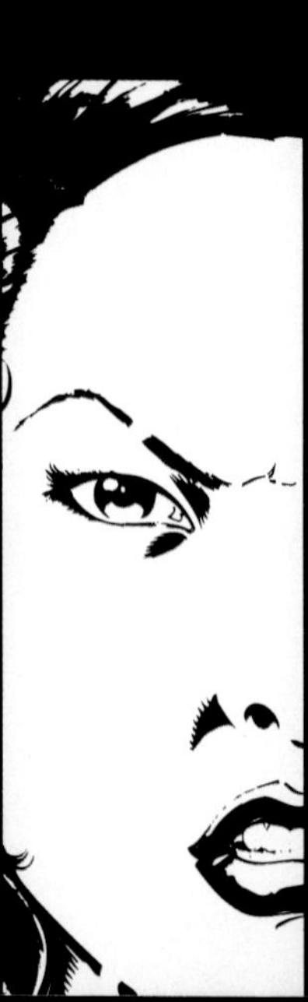

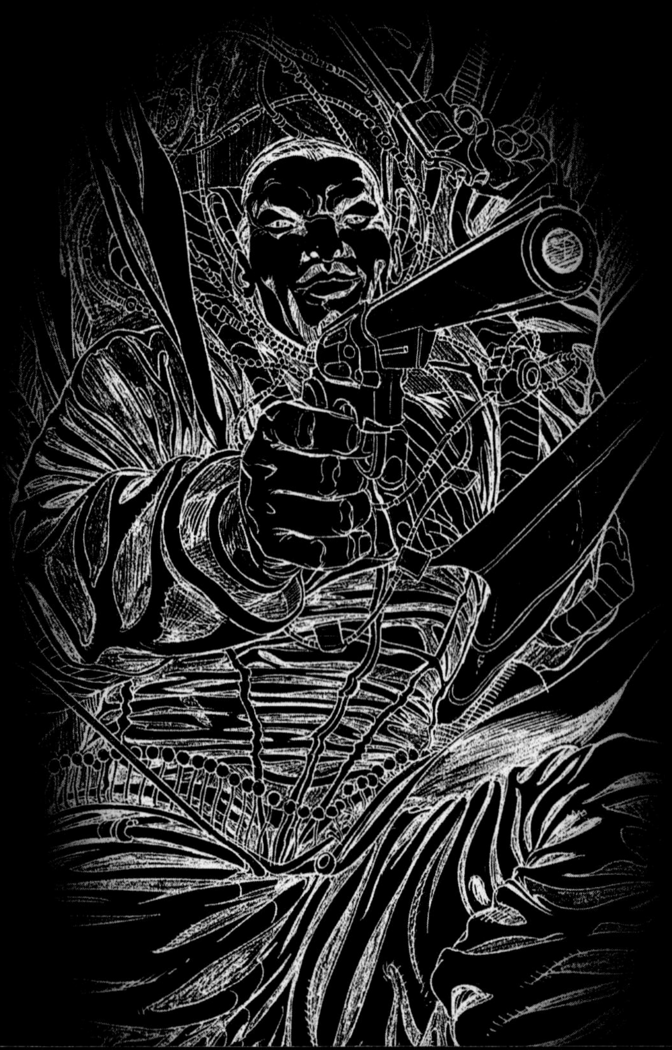

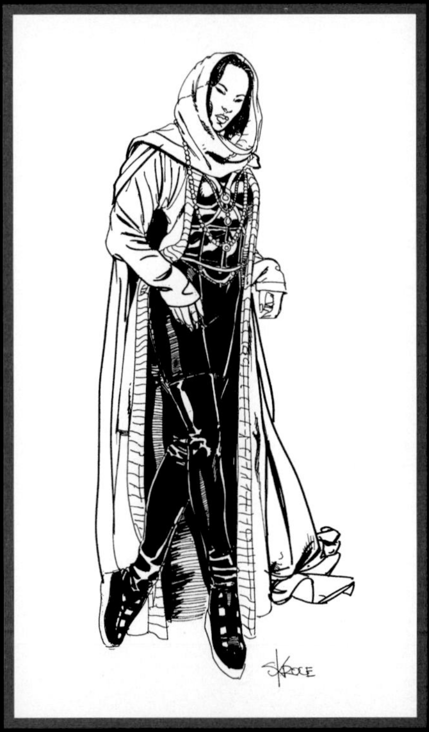

KIA

"With Kia, and the rest of the looks, I definitely wanted an Eastern European, Chinese, and Mongolian style."

"I chose Mongolia because it is a mysterious and not well-traveled place. I thought it would be a great locale, especially in the Marvel Universe, to add some make-believe stuff to."

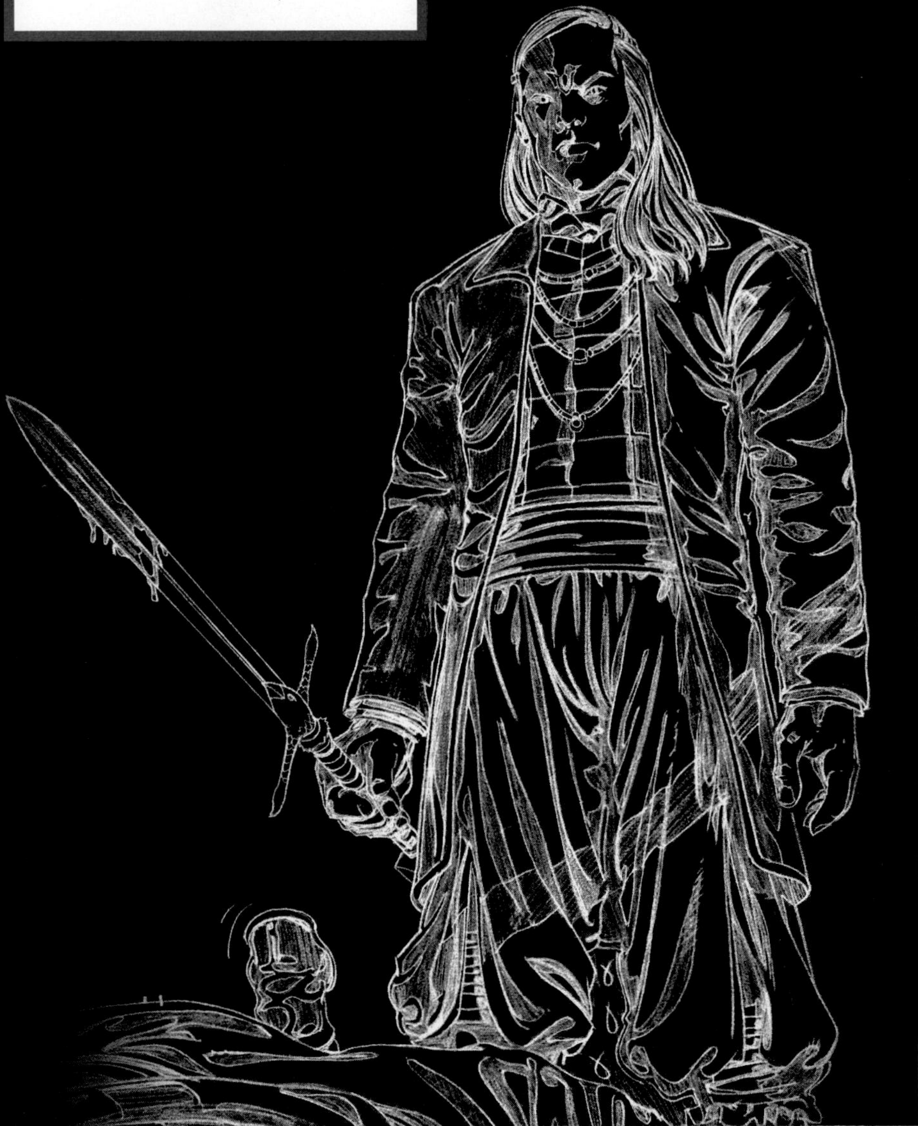

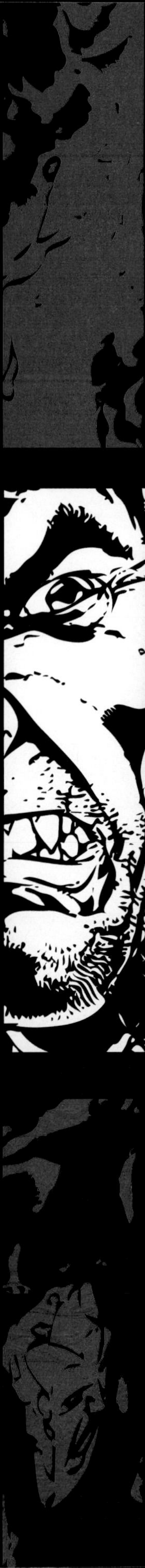

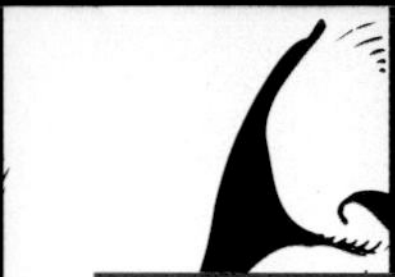

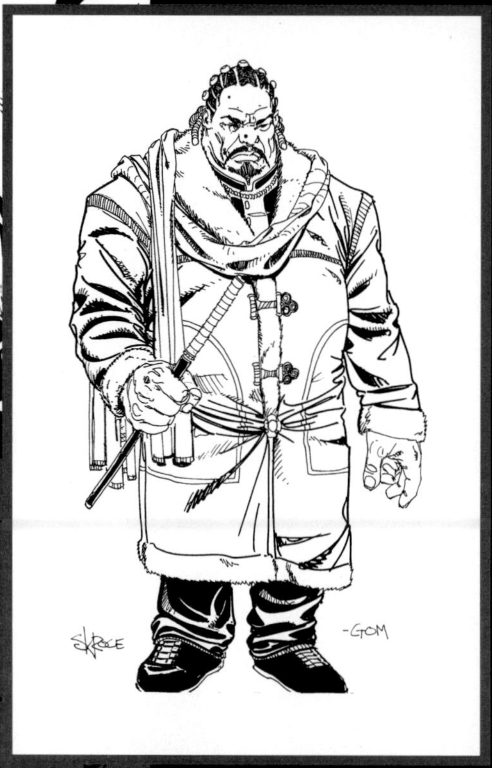

-GOM

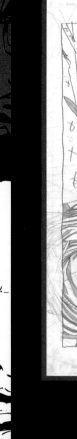

GOM

"As far as his hair goes, the idea came from a Madonna video."

"I gave him a scar over an eye to kind of convey that he is the lesser of the brothers. The appearance I tried to get across was that he was more of the "bean counter" of the family, while Haan appeared to be more of the warrior."

"This is the character that I wanted to give more of a Western look to, and if you notice, there is a bit of a resemblance to the Kingpin."

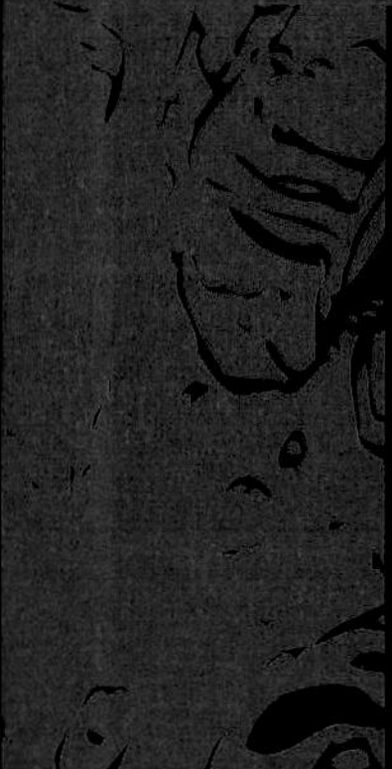

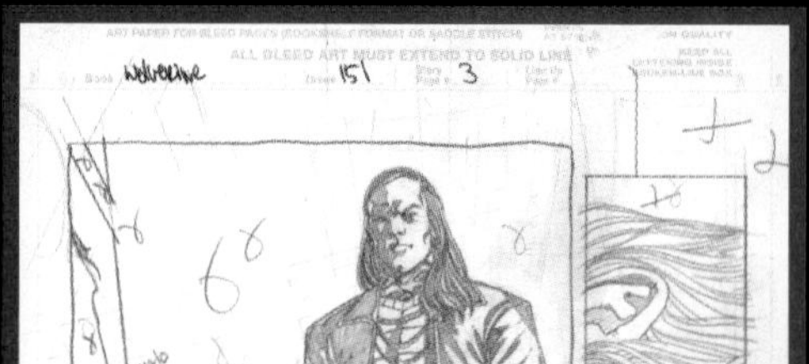

ALL BLEED ART MUST EXTEND TO SOLID LINE

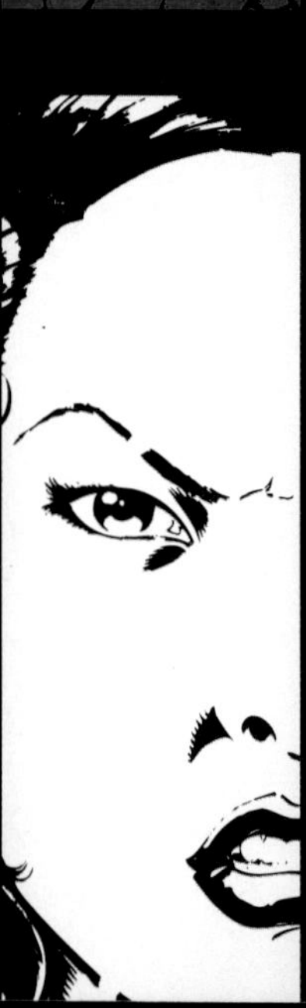

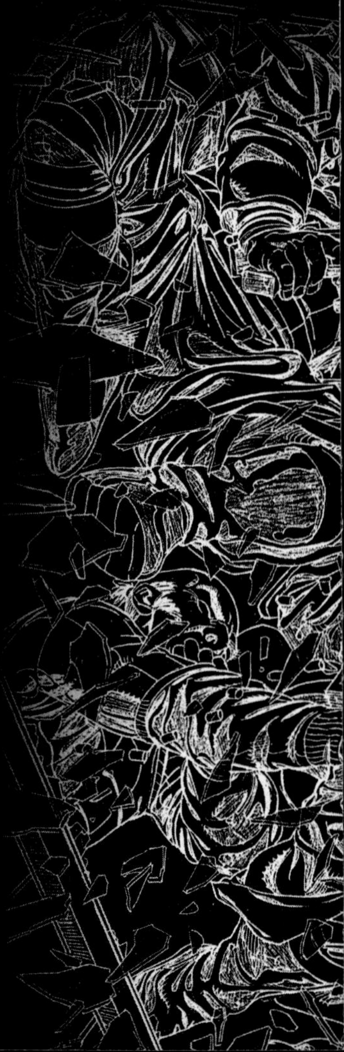

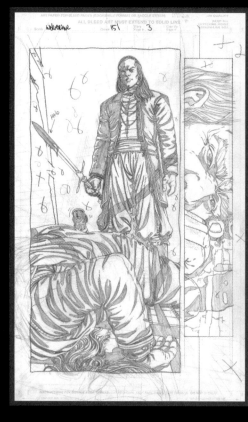

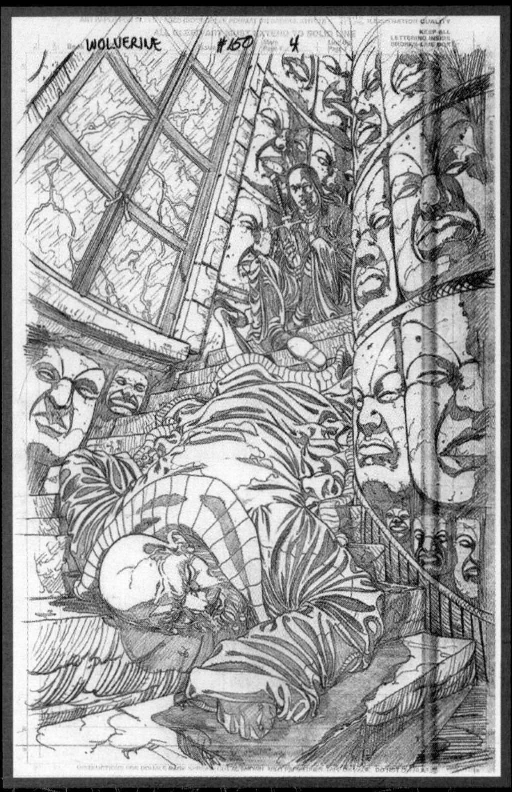
WOLVERINE #150 4

PAGE 4

"The feelin' I was trying to get was that after the death of his father, he (Yolyn) felt an emotion that wasn't expected: regret. It's sort of like you reap what you sow, or what's the payment once you cross that line. The faces on the walls were something that I really liked. The idea behind that was every enemy that the Kiasheks crushed or any hero of that family, their likeness was added to a tower that will be seen later on. What I aimed for was that the murder of the father would take place in this tower, so that the faces could almost act like witnesses to it."

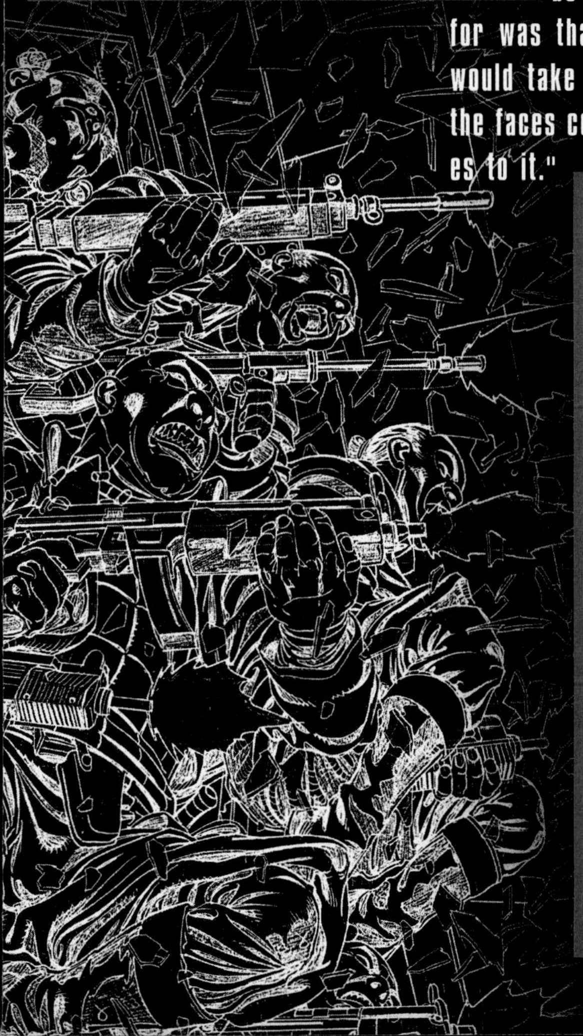

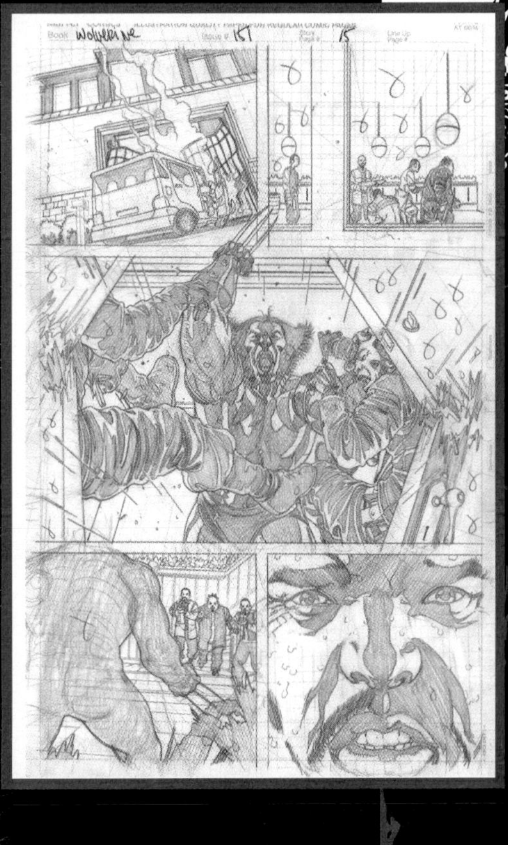

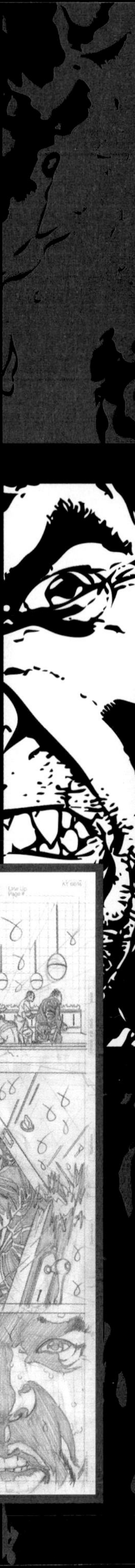

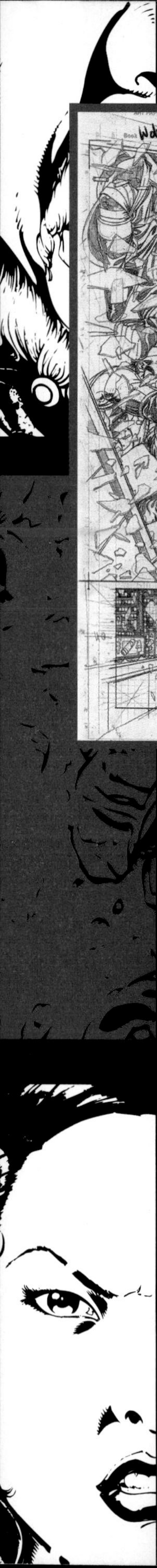

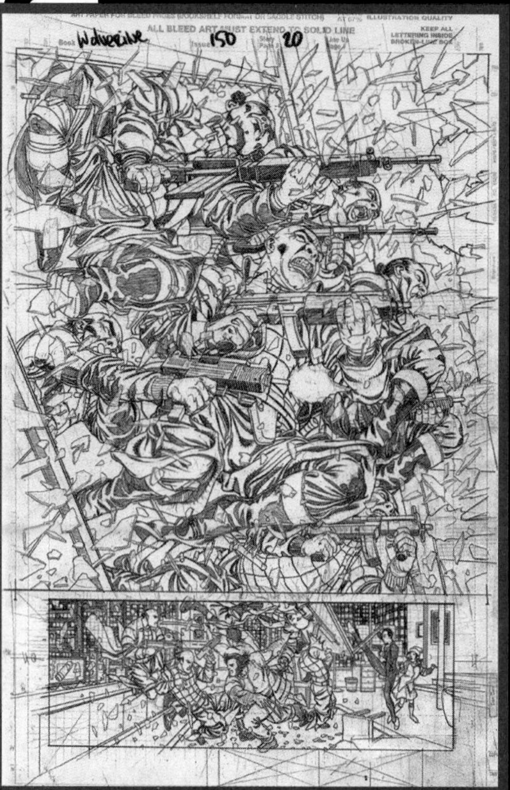
ALL BLEED ART MUST EXTEND TO SOLID LINE
Wolverine 150 20
KEEP ALL LETTERING INSIDE BROKEN-LINE BOX

PAGE 20

"I always thought low angles were cool, and I wanted an impossible shot of a group of characters flying perfectly through the window without smacking into each other. That's what's great about comics, you can do stuff that's insane!"

"I wanted to bring Wolverine into a world closer to our own. No phasers or laser guns!"

"Haan is a confident person, and also a person you really wouldn't want to mess with. Much like on page 20, I wanted an impossible shot of a guy leaping five stories, landing on his feet, and still look like a champ!"

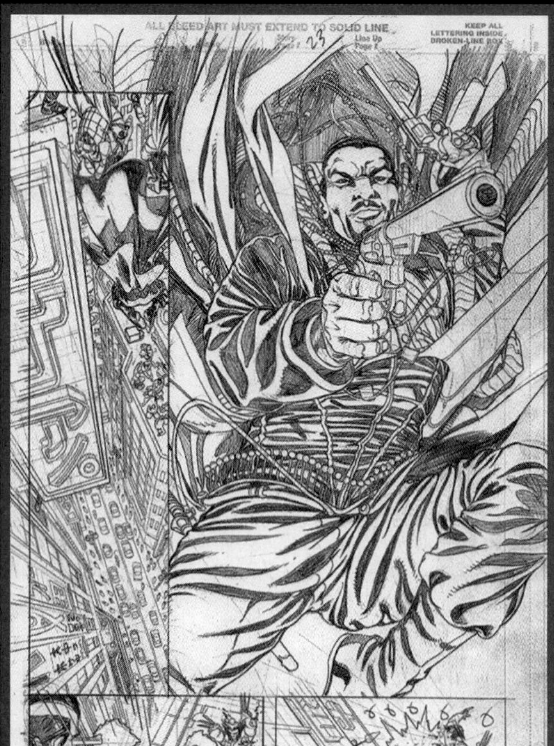
ALL BLEED ART MUST EXTEND TO SOLID LINE
KEEP ALL LETTERING INSIDE BROKEN-LINE BOX

Samurai sketches

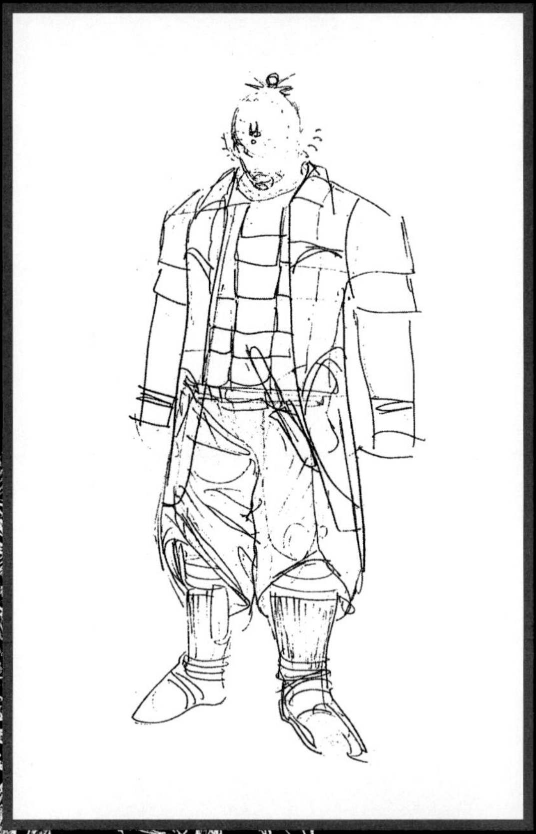

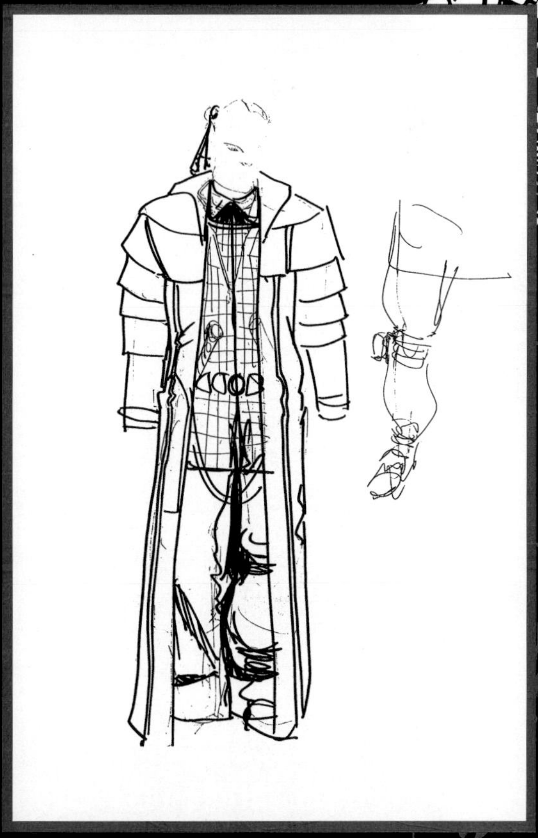

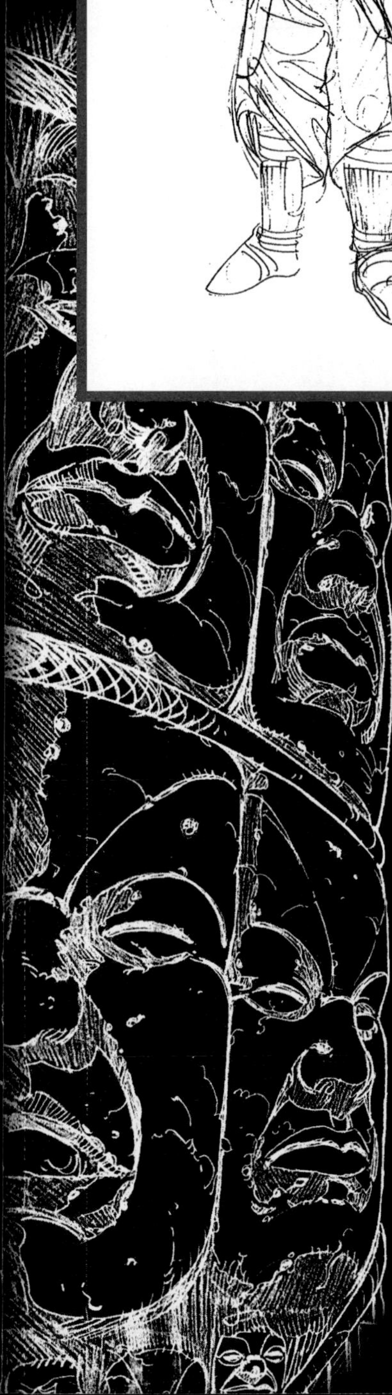

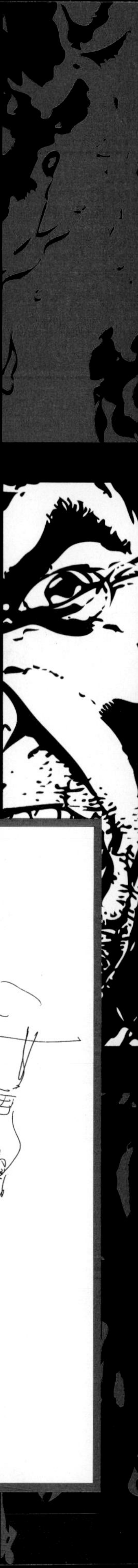

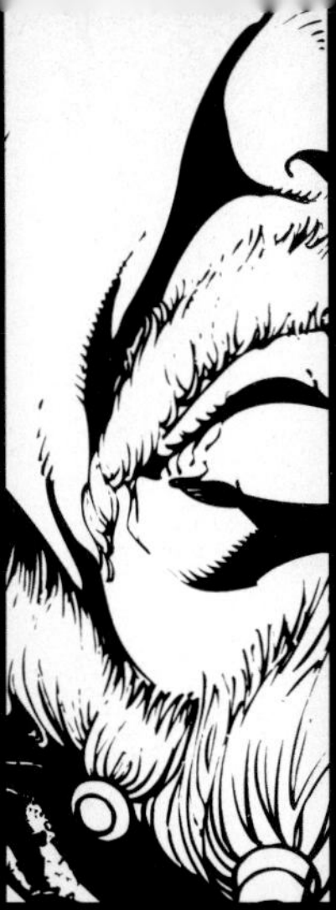

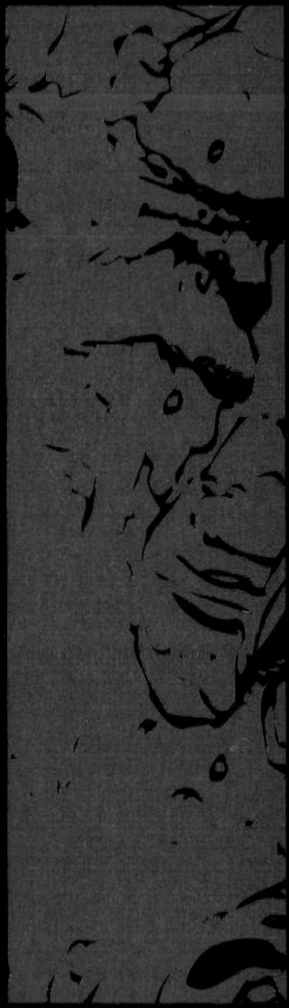

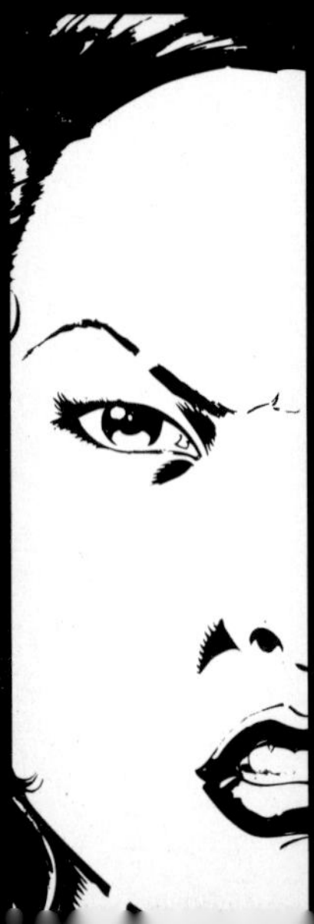

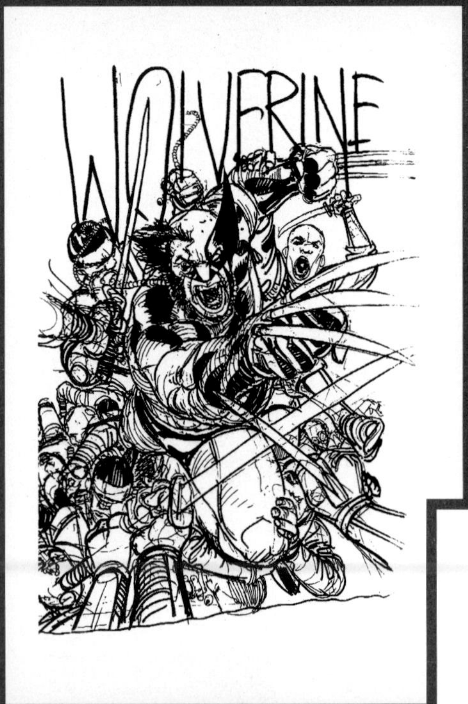
WOLVERINE

Wolverine #150 cover sketch and costume sketches

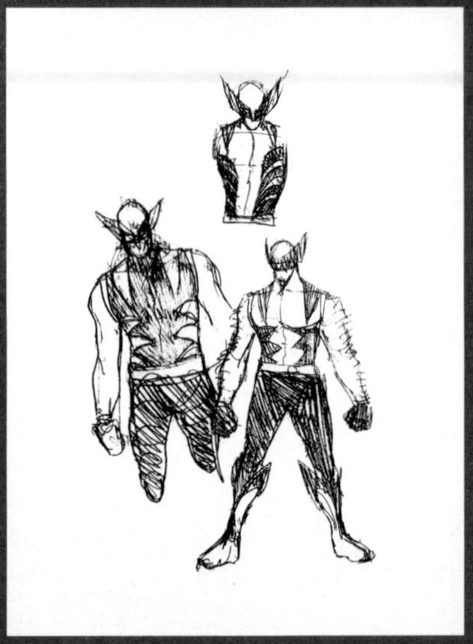

"I just wanted to make a real dynamic and easy to read comic book!"

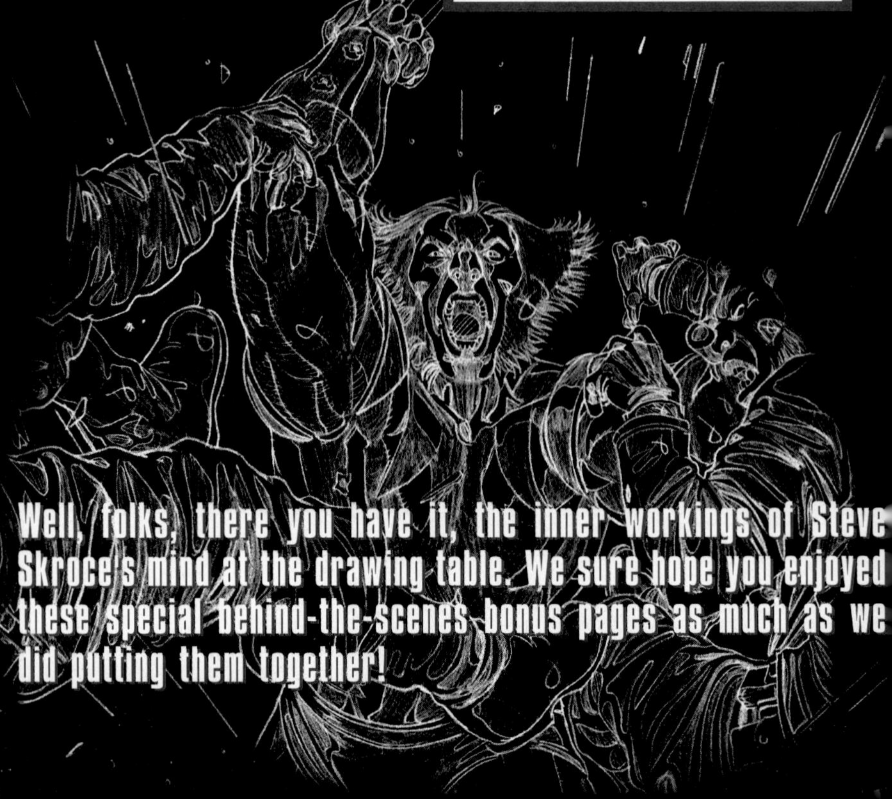

Well, folks, there you have it, the inner workings of Steve Skroce's mind at the drawing table. We sure hope you enjoyed these special behind-the-scenes bonus pages as much as we did putting them together!